WORKWAYS:
SEVEN STARS TO STEER BY
HOW TO BUILD AN ENTERPRISING LIFE

A path for inspiration and renewal which enables the
development of personal leadership in your working life.

Kees Locher and Jos van der Brug

Translators:
Plym Peters and Tony Langham

Hawthorn Press

Workways Copyright © 1997 Hawthorn Press, Stroud
Published by Hawthorn Press, Hawthorn House, 1 Lansdown Lane, Stroud, Glouc. GL5 1BJ, UK
Tel:(01453) 757040 Fax:(01453) 751138

Translated from the Dutch, *Ondernemen in de levensloop,* UCC copyright notice: © 1995 Uitgeverij Vrij Geestesleven, Zeist, Holland

Acknowledgements
Illustrations by Harm van der Meulen
Photographs by Anton Vroom, Driebergen
Cover design by Ivon Oates
Illustrations adapted by Abigail Large
Design and typesetting by Lynda Smith and Frances Fineran
Printed in the UK by Redwood Books, Wiltshire

First English edition, 1997

British Library Cataloguing in Publication Data applied for

ISBN 1 869890 89 2

Contents

PART I
WORKBOOK AND PERSONAL LOGBOOK

Stages:
Seven stars to steer by

Tasks

1 What matters to me?

2 Where am I?

3 What made me what I am?

4 Who am I?

Exercise tips

Explanations

PART II
BACKGROUNDS AND PERSPECTIVES ON LEADING AN ENTERPRISING LIFE

PART I

WORKBOOK AND
PERSONAL LOGBOOK

Getting Going

What have you got here?

What you have here is a workshop in book form. This will enable you to study your own working life and help you make conscious choices in the future. A workshop is aimed at helping you to learn while you work and work while you learn, together with others. This book will inspire you to take active steps, to be enterprising in your life.

It is in three parts.

Part I, the *Workbook,* is the backbone. This contains an interrelated series of thirty-seven tasks. The process that you pass through as you work on these tasks consists of seven stages or steps:

1 What matters to me?

2 Where am I?

3 What made me what I am?

4 Who am I?

5 What do I want?

6 What am I going to do?

7 I learn by doing.

It is best to work on the tasks together with others with whom you are participating in this workshop. We will explain below how to set about this.

Your *Personal Logbook* is included in the *Workbook.* This consists of blank pages in the *Workbook* for your notes and reflections. This is the part that is still mainly empty when you purchase the book, but which you write yourself. It will contain the results of your own study, your experiences and your discoveries. Thus the Logbook is the most valuable part and deserves a special place. You will probably keep it all your life, consulting it again and again, and perhaps adding to it. As well as using the blank pages, users may want to buy a small notebook for further reflections.

Part II contains *Backgrounds,* reflections and observations on the themes which come up in the tasks. These are the personal views of both of us, the authors, which have developed both from the experience of our own lives and work, and from study. They are intended to stimulate the development of your own views, rather than to expound a scientifically supported theory. There is a bibliography at the end of this part.

Who is *Workways* intended for?

It was written for people who are looking for a new relationship with their work and their working life, and for those who wish to monitor this process themselves.

Many people are driven to do this because of the insecurity in our environment. Organisations are no longer the safe havens they were, where work and income were guaranteed for years. Thousands of jobs have been lost as a result of technological developments, and these will not be replaced, even 'when the economy recovers.' All kinds of jobs have disappeared completely; others have changed profoundly or are contracted out to third parties. In the future, organisations will probably provide only a small number of permanent jobs and frequently turn to qualified people to do a particular job for a specific period. In the US, the phenomenon is already described as 'jobless work'.

The world of work is changing in many fields, and all these changes call upon people nowadays to be enterprising. To achieve this, it is necessary to learn to know yourself at a deeper level and to be aware that you must get yourself moving so that you can continue to make a useful contribution to your work.

This leads to questions such as:

– 'How can I find a fruitful relationship to all the changes which are taking place in my organization?'

– 'What is my aim for my future development in my work?'

– 'My job is being scrapped! What can I do, and what do I want to do?'

– 'How can I be useful?'

– 'How can I regain some pleasure in my work?'

– 'Up to now my career has taken its course automatically. How can I make more conscious choices?'

– 'Why is it that I have been passed over several times for promotion? What does this mean for my career in the future?'

These and other questions are the starting point for the workshop.

What results can you expect?

Obviously, the results of the workshop are determined to a large extent by the questions you pose and the situation you are in. Apart from this, they are dependent on what you invest, both in time and in effort. This 'workshop in book form' demands a great deal of self-discipline from a 'do-it-yourself' student or from a small group working together.

Our experience of this workshop is that the end result is almost always different from what had been hoped for or expected in advance, but that it is still very worthwhile. The participants do not usually discover any concrete solutions, but come up with a new view of their own (working) life, and a new direction for the future. Here are some examples of such results:

- 'I became aware of where I would like to direct my efforts in the coming years.'

- 'I have acquired a more realistic view of myself, and feel I can approach the future with more self-confidence.'

- 'I have adopted a different attitude towards all the activities of the organization, with more inner peace, so that I can make a better contribution.'

- 'I have learned to take myself seriously and not to hide my head in the sand when I have to make choices'.

- 'Because I am less restricted by the past, I am now more open to the future.'

- 'Now I know what the following step in my career will be.'

- 'I realized why I had always been such a workaholic, and I am now better able to find a balance between my working life and my private life.'

Apart from this sort of result, the workshop is also aimed at the development of so-called 'life skills', skills which people need in order to find a direction in their lives today. These life skills include:

- being able to live with questions

- making use of other people in a fruitful way

- looking forward and looking back methodically

- observing specific situations

- seeing the effect of one's own actions

- describing and characterizing situations in terms of images

- tracing essential aspects

- producing one's own sources of inspiration

- setting objectives

- making realistic plans

- guiding one's own developmental processes

Who wrote this book?

We are senior partners in the NPI – Institute for Organizational Development in Zeist. This institute was founded in 1954 by Bernard Lievegoed with the purpose of supporting individual and organisational development. Our work is informed by Rudolf Steiner's anthroposophy, which is rooted in Christianity. Central themes in the work of the NPI include process management, co-operation and learning.

Lievegoed can be seen as one of the pioneers in researching the working lives of individuals. This 'biographical' perspective has had a central place in the work of the NPI from the early days.

Besides experience with management consultancy, we now have about twenty years of experience with 'biography work'. This approach helps people take a holistic and creative view of their working lives. Such insights then lead to personal renewal and finding the next step. We have developed the insights and methods which this book reflects, together with our colleagues. In particular, we would like to mention our former colleagues, Erwin van Asbeck, Hans von Sassen and Jerry Schöttelndreier, who did some pioneering work in the Netherlands with their 'biography workshops'. We would like to thank our colleague, Rob Otte, for his many tips and psychological insights.

We owe most thanks to all those people who gave us their trust and allowed us to look into their lives. In particular, we would like to mention the participants in the workshop, *'My work and I'*, which has been one of the courses provided by the NPI since 1991. Many of the examples and statements in this book came from them, and they agreed to the inclusion of photographs of their artistic projects in this book by way of illustration. Their encouragement stimulated us to get on with the task of writing this book. With this workbook, we would like to enable larger groups of people to have access to the biographical study of their working lives, in such a way that they can make use of this independently.

Lastly, we would like to thank Frans van Bussel, who rose to the editorial challenge of our book with admirable perseverance.

Jos van der Brug and Kees Locher

About the authors

Jos van der Brug, born in 1936 in Arnhem.

I have worked for the NPI since 1976. Before that time, I worked for a long time in the field of management and organizational development in two industrial companies, and for a short period in the health sector. I was – and am – fascinated by processes of change, development and renewal, both in individual people, in groups of people co-operating together, and in organisations in society.

In my work at the NPI, the emphasis is on coaching managers who are monitoring the process of change in their organization and on supervising people who are undergoing these changes.

I live in Driebergen with my partner. Her son and my three children are finding their own way as young adults, and sometimes we are intensely involved in this.

Kees Locher, born in 1939 in Bandung, Indonesia.

Since 1968 I have worked as an organizational consultant and trainer in management development projects, first for the consultancy bureau Bosboom & Hegener, and since 1973 for the NPI. I am interested in the way in which people develop, how they bring about changes in society and in their organisations, and how they can initiate these themselves. Recently, the focus of my work has shifted to coaching managers who have to monitor these processes of change themselves, and people who have to or wish to initiate this process in a working situation themselves. Following my studies of mechanical engineering in Delft and working on the problems of vibration and shocks in submarines for the navy, I learned about this field through practical experience.

Together with my 'other half', a historian at the university, I am trying to teach our three children independence and co-operation. Apart from my work and my family, I also like to make stone sculptures.

Important conditions

With others

We strongly advise you to do this workshop together with others. Someone who can listen to you with interest will often, as an outsider, be able to give you a surprising new view of your life. By telling others about things, you place these outside yourself and you can look at them from a greater distance. The experiences and events of your life lose their self-evident quality and appear in a new light.

We wrote the tasks and practical instructions for groups of three to six people working on their biographies together. With more than six people, this becomes too complex and working together takes up too much time and attention. It is also possible to do the workshop together with one other person.

If you cannot find a partner, find someone you know who you can regularly talk to about the things you have come across as you progress, someone you can ask for advice, share your worries, questions, etc. (Where it is a matter of mentoring discussions within the organization, the NPI can supervise these if required, or train people for this purpose.) Workways counsellors can help, or develop mentors for this purpose.

The amount of time required

This workshop requires time. Most of the time, you will work independently. Then you discuss the results of this 'homework' and the progress of your research with others. You should count on 150 to 200 hours, divided over a period of about six months. If you wish to complete the process in half a year, this will require a great deal of self-discipline. This relatively long period is necessary because sometimes things can be quite clear, but at other times they may require more thought and consideration. It may be necessary to sleep on something, forget it and then take it up again. Time has an effect and you can make use of this, but do try to complete the process within eight months. Otherwise it becomes too lengthy and loses some of its effect.

In a group of three people you can discuss two tasks in part of a day (four hours). When you discuss all the tasks together which you have prepared at home, you will need eighteen meetings over a period of six months. This comes to three half days per month. It is a good rhythm to alternate whole days and half days, with a period in between of about two weeks.

You will need extra time to do the support exercises together, to discuss your experiences together with the practical tips which are given next to the tasks in Part I, or to discuss the thematic explanations (Part I) and the backgrounds to the contents (Part II). It is difficult to estimate how much time this will take.

Materials

Blank pages are included in Part I, the *Workbook,* as space for your personal logbook. Apart from a few tables which accompany certain tasks, these pages are empty. These are meant for the tasks in which you work with artistic means, and for notes. The intention is that you record and store the most important results of your study (insights, experiences and plans of action) in this logbook.

However, you will not have the *Workbook* with you every day. Therefore we would advise you to buy a small notebook, in which you can note down the thoughts, ideas, intentions and so on, that come up during the day, so that you can enter them in your *Workbook* later. Often, you can be so taken up by everyday life, that fruitful insights are quickly forgotten. That is why a notebook is useful.

In a number of tasks, you will be working with colour. An ordinary box of crayons will be sufficient for this purpose. For the support exercises, you will need:

- a stick of compressed charcoal;
- a kneadable putty rubber or a block of plastic gum eg Knetgummi: 320, Koh-i-noor;
- a box of coloured crayons;
- soft crayons: dark red, ultramarine blue, pale yellow, two sticks of each colour (or soft pastels);
- seven sheets of drawing paper, A3;
- a block of clay (eg red earthenware clay);
- a sheet of hardboard to work on with the clay (40 x 50cm).

Introducing the seven stages and elements of the workshop

You will find the seven stages of the workshop in this Workbook. These stages contain tasks, explanations, support exercises and practical tips. At the beginning of each stage, we indicate what you can expect.

Tasks

Altogether, there are thirty-seven tasks. Each task consists of three parts:

- the part you do at home ('For yourself');
- the joint discussion of the results of the homework ('In dialogue');
- the rounding off and recording of the most important findings ('Rounding Off').

In addition, the motives or reasons for the task are given for each task, as well as some 'practical instructions' for the dialogue and the homework. For some tasks, reference is made to a thematic explanation in the *Workbook* or to a chapter that explains it in more detail in the *Backgrounds* section. For the quality of the process of your search, it is important that you carry out the tasks in the order indicated. First read through every task fully, before starting on it.

Explanations

The explanations contain practical insights into understanding people which are directly linked to the tasks. We recommend that you start working on a task yourself first, then read the explanation, then return to the task. If you find it difficult to 'get into' a certain task, read the explanation first.

Support exercises

Five of the seven stages include a support exercise. These are exercises using artistic materials (chalk, coloured pencils, soft crayons and clay), which enable you to work on your life with other means than by talking and thinking. They are intended to support your study and, if you like, they can be missed out. Wait to decide about this until you have reached the first support exercise and read through it together with the accompanying explanation. We suggest that you do these exercises in the meetings with the others.

Practical tips

The explanations are accompanied by practical tips, of which there are nineteen altogether. These are tips for small exercises which you can do for a short time during the workshop. They support the work on the tasks. Practice involves repetition, and requires time and perseverance. The tips are in the nature of advice, and can therefore be followed or ignored. This requires a conscious choice on your part.

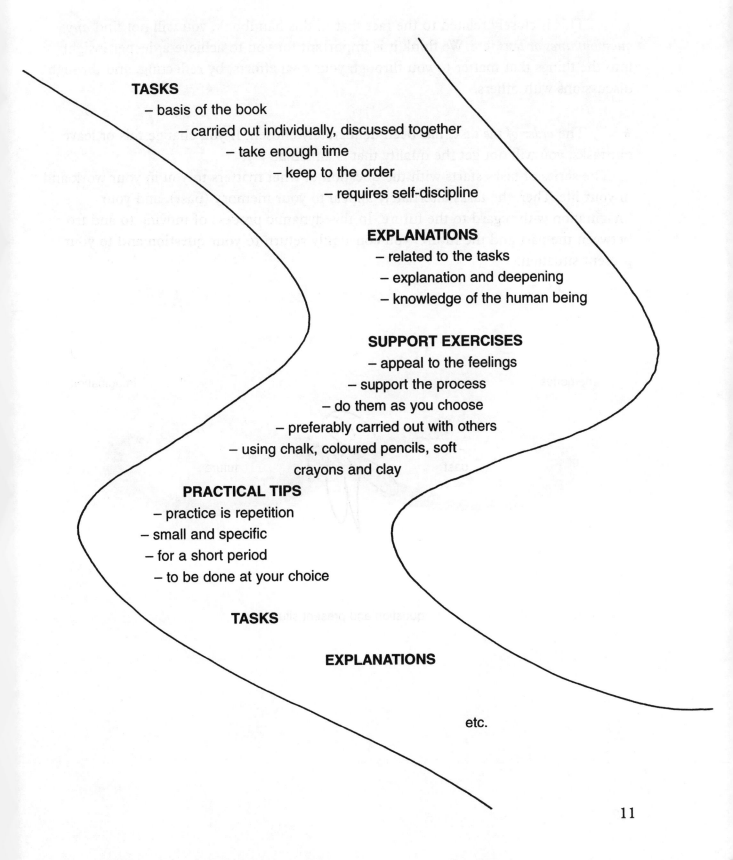

TASKS
– basis of the book
– carried out individually, discussed together
– take enough time
– keep to the order
– requires self-discipline

EXPLANATIONS
– related to the tasks
– explanation and deepening
– knowledge of the human being

SUPPORT EXERCISES
– appeal to the feelings
– support the process
– do them as you choose
– preferably carried out with others
– using chalk, coloured pencils, soft crayons and clay

PRACTICAL TIPS
– practice is repetition
– small and specific
– for a short period
– to be done at your choice

TASKS

EXPLANATIONS

etc.

Finally...

★   You may have some difficulties with certain tasks, because they do not describe exactly what you have to do, or because certain terms are not precisely defined. Do not let this stop you from starting on the task, but feel confident to follow your own interpretation or definitions. We have deliberately not circumscribed the tasks completely, *leaving room for your own ideas and interpretation.*

★   This is closely related to the fact that in this handbook, you will not find *any questionnaires or tests,* etc. We think it is important for you to achieve a deeper insight into the things that matter to you through your own efforts, by reflecting, and through discussions with others.

★   The *order of the tasks* has been deliberately chosen. If you change this or leave out tasks, you will not get the quality that is aimed at.

The series of tasks starts with the question of what matters to you in your work and in your life. Then the tasks alternately appeal to your memory (past), and your imagination with regard to the future. In this dynamic process of moving to and fro between the past and the future, you constantly return to your question and to your present situation.

memories   imagination

past   future

question and present situation

★ Step by step, you will get to know *our way of thinking*. We proceed on the assumption that as a person, you have the potential to guide everything inside yourself and everything going on around you. That is what this workshop is about: to increase or reinforce your own powers of steering. It is equally important to us that everyone has the freedom to choose their own view of mankind and the world and to develop this further.

★ *He and she:* we have opted to write the tasks and the support exercises alternately using the pronouns 'he' and 'she'. We have also tried to vary the examples with men and women.

Editor's note on 'he' and 'she': we have followed the authors' wishes, so that the exercises with odd numbers use mainly 'he' and the even-numbered exercises 'she'. We have tried to avoid cumbersome language so have not used 'she or he' or 's/he'. Since the authors wanted to address readers directly, we have used 'you' where possible. Whilst the examples in the text are varied, we hope that the reader is not confused. No discrimination, bias or prejudice is intended, and we apologise for any offence which may be caused.

What matters to me?

The study of your biography – present, past and future – starts with formulating the question of what you want to work on and creating the conditions to start working effectively. The most important condition is that you have travelling companions on your voyage of exploration. Find them before you start.

Tasks

1 My question
2 Agreements

Explanations

Living with questions
Describing in images

Task 1: My question

Anyone who wants to examine their life, can easily go adrift. It is necessary to find a point of orientation, a beacon to determine the course you must steer. The question of what matters to you with regard to your work and your life is such a beacon.

For yourself

The individual part of this task consists of three stages.

1 Reflect quietly on the following questions:

– What are the thoughts and feelings which I have with regard to my situation at work? What matters to me?

– Where did I get this book? What struck me when I heard about it or when I came across it?

– Why do I want to start working on it? What results do I expect? What are my aims?

2 Now simplify your response – the thoughts and feelings you have about the above questions into one single question: the question about your work and your life which you want to clarify in the near future. In your formulation, keep to the following criteria:

– one short sentence

– containing the word 'I'

– ending with a question mark

– aimed at what you want in the future

3 Now find an 'anchor' for your question: relate it to experiences in the past and specific visions about the future.

– Think of one or more specific situations in the past in which your question played a part. Try to remember what actually happened, where it took place and which people were involved.

– Then try to imagine your situation in the future as it will be if you do not take any active steps and do not work on your question. Where will you be then? What will happen there and who will you be involved with?

Outline both situations on paper with a few key words.
Finally, also note down your question.

Practical instructions

For stage 2: The questions are different for everyone. Examples are:

- Do I want to stay in this organization, now that the mentality has changed so much?

- How can I make a more conscious choice with regard to my work and life?

- How can I continue to be involved in my work if my boss constantly confronts me with faits accomplis?

- What must I learn to influence this situation to get what I want?

- How can I stay healthy in the work I do?

- How can I relax and leave work to others even though it is still so important for me?

- Am I going to continue to specialize or am I going to find a broader field of work?

- How can I make the content of my work meaningful for the next few years until I retire?

- How can I integrate my cultural and administrative interests with the information technology field?

- What should I do now that my job is under threat because of downsizing?

Stage 3 involves memories and a vision of the future.

Memories concern situations in which you were actively involved not so long ago. Although your memory may evoke feelings and emotions, it is not a matter of reliving whatever you liked or disliked. Focus on the factual aspects of the event as though you are looking at them as an outsider. Try to see the situation before you as if it were a film, and concentrate on:

- the time: when and what time, what happened first and what happened next, and how long it took;

- the place: where, indoors or outdoors, colours and smells, light and dark, plants and objects, materials, people and their appearance, movements and gestures;

- the interaction: speaking and listening, question and answer, remarks and responses, verbal and nonverbal behaviour, your own thoughts, feelings and inclinations.

With regard to the *future,* use your imagination to create a specific vision of the situation in the future. Do this in a factual sense as you did for memories, i.e., look at the time, the place and the interaction. Do not say: 'I can't do that.' Follow your spontaneous impulses and trust your imagination. The ideas which you come up with will probably never be reality, but by creating it – a picture of your future – you will come closer to the essence of your question.

Explanation: Living with questions (p. 23)

In dialogue

In the discussions with your partners, everyone takes turns to talk while the other two listen and help. They work as follows:

- The person who is talking formulates the *question* he is working on and describes one or two concrete *situations* from the past which are related to his question, followed by one or two situations from the future. The others listen. They may ask the person who is talking to clarify or add to what he has said.

- When he has finished talking, the listeners indicate what struck them about the situations that were being described.

- Finally, they say what they feel to be the speaker's question in the situations that were described.

Explanation: Describing in images (p. 28)

Practical instructions

Tips for the speaker:

- Try to be as brief, factual and specific as possible. In other words, leave out all sorts of explanations, backgrounds and opinions about people and events. Give an outline of the situation that is so clear and specific that the others can see it as though they were there themselves. This is known as 'a description in images'.

- Do not read out an account that you have written out beforehand, but tell it as it occurs to you now. Because you have to retell a memory or an idea of the future that you will already have thought about, new details may come up so that you are telling a living story.

- Avoid explaining to the others that they have misinterpreted you. Of course, their image of your situation will still be incomplete and distorted for the time being. Nevertheless, whatever strikes them and whatever they see as being your question, may be valuable to you. Perhaps you will not see this immediately. That is why it is important that you write down their contributions.

Tips for the listener:

- Listen attentively and with respect for the speaker, and stay with his question. He is the 'owner' of his question. Some of the common pitfalls are:

- you recognize the situation, because 'you have experienced it yourself'. In this case, you run the risk of falling back on your own memories rather than focusing on the speaker's own unique situation;

- you give explanations because you 'see' what is happening in the speaker's situation;

18

– you give solutions and advise about what the speaker should do;

– you judge the speaker or his situation.

If you fall over these stumbling blocks, you remove the question from the speaker.

– Ask only those questions which help to make the picture clearer and more specific. The aim is not to satisfy your curiosity, but to reveal how the speaker relates to his question.

– Then say what struck you about the situations described, bearing in mind the speaker's question.

– Finally, 'give him back' what you see as being his question. This is the most subjective part of your role, even more than the previous point. Try to leave the speaker free to do what he wants with your contribution.

Rounding off

It may be that after this discussion, you will be able to formulate your question more accurately or more concisely. Note it in this form in your Logbook on the next page, together with what you learned about yourself in the discussion.

Living with questions

Living with questions is often more important than giving the answers.

This quote may seem rather strange at first sight. After all, most people tend to think answers are more important than questions. With regard to solving practical problems, that is certainly true.

However, in life itself, it is the questions which get people going and keep them moving. They are the motor behind the processes of personal development, while the answers often stop this motor running. When you have found the answer or the solution, you do not look any further and the process stops. People who always have a solution to everything are not always the most interesting people. They are at risk of stagnating in their development, while those who understand the art of living with questions have the possibility of making new discoveries all the time, both about themselves and about their environment.

Children never stop asking questions. One four year old asks his father, 'How does that huge horse fit into my little eye?' Another asks, 'Mum, why is the sky blue?' The vague and abstract answers of adults are one of the reasons that we soon learn not to ask real questions and start copying adult answers, answers to questions we did not ask ourselves.

As a result, our own questions disappear. We don't even know that we had them any more. We are astonished when someone asks us what questions we are working on. We don't have any! And if we do have them, we call them, 'problems'. Of course, we want to get rid of these as quickly as possible, because it is intolerable to walk around with an unsolved problem.

In the art of living with questions, it is a matter of giving the question its proper place. This means that we should not suppress the question, but must leave it 'be'. It should not turn into a problem that quickly has to be solved, but it should become a reason for going in search of things, taking initiatives and making discoveries.

It is possible to learn this art.

Breaking through the self-evident

It is a characteristic of the human being that he or she asks questions. In contrast with animals, we are able to distance ourselves from our environment and ask questions. Animals are as one with their world. Their bodies and all their instincts are geared to this. In this interconnection, there is no room for questioning consciousness.

As people we also, of course, live partly in a self-evident world. We do our work, and go back home, read the paper, drink a cup of coffee, have a chat with the neighbour, and go to bed – without asking any questions about this. That is just as well, because our lives would become very stressful if we did. However, sometimes –

because of an unexpected external event or because of an inner mood – this self-evident connection with everyday life breaks down and we ask ourselves questions.

For example, a nurse in a psychiatric hospital asked herself the question, a few years ago, why the patients were removed from their own environment and admitted to hospital. Up to that time, this had been as self-evident to her as it had been to others. The first reactions from her colleagues were that she should stop being so 'difficult'. However, in the end, her question resulted in a new admission policy, and a change in the treatment of the patients who were admitted.

Questions arise when there is a breakthrough in what was self-evident, either by ourselves or by the world around us. Questions can sometimes make us so restless that they stop us sleeping, and can also continue to occupy us all day long.

Once questions have been raised, you cannot really ignore them. They 'work' in you. A real question, which is given true recognition, will sooner or later lead to a new development.

In doing biography work, the self-evident nature of your daily life gets interrupted. Such reflection offers a point of rest in the course of your life. You stand still for a moment and ask yourself a question. The most profound questions which have concerned people for thousands of years have never changed. Who am I? What am I doing here? What do I want to do with my life?

Connecting the question with yourself

Many questions which you hear in daily life are questions for the sake of asking questions. They are interesting questions, clever questions, trick questions, polite questions and so on. In certain situations these may be useful, but they are of no importance in stimulating and continuing your personal development. For this purpose you need questions which are anchored more deeply. True personal questions originate in the emotions.

Feelings are concerned with and give indications for the breakthrough of what is self-evident. The balance between our inner world (containing our views, ideas, values, norms and intentions) and the outer world is disturbed. The emotion which arises may be a vague sense of restlessness, a vague feeling of lacking something, or an overwhelming fear with all sorts of degrees in between.

In his book, *Oordeelsvorming in groepen (Arriving at Judgements in Groups)*, our former colleague, Lex Bos, pointed out that this emotional signal can point in two different directions. It can be a feeling of surprise and wonder about what 'is', about what exists. This feeling leads to questions aimed at 'knowing', at 'insight'. For example: 'Why is it that I keep going in a job when I know perfectly well that it is a failure?' However, it may also be a sense of imprisonment. This leads to questions for the future: 'What should I do now that my company no longer needs me?' These questions are not so much aimed at gaining an insight, as at a choice which has to be made, a decision which has to be taken.

In our biography work, we are concerned with both sorts of questions. Most people who start on this sort of self-study are looking at the future and have questions about choices. But in order to make the right choice, you also need insight: insight into who you are, what suits you, what you are able to do. Questions in this direction, described by Lex Bos as the 'path of knowledge', are also part of this.

To reiterate: every question is based on a feeling. This feeling has to be formulated. This can be a difficult task, because you have to translate a personal experience into universal words and concepts.

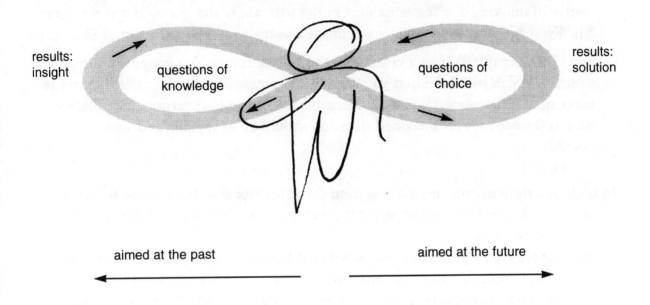

results:
insight

questions of
knowledge

questions of
choice

results:
solution

aimed at the past

aimed at the future

There is a tension between these. On the one hand, you may become stuck in your feelings so that you cannot ask a clear question. On the other hand, you may become too separate from the original feeling, so that the question becomes too general and abstract.

Try to formulate the question so clearly that you can work on it, while at the same time it remains linked to the original feeling which produced it. In order to achieve this balance, you often need a partner to help you formulate your question. This should be someone who listens, and 'reflects' what he hears in your words.

It is hardly ever possible to come up with the right question straightaway. What do we mean by the 'right' question? The question is always a provisional question. It often changes in the course of the process of self-study. Or you may discover another question behind the original question which may be even more important for you. However, the initial question should be clear enough for you to be able to start working on it.

In working on your biography, this initial question acts as a support. The biographical material of your life is infinite. You could easily get lost in it by constantly seeing new interesting aspects and connections. However, the question should keep you on track. It indicates the direction in which you are searching and with which you are examining your life. It also acts as a magnet, attracting the relevant information for your question.

Connecting the question to specific situations

At first, a question arises in my inner world. Even if it has been formulated very clearly – e.g., 'Why is it that in every new job, I come into conflict with my boss after a few years?' – it still concerns a more or less isolated experience in your own soul. In order to start working on the question, it is important to relate the question to the outside world, i.e., to specific situations in which the question applies. This happens in two ways, which we also use spontaneously in everyday life:

– You connect the question with specific situations from the past. In doing this, it is a matter of thinking of a few situations in the past where the question was relevant. Then you describe these situations in images, so that you produce a sort of film image.

– You relate the question to a vision or image of the future. You imagine a future situation which will develop if you do not take any action, but just allow things to happen; in other words, if you allow the outside world to determine completely what will happen. This imagined situation should be as specific and visual as possible.

In both descriptions, you are moving from the inner world to the outside world. Because the descriptions use images, others can see the situation and tell you what strikes them about it.

It is not always easy to make this movement from the inner to the outer world. You may have shut yourself up in your inner world, because of the emotions which accompany your experiences. It may also be the case that relating your question to specific situations evokes a resistance in you because it inevitably means stepping back, being objective, looking at the situation through another's eyes. Sometimes it is easier to express your emotions. Perhaps you should do this first, because this will probably give you a clearer view of the facts, circumstances and actions concerned.

Others may be able to help you to describe specific situations, by asking questions which 'clarify' the picture. Furthermore, by indicating what strikes him, in the situations that were described, the other person may be able to shed a surprising light on your question. This may result in the first shift in the question you have asked.

By linking the question to specific situations in the past, you gain a better insight into what is basically happening, and by linking it to a vision of the future, you can strengthen the will to work on it.

To summarize, the art of living with questions consists of:

- breaking through the self-evident nature of your life or of the events taking place around you and posing a question;

- allowing the question simply 'to be', without immediately looking for an answer or a solution;

- linking the question to your personal experience and not allowing it to 'disappear' in an abstract formulation;

- linking the question to specific situations in the past and in the future.

Exercise tip

Choose someone in your own environment and observe them attentively at particular moments for a week. Then ask yourself: what is his or her question? Do the same thing with one or two other people.

Describing in images

Fortunately, the world is organized in such a way that a dew drop on a blade of grass can reflect it.

Harry Mulisch

Images appeal to the imagination. According to an old Chinese proverb, a well-chosen image says more than a thousand words. But you do have to understand the image. Images from dreams, from effigies, in paintings or in stone all have their own language with which you can trace their meaning. You could say that it is possible to distinguish subsidiary languages in imagery, just as English has many 'subsidiary' languages, such as the language of newspapers, legal language, computer language, builders' language, management language, medical language, the language of personnel, and of developers. Which language do we mean when we talk about 'describing using images'?

This workshop makes a great deal of use of images in the memory and vision of the future. The examination of your life, after all, concerns experiences from the past and wishes or desires for the future. In order to discuss situations from the past, you need memory. In order to look at future situations you use your imagination.

In a 'description in images', you relate the specific situations in such a way that others can see it as though they are looking at a photograph or a film on which the outside world is recorded.

The advantage of a photograph is that the image stands still and you can look at all the aspects: the place, the objects and the people. It is a matter of their appearance, their position in the image and their interrelationship. The added value of a film is the change over time: movement, action and interaction, what takes place consecutively and what takes place simultaneously. This interaction also reveals the culture of the organization or the type of conduct of the people present. This is expressed in a verbal and non-verbal way. In a description using images, you can use all the organs of perception, such as eyes, ears and nose. An example of a description using images is given below.

An example

'The door is red... a shiny, peppery red... It is always closed. I press down the aluminium knocker and step inside. This is the staff room. In front of me, there is a table across the room, 4 metres long, more than a metre wide, and with 16 chairs standing around it, without armrests. I am looking at the backs of Henry and William... they are leaning forward, talking loudly to a deputy head... opposite Henry. Maria and Irene are also talking at the head of the table, to the left of Henry. Two rather older colleagues are sitting in front of me to the right, next to the deputy head on the other side of the table and are also taking part in the discussion.

When I open the door, the deputy head looks up and cries, 'Hi young man!' Wait a minute, this deputy head always introduces himself like this: 'Mr. P.J.L.M. van Vledermuis, call me Peter'. He is a rather small man with dark curls, light coloured spectacles, a pale face and a bit of a belly. He slouches in his chair. 'Well, young man, have you washed behind your ears? You won't get far like that you know, with the girls! Just look at that.' His small, grey pupils check me out from top to toe. The others burst out laughing and turn towards me. Seven pairs of eyes examining me from top to toe and the remarks follow in such quick succession that all I hear, is 'Well, well, what a youngster, and that for 5A'.

This was a famous class at the time, one of the most difficult, and after lunch I would have my first lesson in that class. I was not looking forward to it. I had not had much experience, and it was true that I was wearing a sloppy sweater; it made me feel comfortable.

As their eyes examined my clothes, I saw some of my colleagues looking rather shocked at the other end of the table. There it became rather quiet. The other deputy head is seated at this end of the table to my right. This deputy, John, has big blue eyes, slightly greying hair and long slender fingers. He sits up straight, peeling an orange.

In the middle of the table, on the other side, sits Rob. When everyone laughs, he moves his things to one side and passes to the next chair... so that there is a place free to his right seen from my point of view.

I look one by one into each of the seven pairs of eyes in front of me and think, 'Wow, you're a lot of fun', and I walk to the right, to the place next to Rob. 'Shall I get you a cup of coffee?' he asks. 'No, thank you', I answer, 'I'll do it myself'. Then I walk behind Peter to the coffee jug on the side board... to the left of the door as you come in.'

Thus a description using images is like a film of a memory or of a situation in the future. In this way you bring a memory to you. You bring the past closer, and a vision of the future can be created from your free imagination. In your imagination, you make fantasy become concrete. Describing the situations in the present tense is a good way of achieving this. It helps the images to come alive, here and now, for yourself and for your listeners.

Describing things in images does not happen automatically. It requires concentration and a conscious effort. You create an image of the future which does not yet exist. Raking up an image from your memory can also be difficult. You try to answer questions such as: 'What did I see? What did I hear? What did I smell?' If the memory has disappeared, this means searching and digging. If the memory is still very much alive, it means choosing and selecting what is important. If you say too little, the situation will not come alive and the listeners will not see it. If you say too much, the listeners will lose sight of its significance, for example, its relationship to your question. In the example given above, the speaker's question was, 'How do you integrate two cultures after a merger?'

What results do you achieve with this?

- As a speaker, you learn to distinguish between the actual situation and the emotions, views and opinions which the situation evokes in you. By describing in concrete terms what is happening outside you, the interconnection between the inner world and the outside world becomes looser. You introduce a measure of objectivity into your situation and this gives you more freedom to steer a course.

- By describing a situation in images for someone else, you give the other person the space to make his own evaluations.

- You do more justice to things by describing them factually, irrespective of what you think of them.

- You practise achieving an objective interest in the situations you find yourself in. By saying that someone is wearing a tie, you become aware that he usually walks around without a tie, or of the sort of ties he usually wears.

- By describing things in images, you also practise thinking in images.

Stumbling blocks in describing a situation

If we ask someone to describe his situation, we often hear comments such as:

- 'Look, there are a few things you ought to know first. We just had a reorganization, with a new management structure, and a few divisions. This was necessary because immediately after the merger, the number of pupils increased rapidly and so the number of teachers did as well. In addition, buildings were being converted and new buildings were being added, so that...' and so on.

- 'After the merger I had been given a number of hours for coordinating and supervising the integration of the cultures of the two organisations. My central question was and still is, how do you do that?'

- 'It was a terrible time. They tormented me, tried to get me down because I did not always do their thing. The others were no help at all. They did not lift a finger to put me at my ease. It was a hopeless case. What could I do there?'

The first statement is full of explanations, elucidations and background, the second statement is full of generalities and the third statement is full of emotions and judgements. But the listener does not see anything. It is only when the speaker is forced to choose one or two characteristic situations and describe them in concrete terms that he finds an anchor for his statements.

By describing something in images, the situation becomes very ordinary. All sorts of fine ideas, such as 'I supervise and co-ordinate the integration after the merger' become irrelevant: 'Two styles of relationships round the coffee table and me in the middle.' Often describing one situation is enough for this, because that one dewdrop reflects much more. You just have to stand still a moment to see it. Some people have a strong resistance to this, to standing still and looking, or to the ordinary, factual aspects of things. This is a handicap for describing situations in images. However, a handicap is also always the starting block for a new skill.

Exercise tip

At regular intervals, try to describe in images a situation from the day you have just had.

Task 2: Agreements

Co-operation is based on agreements. Making clear, unambiguous agreements and keeping to them leads to mutual trust and is the basis for every form of productive co-operation. How do you deal with agreements in your work?

For yourself

Examine two situations:

1 For a number of agreements which you made in the past, describe the way in which these came about. Do this by looking, for example, at the following questions.
- Who took the initiative?
- How 'strong' was your inner decision?
- Were you able to keep to the agreements? If not, why not?
- What do your colleagues think of the way in which you deal with agreements?
- How do you react if other people do not keep to agreements?

2 Look at your diary and your work load for the next four to six months and see how you can work on this book during that period. You should count on 150 to 200 hours, including the meetings with your speaking partners. Examine the following points.
- When can you make time for this?
- What arrangements will you have to make in your work and in your private life to make enough time?
- What will you have to leave out, put aside or postpone?

Practical instructions

The above questions are not intended to be answered as a questionnaire, but should be seen as suggestions for your own study.

The *arrangements in the past,* are not concerned so much with official agreements, but above all agreements about working with others on a day-to-day basis. Look at the specific situations in which the agreements were made. Prepare to describe these in images.

For the *agreements for this workshop,* you should imagine how you wish to achieve these in the most specific terms. Take your diary and set aside some time. In this way you will reach an inner decision that is as strong as possible.

In dialogue

Not every task has to be discussed with others after the work you do by yourself. How many tasks you wish to discuss together depends in the first instance on the amount of time you want to spend on this together. Decide together which tasks you will discuss and which you will not. (As you go through them, you may find that, on closer consideration, there is a particular task that you do want to discuss together. In this case do not hesitate to adjust the agreements.)

Practice has shown that it is important to discuss at least a number of the tasks. The tasks for which it is not absolutely necessary are introduced with the words: 'If you discuss this task together...'

The discussion on the task *Agreements* consists of 2 parts:

1 *Agreements in the past*

If you discuss this task together, everyone takes turns to describe the situation(s) they have chosen from the past, while the others listen and help. They follow this procedure:

- The speaker outlines one or more situations without adding any explanations. The others allow the images to affect them without responding, and they make a note of what struck them about these images.

- The others recount their impressions one after the other. The speaker writes them down without commenting and tries to understand the impressions (she may ask the others to clarify what they said).

- The speaker responds by saying whether she recognizes the impressions, and whether they are close to her or far away from her.

2 *Agreements with regard to this workbook*

- The speaker describes how she wants to achieve working on the tasks in this book (using images which are as clear as possible). The others listen without commenting, compare this summary with the previous one (about agreements in the past), and try to gauge how firmly the speaker is linked to her plans for what she wants to achieve. When they have finished, they make notes.

- Then the listeners take turns to say what they thought. The speaker makes a note of their contributions without commenting on them, but she may ask questions if there is anything that is not clear to her.

- Finally, the speaker responds by saying what she recognizes in these contributions.

Practical instructions

As the speaker, you should be as factual as possible, describing situations in images wherever possible. As the listener, you should withhold your own views and judgements as much as possible. Try to find what is essential or characteristic in the images used by the speaker, and tell her what you found.

Rounding off

When you have written down what you wish to remember, you can now make agreements together about the meetings.

Where am I?

In this stage, you will map out your present situation on the basis of your question. This is always in a dynamic balance between the past and the future. Your working situation is the key theme of this book, though it cannot be seen separately from the rest of your life.

Tasks

3 My mood about my present working life
4 Between yesterday and tomorrow
5 My working life, beginning and end
6 How I spend my time
7 My clients
8 My boss says
9 Results and learning so far
10 My question again

Explanations

Working with colour
Characterization
Support exercises
Development

Support exercise

Development

Task 3: My mood about my present working life

Moods often have a complex emotional background. In order to prevent yourself from becoming trapped in a mood, it is a good idea to express these moods and examine them. This allows you to see them objectively and to make them instrumental. Other people can be important in helping you to do this.

For yourself

Express your mood about your present working life in colour on a sheet of drawing paper.

Practical instructions

Use a blank page or take a separate piece of drawing paper, the soft coloured crayons and the stick of charcoal. Experiment with the colours on a piece of rough paper. Before you start, concentrate on the feeling which you have when you imagine your working situation.

Do not think too much when you are carrying out this task. Trust in your hands and the spontaneous choice of colours. Allow whatever surfaces to come. You do not have to make a 'work of art'.

Avoid specific images, such as a house, tree, animal, or other signs and symbols. Work freely, with movement, so that you do not construct the image or work towards a preconceived result. Trust in your feeling.

Explanation: Working with colour (p. 42)

In dialogue

Everyone takes turns to show the image of their mood, and the others look at it and characterize it. They adopt the following procedure.

1 The person who made the image of his mood shows it to the others without explaining it. The others allow it to affect them, without commenting on it, and write down what they think is characteristic about this image. We call this 'characterization'.

Explanation: Characterisation (p. 44)

2 The viewers now describe the characteristics they saw in the image. The person who drew the image listens to these characteristics, writes them down, and tries to

understand them in terms of the image he made. If necessary, he asks the others to show the place in the image to which a characteristic refers.

3 The person who drew the image tells the others if he recognizes the characteristics, whether they are close to him or not, and which characteristics surprise him.

Practical instructions

For the person who drew the image:

– When you show your image, do not explain how it came about, what you think of it or what it means. This will stop the others from responding in a natural way and deprives you of the possibility of hearing something new.

– Listen carefully to the content of the characteristics and their relationship to the image of your mood. Ask questions if you do not understand the characteristic 'in relation to the image'. Take particular note of unknown or new aspects. Don't be too ready to say: 'That seems more or less familiar to me.'

– Write down the characteristics – in actual words, if possible, so that you can read through them again at a later stage – including the characteristics which seem strange, inaccurate or unpleasant! It is quite possible that these will be of more use to you than the 'familiar', 'correct' or 'attractive' characteristics.

For the viewer:

– When you look at the image, withhold your views, explanations, and analysis. Allow the image to have an effect on you and ask yourself, 'What are the characteristics and individual aspects of this image?'

– Write down your characteristics straightaway so that you do not lose your original impressions when the other viewer talks about his impressions.

– Give equal value to the characteristics of the other viewer.

– Use your own formulation, even if it is similar to that of another viewer. Make sure that you can show the part of the image to which your characteristic relates, if you are asked to do so.

– Do not force your characterization onto the person who drew the image of the mood.

Rounding off

Write down in your Logbook what you wish to remember.

Working with colour

Colour and mood

There are many ways in which you can express your mood. The most common way is in a verbal form. You tell a friend or a colleague what matters to you. You describe the trip to Canada which you might be hoping to make at last in two years' time. Or you complain about the absurd policy on promotion in your company. The other person hears what you are saying. However, it is not only your words which express your mood; often, the sound of your voice says much more. Other non-verbal signals such as gestures, mimicry, and the way in which you move your shoulders or your body, also play an important role. The listener observes these consciously or unconsciously, and responds to them.

In order to become aware of your own mood, you could keep a record of the way in which you express it, for example, with audiovisual means, and then look at these. Another way is to work with the means used by an artist, such as colour.

There is a direct relationship between colours and moods. An orangey-red sun, surrounded by pale yellow bits of cloud against a light blue sky, or leaden clouds, above greyish-blue water and dark green fields – these images evoke very different moods. Your feelings respond immediately to different colours or shades. Conversely, it is possible to convert your moods and feelings directly into colours. It does not take much time to produce this sort of image of a mood. However, it produces a permanent result which you can then examine at your leisure any time you wish. That is why we opted for this form of expression.

For many people, the use of colour is something new, a method that they have not used since they were toddlers. (For the odd amateur painter, who is used to working with colour, the procedure used here may still be quite new.) Therefore, the request to sit down at the table with a sheet of paper and soft crayons can easily evoke a response of hesitation, shyness or even irritation. These responses are quite understandable, particularly in view of the achievement and result-orientated culture we live in. Where the medium of colour is used in this workbook, it is not a matter of your performance or of producing a 'work of art'. It is a matter of expressing your mood in a perhaps rather unconventional way. You can work with any results that are produced.

Procedure

Producing a colour image is based on spontaneity: your feelings and hands do the work. You start somewhere on the paper with one colour. You see what is created and then you continue with this, or introduce a different movement. Or you take another colour and evoke a new mood with this, a different movement within the image. In this way a spontaneous colour image is created. The process is obstructed by clearly defined representations, ideas of specific objects or situations. You work with areas of colour, different depths of colour, and mixtures of colour and movement.

Red, yellow and blue are the basic colours (primary colours) with which you can make many other colours. Red and yellow make orange, yellow and blue make green, blue and red make purple. It is possible to create countless shades. Red over yellow produces a different orange from yellow over red. You can also mix the colours with the black charcoal stick.

Soft crayons

In technical terms, the ultramarine blue is the weakest crayon. If you press too hard, it will easily pulverise. If you leave the crayon in its blue wrapper, the chances of this happening are smaller. If you want a broader area to work on, you can take off the paper wrapper and move the crayon flat across the paper. You can also produce beautiful effects by wiping the colour over the paper with your fingers. This means that the colour is less bright.

Do not wipe any powder you have spilt on clothes or the carpet with a wet cloth, but blow it away or vacuum it up. In fact, it easily washes out in the washing machine.

You can fix your completed work with hair spray or with a special fixative.

Characterization

Characterizing is a skill, which can be useful to you, perhaps even more so than describing things in images. When you describe a situation in images, you are practising to get a real interest in those situations and what is happening, while in characterization, you try to define the characteristic or typical feature of a situation or an object.

For example, how would you characterize a tree? You might like trees, or you might not. You might think them useful, or picturesque, or not. You might think that a beech tree is more beautiful than a birch tree, but this says more about you than about the tree. You can also perceive the tree in very factual terms and describe it in images. In characterization you go one step further.

For example, if you look at a birch tree and a beech tree as mature individual trees, you will notice that they have very different characters. Try to formulate some of the individual qualities of these two trees, and you might arrive at the following characteristics:

The birch	*The beech*
airy and light	quiet strength
delicate and playful	protective
modest presence	firmly rooted in the earth
	clear presence

Characterization always has a personal aspect. That is why not everyone will immediately recognize our characteristics of the birch tree and the beech tree. Nevertheless, it should be possible in principle, because the characteristic feature is in the object you are looking at; so that others should also be able to find it. This applies all the more when you master the art of characterizing things and you can identify what you see better. For example, what do you see in a birch tree and a beech tree?

In a *birch tree,* we look at the almost straight trunk with its white bark, which is interrupted here and there and curls at the edges. Then we look at the delicate ends of the twigs which hang down slightly and the small, light-coloured leaves that the wind plays with. The crown of leaves is transparent: the light falls through it and you can see the sky behind. A birch tree never stands alone and does not immediately strike one between the other trees and bushes – only its white trunk attracts attention.

In a *beech tree,* we look at the powerful roots and the trunk rising up from them, often straight and round, with vertical ribs and fairly smooth bark. The leaves are dark green or reddish-brown. They are almost motionless, even in the wind. The crown is dense and sometimes forms a beautiful round dome. Under, it is pleasant to sit for a while on the roots by the trunk. It is rather dark and pleasantly cool in summer. Nothing grows under a beech tree, and a beech tree growing alone in the woods is very striking.

Characterizing an image or story

Apart from describing things in images, characterization is an activity that comes up frequently in this workbook. One person tells a story, the other characterizes it and helps the speaker to find the characteristic aspects of what he has related. For example, in the description given earlier by the young teacher entering the staff room during a break *(p. 28)*. The speaker was told that this description contained the following characteristics, amongst others.

– About the situation: insecurity and security, challenge and a sense of calm.

– About his position: in the middle, just over the midline on the calm side of the table. He was particularly surprised by the last characteristic. He saw himself as an enterprising person who sought challenges. His first reaction was to say: 'Moreover, Rob moved to the left so I had to sit on that side.'

One situation – what can that tell you? If you do not give it any further thought, it doesn't tell you anything. On the other hand, if you ask yourself what this apparently coincidental event means, you may stumble upon something that is characteristic of you. That is what happened in this case: the speaker discovered that he did seek challenges, but hesitated in the face of the insecurity related to this. He felt at home in quiet, secure situations, but at the same time he felt that he wanted to escape from the tedium which this entailed. By becoming aware of this dilemma, he saw the 'macho' side of being enterprising and seeking challenges in relative terms. What he thought he was already, now became a more realistic aim for his own development.

Exercise tip

For a week, look at a different plant, shrub or tree every day and try to characterize what you see.

A number of tasks in this workbook have a non-verbal result, such as the 'mood image' in colour. It may be an unpleasant prospect to think that others will look at the results of your work and characterize it. What will they do with the feelings you express? How careful will they be with these feelings? Will your feelings be analyzed, judged and explained?

There is certainly a danger of this happening. You fall into this trap if you respond to the mood image shown in Illustration 3 *(after p. 280)* with a interpretive comment like: 'A typically divided personality,' or 'You are struggling with sombre feelings,' 'An introvert,' and so on.

Characterization is aimed at avoiding this. A characteristic is bound to a particular place and time and is restricted to what is seen here and now. Characteristics are not permanent truths, unless the maker recognizes them in several places in his life. Even then, they say something only about the past.

Characterization is also clearly an individual activity. Everyone is struck by different things in the same image. In this sense it is subjective, i.e., linked to a particular person. But at the same time, it is an exercise in objectivity. The observer tries to see and to formulate through his own eyes what is expressed in the maker's mood image. The characteristics that are found may be very different, but they can also be similar or point in the same direction.

For example, the following characteristics were given for the mood image (Ill. 3):

'Limited and divided; different layers; not enclosed; three directions: from top to bottom, from left to right, and from front to back; strength and delicacy; light as a background, dark in the foreground; a place which glows but also burns; determined and seeking.'

'For me, there is a striking tension, on the one hand, between the fresh, light spots which seem young, and the black outline with the division through the middle, on the other hand. There is also tension between the fiery spark by the light spot on the left and the veiled area on the right.'

When the person who made this image heard these characteristics she responded, 'Yes, I recognize most of this. I'm stuck in all sorts of ways, at home and at work. This stops me from actively searching. And yet that is what I should do really, because there is a threat that I will be dismissed. I don't want to be because I'm very close to a number of people and involved in the work. That red area is pain rather than anger, after the last discussion with my boss. What surprises me is the light, fresh background. Perhaps that is right, but 'determined and seeking' certainly is not.'

Exercise tip

Characterize the mood image referred to (Ill. 3) three times, for example, at intervals of a week.

The rules for characterizing

The most important rules in characterizing are:

- Keep to the story that you hear, the image you are shown.

- Consequently, do not extend the characteristic to the maker or speaker, and do not say: 'You are…' or 'It's typical of you…', and so on. Of course, it is possible to say something about the maker as a maker in the way he told the story or the speaker as a figure in his own story, e.g., 'It strikes me, that in this situation, you…'

- Name the most characteristic things. Try to formulate these briefly, so that they have the character of the title of a book or a film. Even if this does not always work, it is worth trying.

- Do not focus on the skill of the maker or the speaker; it is not a matter of how beautiful the work is, or how witty or fascinating the story.

- Do not start discussing whether the characteristic is correct, though you can discuss whether it is a characteristic and not a judgement, for example.

- Leave the person who told the story or made the image free to accept the characteristic or not, or to use it in their study.

Summary

Characterizing starts with observing without any preconceptions. You take the image that you see or the story that you hear for what it is. You take it in as though it is air that you are breathing in. Then you recreate the image inside you and allow it to go through you again. When you do this, you withhold your own opinions, such as 'ugly' or 'beautiful', 'agreement' or 'disagreement.' This results in a turning point. You become aware that you are responding to certain aspects with your feelings. It is as though you feel, 'Hey, that's special!' or 'What's happening there?' Your attention moves away from the outside world to what is happening inside you. This is the turning point. Then you try to put this experience into words. You move from the experience to the image and back, seeking for the way to formulate it. You explore the connection with words. The characteristic you discover and the words you use to express it say something about you and something about the object outside.

This is an important point. Characterization is not a purely subjective activity. It is rather like wine tasting. The experienced wine taster distinguishes and describes true qualities. He looks and smells, takes a sip, tastes and then swallows the wine and tastes the aftertaste. Essentially this is the same process as characterizing a tree, a story or a mood image on paper. Distinguishing and naming the characteristics is an activity of the 'self'. The self observes, separates itself from opinions such as delicious or disgusting and describes the true character of the wine. This activity of the self requires a conscious effort.

Task 4: Between yesterday and tomorrow

In life, your perspective constantly alternates between two directions: memories and visions of the future. You determine the shape of the present with both these orientations. The past contains your successes and your disappointments, your experiences: your baggage. For the future, you have plans, desires, expectations, and perhaps fears. The course of your life develops between the two. Often you may not be clearly conscious of either your memories or your desires.

For yourself

1 *Seven years ago*

Go back in your memory and look at your working life seven years ago, using the following questions. Think of more questions yourself. Trust in the things that occur to you and try to recall some specific memories as you search.

- Where were you working at the time?

- With whom were you working?

- What happened? What was important?

- What were you doing? What challenges were facing you?

- What were your feelings about all this?

- Finally, was the question you are working on now – the question for your study – relevant at that time? If so, how? Did you have any other questions? If so, which ones?

2 *Seven years ahead*

Now put yourself seven years into the future and imagine your working life with the help of the following questions. Again, think of your own questions as well. Trust in whatever occurs to you and try, using your imagination, to achieve a concrete vision of your future working life.

- Where will you be?

- With whom will you be working?

- What's happening? What's important?

- What are you doing?

- What are the challenges in your work?

- What are your thoughts about all this?

- And finally, what will have happened with your present question? Will it be relevant? If so, how? Do you see any other questions arising? If so, which ones?

Practical instructions

For 2: It may be that the point of early retirement or retirement is not far off. This means a future without a permanent job. In this situation it is a good idea to work on this 'hole' in your life, to consciously consider the new situation. Of course, 'work' can also be considered separately from income. If necessary, you could call it 'activity'. What will you do in the future, with and for other people? What is important for you in this? And so on.

As we have said before, you should not allow yourself to be hampered by objections, such as, 'How can I know what the future will be like?' It is a matter of trying to produce visions of the future with your concrete imagination.

The questions we gave as examples are not all intended to be answered exactly. They are given as suggestions for creating images. Perhaps you will be able to find different, more suitable questions yourself.

The intention is that you can describe these two situations together in factual and concrete terms in no more than seven minutes.

In dialogue

The roles in the discussion again divide into 'speaking' and 'listening and characterizing'. Everyone has a turn telling her story. The two situations which are described are characterized separately, but the differences between the two are also mentioned.

Practical instructions

An image is easier to characterize if it is told factually. The more powerful and succinct the characteristics, the more effective they will be.

Rounding off

Finally, write down what you want to remember. In doing this, make a note of the difference in the experience of describing the past and the future. What is your mood when you focus on the one, and when you focus on the other?

Task 5: My working life, beginning and end

The way in which you started your working life often has a great influence on the questions which you encounter later on in your work. Equally important are the expectations, hopes and desires which you have with regard to what you want to achieve in your work. At the end of your working life, these will also count in your evaluation of that period. How did you start and what did you want to achieve by the end?

For yourself

Focus on three situations: your *first work experience,* the *end of your working life* and your *present working situation.* Prepare to describe these situations in images.

1 *First work experience*
Go back in your memory to your first work experience. Describe it in images as clearly as possible in your logbook with the help of the following questions:

- How old were you then?

- In what environment did you have this experience?

- Who was involved?

- What happened?

- How did you respond with your feelings and thoughts?

- What did you want from this situation?

2 *The end of your working life*
Imagine that you are retiring, and that a more or less formal speech is given upon your retirement. First, write down what you would like to be said. Mention the things which you have achieved between now and the time of retirement and that you can look back at with a certain degree of pride and satisfaction. Describe these in the most concrete terms possible.

3 *Present working situation*
Now focus on your present working situation.

- What do you recognize in your present profession, job and organization in connection with your first work experience?

- What possibilities do you see in your present working situation for what you still want to achieve? Or what is necessary to make this possible?

Practical instructions

For situation 1: Your first work experience
The work you have experienced may differ considerably. We give two examples.

'It was November 1957. I was twenty years old and had just left military service as the reserve second lieutenant. I started working for a large industrial company as an assistant in the personnel department. I did not have a clearly defined task, and I had to learn the job in personnel by being prepared to do whatever was necessary. I ended up in the personnel office working with four employees who were all much older than me, and the head of department. The desks of the other employees, who did simple administrative work (work clothes, coupons, bus transport and dentists' cards) were opposite each other. The head of department's desk was placed diagonally behind them. When he wasn't there, the employees would start talking or reading the newspaper, but it quickly disappeared into the drawer when the head of department returned. I knew my place in relation to this head of department, who had been a captain in the army. As regards the other employees, I didn't know if they were above me or below me. I didn't know how you could see this, as you can in the army. Should I address them formally with a title, or informally by their surnames as they did amongst themselves?'

'I am ten years old and I am kneeling on the lawn, about 20 square yards, between our house and the church next door. The tropical sun is burning my bare back. It's after the siesta, about 4 o' clock. I am cutting the grass with a long knife made of sharpened bamboo as I have often seen the local boys do. I want to be able to do this quickly and skilfully like them. But everything hurts, my wrists, my arms, my back. Behind me there is a small stretch of short grass, and in front of me, an endless stretch of long grass. I don't want to give up, because I don't want to lose face with the local boys – or my father, who thinks you should finish whatever you start. The sweat is dripping down my face, which is not unpleasant. The whitewashed walls seem to be laughing harshly at me.'

For situation 2: The end of my working life
For the sake of convenience, we have chosen the moment of retirement as the end of the working life. This does not have to mean that you do not work afterwards, but it does mean that you conclude a particular section of your social career.

A common and understandable reaction is, 'I don't want a speech or any of those formalities; I'll simply shut the door behind me and go home. Why should I do this task?'

But whichever way you approach it – whether in an extrovert way, or very quietly – saying farewell is essential. If you do it properly, it gives you freedom to do something new. When you say farewell, it is important to look back at the period behind you. What did you do, and what are you leaving behind? Are you satisfied with it? And, as this moment is still in front of you, what would you like to do to ensure that you will be able to look back with satisfaction? These are the questions with which these tasks are concerned.

In dialogue

The roles in the discussion again consist of 'speaking' and 'listening and characterizing'. Everyone has a turn to speak. The two situations that are described are characterized separately, but the differences between the two are also characterized.

Rounding off

Finally, write down what you wish to remember.

See Part II, Backgrounds: My work and I (p. 260)

Support exercises: introduction

This workbook contains five support exercises, the first of which follows on the next page. These exercises, which use methods from the visual arts, have a double purpose.

- They employ a number of skills which are extremely valuable for biography work – and, in fact, for a creative approach to your life. These skills are: thinking in developmental processes, observing the past, being active in determining the course of your life, imagining the future and making plans.

- They make biography work a more vivid and profound activity so that you are working with these skills in a non-verbal way.

You develop skills through repetition. Conscious repetition is practice. Practice produces art.

The skills we are referring to here are inner skills. Therefore the exercises are aimed at an inner learning process and not at the sort of skill which results in 'artistic' achievement.

Repeated practice requires motivation. The repetition of the support exercises can be an important aid to your study, but is not necessary. However, we do recommend that you do every exercise at least once.

The things which you work with in the support exercises are black and white, colour and clay. These produce permanent results, which you can examine at your leisure and at any time you like.

Support exercise:
Development

For yourself

Take a sheet of drawing paper (A3) with the short side towards you, and get a stick of charcoal and a putty rubber ready.

Make sure you are sitting comfortably, and try to relax. Breathe calmly, breathing out thoroughly.

Now read the following description and note the inner image this evokes in you.

Image

It is autumn. The seeds of trees are lying on the damp ground. The leaves are starting to fall. They swirl round and lie still. The seeds rest under this blanket. It is dark. Nature falls quiet and is cold. Then, when the sun warms up again, the seed comes to life. It swells up, breaks open and the roots penetrate the earth to the side and downwards. Then a stem rises up, through the blanket of leaves towards the light. Alternating bursts of growth push the roots into the earth and the stems into the air. The stem produces sideshoots and turns into a trunk. The tree grows, rests in winter, grows and rests and grows until it is fully grown and flowers and produces more seeds.

Hold on to this image for a moment and allow it to have an effect on you.

- Now take the stick of charcoal and use it across the whole width of the paper, starting at the top. Make the paper gradually darker and darker: as light as possible at the top and as dark as possible at the bottom. If it doesn't work the first time, start again from the top.

- When the darkness at the bottom of the paper is dense enough, create a small light spot in the middle of the dark area. You can do this by pressing the putty rubber on the black and then removing it with a rotating movement. Make sure that there is enough space between it and the bottom edge of the paper. From this light spot, work alternately downwards/sideways and upwards. By erasing the black in the dark area with the putty rubber, you create roots. In the lighter areas, you create the trunk, the branches and so on, with the stick of charcoal.

- When your tree is fully grown, you have finished. Do not give in to a tendency to make stylistic improvements.

Practical instructions

Before starting, read the account of the image described above again.

When you start work, trust in your hands. Get away from the feeling that you have to make a 'work of art'. Allow the image to emerge by following the process described above. Thus you should not have a preconceived idea of the final form that you are working towards. Trust your inner image of the growth and development of your tree to guide you as you work.

The charcoal stick may smudge, but it is easy to wash your hands.

In dialogue

Everyone shows their work in turn, and the others look at it and characterize it. After characterising the work, they discuss the following questions.

- How did you go about working on this? For example, did you manage to allow the image to develop? In other words, did the image develop of its own accord, step by step?

- With regard to the previous questions, what did you come across in yourself?

- Does this say anything about the way in which you conduct yourself in your working life?

- What does this mean for your question in your study?

This exercise relates to the following skills or inner abilities:

- the ability to 'be moved' by a task;

- allowing an inner image to develop without fixing it in your imagination;

- working towards an end result through a process, i.e., allowing the end result to develop as you work;

- experiencing growth and development.

Explanation: Development (p. 62)

Rounding off

Finally, write down what you want to remember.

Examples of this exercise: Ill. 4 (after p. 280)

Development

Life is movement, and everything always changes.

Marten Toonder.

Time and change belong together. Life is change through time. In his book, *Phases,* Bernard Lievegoed says that life means that there is a pattern in this change. Growth is systematic change in which a living organism increases in size or weight. But an organism does not merely grow. At certain critical moments, the constant growth requires a restructuring of the organism's inner order. When this happens, Lievegoed refers to development. Thus development comprises growth, restructuring, growth. Restructuring means letting go of the old order, followed by a shorter or longer stage of uncertainty, during which a new order crystallizes with new possibilities of existence. Then the growth can continue again.

Here are some examples of development:

The tree. First, there is a seed, which is enclosed within itself, and which does not reveal the figure of a tree when you cut it open. This seed grows, swells up and breaks open. The stem and roots grow. Buds form on the stem as a new sort of seed. The leaves unfold from these buds. Then the growth goes on: stem, root, leaf – stem, root, leaf. The main stem becomes the trunk, the other stems become branches and twigs. Then more buds form and produce flowers. The flowers produce seeds, which are each the beginning of a new tree. Four times, there is growth and restructuring.

The butterfly. The egg 'restructures' itself into a caterpillar, which eats and grows, and eats and grows. Then the caterpillar spins itself a new sort of egg from which the butterfly emerges completely formed. Then the butterfly lays more eggs.

Man. After conception, the single cell egg multiplies into more cells. This cluster of cells restructures itself into three clearly distinct parts, and then these parts continue to grow, the fruit differentiates itself again, and so on, until the child is born. The child grows up to become sexually mature. Although the propensity is there at an early stage, it could be said that during puberty, the body is restructured. This 'new' body produces new fruit.

Development does not lead only to flowering. Decay is also part of development. Plants, animals and people are created and die. Growth and destruction – both these forces are present. In the course of seven years, all the cells in the human body are broken down and renewed. Nevertheless, you recognize the same person over the years. He or she has merely become older. You could say that they are marked by life. You can see this in the skin and in the figure as a whole. The body expresses the stage of development.

But a person is not merely a *body*. You also recognize the aging process in people's thoughts and attitude to life. They are formed by their experiences. What was once present as a seed has flowered. But once beautiful flowers also wither to enable new things to develop. Qualities which were present disappear, such as a sharp eye, the ability to analyze things quickly, or a strong talent for organization. This is often painful, but development is not possible without loss. Looking on the positive side, we refer to 'the mature personality', or say, 'Hasn't she become easy going?' This refers to something other than the body. We call it a person's psychological development, which does not have to run parallel with his physical development. Sometimes it may be far in advance, sometimes it follows slowly behind. We talk about people being, 'precocious', a child as being a 'little woman', 'a mother's boy', 'What a little old lady she is already', 'Goodness, how young he is still', and so on. The psychological development, or in other words, the development of the *soul*, has its own dynamics. Although the body and the soul are closely interconnected, they reveal different aspects.

Psychological development is also dependent to a large extent on a person's *spiritual strength,* his capacity to cope with setbacks, or to look beyond a given situation. You can see this as a task which applies throughout life, but becomes crucial after the age of forty when destructive forces gain the upper hand in the body. It appears that at about this age, a restructuring is necessary: from the spiritual strength which is supported by physical vitality, to a spiritual strength which finds its source of energy separately from this declining vitality. In old people you see very clearly which path they have taken. One goes towards physical destruction complaining; another refuses to be brought down by it, and may be present in a very stimulating way, despite his dwindling energy. In this sense, man's development is open-ended.

Thus, you can distinguish between a person's body, soul and spirit, each of which has its own development, but also influences the others.

Development is movement through the process of time. The human being develops through time as a traveller between creative and destructive forces, which interact with the environment. At the same time, a person has a constantly changing attitude to the phenomenon of time throughout his or her life. An inscription on the cathedral clock in Chester, England, reflects this as follows:

> *When as a child I laughed and wept,*
> *time crept.*
> *When as a youth I dreamed and talked,*
> *time walked.*
> *When I became a full grown man,*
> *time ran.*
> *And later as I older grew,*
> *time flew.*
> *Soon shall I find while travelling on,*
> *time gone.*
> *Will Christ have saved my soul by then?*
> *Amen.*

The relationship with your environment also develops between the creative and destructive forces, as does the relationship with yourself. An inferiority complex is an example of a destructive force, as is arrogance. Seeing yourself as someone with skills and darker sides and observing this as objectively as possible so that you can work on this basis, is an example of a creative force. You see yourself as a developing person, becoming who you are. That person is already present in the form of a seed.

> *'Life is movement from within.'*
>
> Thomas Aquinas

It is a matter of allowing what is in you to appear, to develop from the folds in which it is wrapped – unfolding yourself. This is referred to in

> *'the unused wings, folded in our hearts'*
>
> Christopher Fry

Exercise tip

Look, for example, at a snowdrop, a tulip or an autumn crocus, and try to imagine how the plant or the flower came into being. And go deeper; try to imagine how it will wither and die. Do this three times with different plants.

Task 6: How I spend my time

A person's priorities are evident from what he or she does. Suppose you put Monday morning aside for study. If this time is constantly used for doing other things instead, it is clear that the study was not so important to you. How do you really spend your time? And what choices are revealed by this?

For yourself

1 Take your diary, look at the past three weeks and summarize what you have done. What matters is what you actually did, not what you should have done, or planned to do. Also, make a note of the number of hours you spent on different activities. Ask yourself: were there times when I made a choice, and what was my decision?

2 Look at the summary and ask yourself what the way you spent your time has to do with your attitude towards your working life.

3 Do the same in relation to the question of your study.

Practical instructions

If the past three weeks were different from normal, for example, because you were on holiday, look at another three weeks not so long ago.

First, write down everything in a row: activities and hours. Then classify them in your own way, for example, meetings, dictating letters, administration, thinking as you walk around, job orientation discussions, telephone conversations, partner, children, household, friends, relaxation, sport, culture. Try to create clearly distinct categories. If you have too many categories, the overall picture becomes confused. If you have too few, it remains too vague.

Arrange the various activities under these categories, so that you get an idea of the real way in which you spent time in the past three weeks.

In dialogue

If you discuss this task together, follow the procedure, 'speaking and characterizing'. Everyone has a turn to speak.

Try to help the speaker to describe the situations she has chosen in images as clearly as possible. Characterize these in accordance with the usual procedure. In discussion with the other 'helper', then try to trace the views which are behind the speaker's choices. The speaker herself listens. Finally, the speaker says to what extent she recognizes the views that were put forward.

Practical instructions

As a speaker, try to be as factual as possible, using images wherever you can. As a listener, you characterize the image of the way in which the speaker spent her time and the way in which priorities were actually achieved. In addition, you try to listen to the speaker's considerations with a degree of empathy. What views are revealed by her choices? Examples of such views are: 'I have to talk to all the people in my department every week' or, 'Whatever happens, Tuesdays and Wednesdays are for the children' or 'one of the things about this job is that you have to take your work home', and so on.

Rounding off

Finally, write down what you want to remember.

Task 7: My clients

The clients' demands determine the organization's existence and that of the work that is done there. You always work for your clients, even if you cannot see them. In addition to external clients (those of the organization as a whole), there are also internal clients. These are all the people in the organization who 'do something' with the results of your work. Who are your clients, and what do they want from you?

For yourself

1 Look at what you are doing at the moment and for whom you are really working. Look at this in terms of the facts, and not in terms of your job description or in terms of your tasks. Who are your clients? What do they want from you? What do they need from you? Do you give them what they want? What do they do with the results of your efforts? Make a list of your clients in the order of their importance.

2 Look at the list you have drawn up and ask yourself how this is related to your attitude to your working life.

3 Do the same thing in relation to your question.

Practical instructions

By clients, we mean all those who are involved in the results of the work you do. These may be the clients of your organization, your department, work unit, your own central task, and subsidiary tasks. The more closely connected they are with your task, the better.

A client may ask you something explicitly, but his requests may also be implicit; an example of this is the daily delivery of the mail. People do not ask for this to be done, but they do expect it.

When you draw up your list of clients, try to imagine real people, i.e., not abstractions, such as the consumer, the management, the patient, the 'sale', etc. Who are these people? How old are they? What do they look like? What situation are they in? What are they doing? These sorts of questions will help you to form a concrete image of your clients.

It is possible that you have known people for a long time, but still know very little about them. Do not give up too quickly. The effort you have to make to give answers is important. The effect of these is that you become more aware of who your client is and what he needs from you.

In dialogue

If you discuss this task together, follow the procedure, 'speaking and characterizing'. It is a matter of clarifying the speaker's relationship to his work and to the people he works for.

Rounding off

Finally, write down what you wish to remember.

Task 8: My boss says

There are moments in your working life when you wonder how your job is still related to the person you are. Often, a factor which plays a part in this is what your boss is like as a manager; for example, whether she supports you or not, or whether she allows you to take the initiative or not.

What is the policy which determines your boss's actions? What is her view of the organization's future? How does she see you and your colleagues from this perspective? Like it or not, you can learn something from what your boss 'sees'.

For yourself

Ask your boss for a meeting and ask her, for example, the following questions.

– 'What developments do you anticipate in the next few years in relation to our clients? What do they need, and what can we do to meet this need?'

– 'What are the consequences of this for our organization : the processes in our work and financing, the working climate and the staff needed?'

– 'What does this mean for my job description?'

– 'What demands does this impose on me as a person?'

– 'What knowledge, skills and qualities do I have in this respect, and which ones will I have to acquire?

– 'How do you see my potential development as a person, and what are my career opportunities within our organization?'

Give her the questions in advance, so that she can prepare herself. Make sure you are prepared with regard to these questions as well. In the discussion, try not to defend yourself, but remain as open as possible to what your boss has to say.

Practical instructions

We are concerned here with the image your boss has of you and your working life. Of course, this comprises an opinion about you, and about what she considers necessary for the organization. Perhaps you are already aware of this in broad terms, for example, from job orientation or appraisal discussions. But how accurate are your views, and how certain are you about this? In our experience, the question 'What did she say in concrete terms?' often remains unanswered, or is answered in very general terms. The answers also often reveal an opinion only about the way you are performing at the moment, and the requirements are not usually mentioned explicitly and have to be derived from the opinions. Ask your boss for specific evaluations and feedback.

The above questions, which you can amend or add to as you think fit, are a way of helping you to link the demands imposed on you to concrete processes at work and not going by your boss's personal likes or dislikes. This allows for a greater measure of objectivity. The questions will also help you to think in terms of development. It is not so much a matter of what are your weak and strong points, but more of the potential for development. Finally, it is also a matter of the development of the work which has to be done.

If there is tension between you and your boss, find a third person who can be present at the discussion. Ask your boss whether she will agree to the presence of this person. Also arrange in advance what role this third person will play, (or at least what she will certainly not do during the discussion).

If the tension between you and your boss is so great that you are unable to arrange the meeting with her yourself, find a third person to do this for you. Is there a person who has your trust, as well as access to your boss?

If you do not have a boss, try to organize a discussion with your last boss or with someone else you know well in your working life, but who still has a critical view of your performance.

In dialogue

If you discuss this task together, follow the procedure, 'speaking and characterizing'. Everyone gets a turn to speak.

- When it is your turn, describe how the meeting with your boss was arranged and how it went, in images, as clearly as possible. Try to avoid expressing your attitude, opinions, and so on, as far as possible. The others will help you to remain objective and will characterize your account.

- When you have indicated what you recognize in these characteristics, there is a discussion about your relationship with your boss and what she told you.

Rounding off

Finally, write down what you wish to remember, particularly in relation to your question.

Task 9: Results and learning so far

You learn by doing things. To some extent, this happens automatically. However, if you wish to learn from what you are doing in a conscious and directed way, it is a good idea to stand still and reflect at regular intervals on what you have gained from the activities so far.

For yourself

Look at the material that you have acquired in this workshop up to now, and ask yourself what it has done for you so far. What are the results of your study? Focus particularly on the following aspects.

Discovery
You have heard or experienced new things which are important to remember. These may be thoughts, feelings, habits or working methods.

Awareness
You have become (more) aware of something that was present in you for a long time. You were already vaguely aware of it, or working on it unconsciously. Now you are better able to formulate it, or to admit or apply it.

Confirmation
What you already knew or felt or were able to do has been confirmed. This makes you feel more certain about your opinions, more confident about your feelings or particular skills.

Questions
You have started asking different or new questions. Your study starts with a question and ends with an answer. These may be questions for knowledge and insight, or related to skills. They may also be questions about your philosophy or your attitude to life.

Practical instructions
Read the above as suggestions to encourage your search for results. It is not the intention to suppress findings which well up spontaneously.

Collect your learning results without focusing specifically on your question from Task 1. It is inevitable that you will remember this question, but try to keep it in the back of your mind, semi-consciously. What you come up with will be more selective and therefore less productive if you reproduce your question word for word in advance.

In dialogue

Discuss what you have all discovered. The listeners can add to the speaker's account on the basis of their experiences during previous discussions.

Rounding off

Write down what you want to remember.

Task 10: My question again

The question you are struggling with may become pale in the course of time. You are swept along by life, and other things come up. New questions arise, or the old question shifts, revealing a more profound theme. Therefore it is a good idea to take a new look at your questions from time to time, or to formulate them again.

For yourself

1 When you have collected your results from Task 9, formulate your question again with regard to your life and working situation. Ask yourself why you wish to go on with your study, and what results you expect from it now. Formulate this in a single question.

In the formulation, again use the following criteria:

- a short sentence

- containing the word 'I'

- ending with a question mark

- aimed at what you want in the future

2 Compare the question you have formulated now, with the original question. What has changed? What led to the new question?

In dialogue

One person speaks, the others listen and characterize what is said. The speaker should use concrete situations to which the question applies.

Rounding off

Write down what you want to remember and if necessary adapt your question again.

What made me what I am?

After reflecting on your present situation, it is time to look back with an enquiring eye. What are the factors that have had an effect on your life up to now? The study of the past is one way of gaining a better insight into yourself.

Tasks

11 My mood about my life
12 A wider biographical perspective
13 Events in my life
14 Stages in my life
15 The spirit of the age
16 Results and learning so far
17 My question again

Explanations

Birth and death in the cycle of life
Study of the past
The stages of life and work

Support exercise

Observation

Task 11: My mood about my life

Moods – both positive and negative – determine a large part of your life. If they are stubborn, you get up with them in the morning and go to bed with them at night. At the point that you are able to express them, and look at them separately from yourself, you have the space to relate to them in a different way and allow other moods to enter.

For yourself

Express the mood which you feel emerging when you think about your whole life up to now. Do this in colour and movement on paper.

Practical instructions

Take a blank page or a separate sheet of drawing paper, the soft crayons and a stick of charcoal.

Before you start, concentrate on the feeling which arises when you look at your life up to now.

Do not think too much when you carry out the task. Trust in your hands and the spontaneous choice of colours. Allow whatever is in you to come out. Do not work towards a result you envisaged in advance, and avoid representation, such as signs and symbols.

Explanation: Working with colour (p. 42)

In dialogue

Everyone takes turns to show his mood image without indicating how it was created, what he thinks of it, what it means, and so on. The others look at it and characterize it. When the person who made the image has responded to the characteristics, there is a discussion about the question of which aspects of the mood image refer to the present mood or the present situation, and which aspects refer more to the basic attitude of that person's life.

Rounding off

Finally, write down what you want to remember.

Task 12: A wider biographical perspective

Working is only part of life. The working period is contained in a longer time span which stretches from birth to death. The beginning and end have an effect on the life in between. You can become more conscious of this effect by going back in your memory as far as possible and forming a concrete image of the last moment of your life.

For yourself

Prepare to describe the following two situations in images:

1 *Earliest memory*

Go back in your memory and try to recall the first experience you remember. Try to visualize this as factually as possible: the people, animals, plants, objects, sounds, colours and smells, etc.

Write down a brief description of this memory in your Logbook, using the present tense.

Practical instructions

Search your own memory: do not rely on what you have been told, or what you have seen in photographs. Some people can remember an event from when they were two or three years old; others cannot go back further than the age of fourteen. If you cannot come up with an early memory straightaway, try it again and you may be able to go further back.

Two examples of an early memory:

'I am standing on a balcony, holding onto the railings of the fence. My head is leaning against two railings. I am looking down and I can see small people and cars moving by. Then there is a roll of thunder and the sky turns a leaden grey colour. I am frightened by a blue flash that shoots down and start to cry. Behind me, the light in the room is switched on and my mother calls my name. I am about four years old. It must have been in the 'concrete' district in Amsterdam.'

'I am standing between the garage and the house with the sun in front of me high in the sky. The white wall of the garage is to my right. On the left, are the tall open doors of the house. In front of me, the drive goes to the right and then down the hill with a bend to the left. I see a hedge of large bushes next to the drive with dark green leaves and a sea of deep red flowers. In front of me there is a hole in the hedge, and I know there is a broad flight of steps going down the hill behind it. It is beautifully warm with shining yellow light'.

The experience can be a happy one, but it can also be sad. If it evokes strong emotions in you, it is probably a good idea to talk about it with a partner.

2 *Last experience*

Now move into the future to the moment of your death. Imagine the situation where this would happen if it was up to you. How would you prefer to die?

- At what age?

- In what environment, and how?

- Which people are around you? How near are they to you? What role do they fulfil? Imagine this as realistically as possible without making any notes. Then describe it in your logbook, again using the present tense.

Practical instructions

There are many reasons which might prevent you from focusing on your last moments. The profound, possibly religious sense, that it is not up to you to determine that moment, or a horror of death, or a feeling that you are in the middle of life which you enjoy intensely. By focusing on that last moment, you can become aware of these sometimes profound reasons. This in itself is a positive aspect.

Remember that your ideas about the future often say a great deal about how you are relating to life now. Depending on your mood, you may find that you see it in a very different way. Nevertheless, all these views contain aspects of yourself. Becoming aware of this gives you greater freedom to act.

Death is the moment of departure. How do you prepare for it? What is your attitude to saying goodbye in general? How do you say goodbye?

Two examples of a 'last experience' .

'I am lying in bed at home with my husband, my children and a good friend sitting near me. I know that I am near the end and I'm glad that they've all come. I am seventy years old. The sun is high in the sky. I have had the window open and I can feel the cool wind on my cheeks. The autumn colours outside and the faces inside alternate before my closed eyes. I feel weak, very small, and terribly tired. Then I slide away.'

'I have gone to the beach alone, the extreme western beach in Brittany. The ocean is rolling in with its long, black waves. The surf murmurs softly. It is dark, there is no moon, but there are stars. I am eighty years old, and I swim to the horizon wearing my clothes until I am too tired to go on or to go back. I panic, swallow water, try to breathe, fight until I give up, and then I surrender. For a moment I feel the rocking water and the cold.'

If this task evokes strong emotions in you, it is perhaps a good idea to talk about it with a partner.

Explanation: Birth and death in the life cycle (p. 92)

In dialogue

The roles in discussion are 'speaking' and 'characterizing'. Every speaker takes turns. The two situations are characterized separately, and so is the difference between the two.

In the concluding discussion it is possible to explore the question of what this means for your present situation. For example, what do you recognize in the way in which you say goodbye and begin on something new? In this respect, you can also turn to Task 5.

Rounding off

Write down what you want to remember.

Birth and death in the life cycle

A human life is marked by two borders. A person enters his earthly life at the border of birth. This moment of birth is preceded by life in the mother's womb. What comes before that is shrouded in mist and concealed from human consciousness. Some people believe that there is nothing before this; others speak of man's life before birth in a spiritual world. We share the latter view.

A person leaves his life on earth through the gate of death. A physical body from which life has disappeared remains behind in a visible form for a number of days and then disappears for ever, after burial or cremation. There is also uncertainty in our time about what comes after death. Some people see death as the definitive end. Others see a life after death in all sorts of different forms.

We believe that birth and death are not borders, but gateways between which our life runs its course. Within these, we live in a tangible, physical reality. Man is present there with the clarity of consciousness, which sheds light on himself and on the surrounding world. This light disappears behind the two gateways.

Everyone knows from day-to-day experience that objects which are weakly lit up are difficult to see next to objects which are brightly lit. For example, the strength of the sun makes the stars invisible by day, although they are just as present as they are by night. In the development of mankind, the light of consciousness has constantly strengthened mankind so that in our time it has become a sort of spotlight. This means that many things have become visible which were concealed in the past. But this light also makes many other things invisible – as sunlight makes the stars in the sky invisible – and in the past, these things were experienced as reality, in an intuitive way, based on feeling.

The gateways of birth and death were not the dividing walls that they are nowadays. People felt a connection with the unborn and with the spirits of the dead. Stories were told about what happened behind these two doors. In our own time, vestiges of this can be found in the cultures of countries of the third world. The book, Segu, by the African author, Maryse Condé, is a beautiful example of this. We quote from this book:

'Invisible to the eye of ordinary mortals, the Urubu of death came down in a tree of the family enclosure and spread his wings. He was exhausted (...). He had a task to carry out. Naba had died a long way from the land of his birth. His body was resting in foreign earth, denied the customary burial rites. His relatives had to be warned that his spirit would be doomed in future to wander through this desolate wilderness, unable to be reborn in the body of a little boy, or to become a protective ancestor and subsequently a god.'

If modern man wants to become aware of his journey through life, and he asks questions like 'Where do I come from?' and 'Where am I going?' he will sooner or later come up against the gateways which mark the course of his life, and will seek a relationship to them.

However, the striking fact is that we know these two gateways only from the outside. We do not have any experience of our birth – leaving aside experiences of regression, and so on. We know of birth and death only by attending those of other people.

Furthermore, it is clear that the birth of a child is usually an extremely joyful occasion for those around, while the moment of death often fills the survivors with grief and sorrow.

We do not know whether the moment of birth is such a joyful occasion for the child itself. After all, it is emerging from the warm, safe environment of the mother's womb into the cold of life on earth, the umbilical cord is severed, and suddenly it has to start breathing itself and start using its lungs; its digestive system and circulation have to be completely switched round. At this point an inconceivable number of things are happening, and it is just as well we do not have to experience all this consciously, because it would fill us with dread. The embryonic life is cut off, and life as an independent person begins. At that moment, birth and death are one.

Similarly, we do not know whether the moment of death is such a sad moment for the person who is dying himself. In the last few years, a great deal has been written about people who have had near-death experiences. Ritchie writes about this in his book, *Return from Tomorrow*, and Moody does the same in his book, *Life after Life*. These are the testimonies of ordinary people of our own time who tell us what they experienced after they died, but then returned to their bodies. According to most of the people interviewed, death was a joyful experience, entering into a whole new world of colour and light, where they met beings who welcomed them with great love and warmth.

Viewed in this light, the moment of death could also have the character of birth. Life on earth stops, but at the same time, a new life is beginning. In this case, death and birth are one. The processes of birth and death do not take place only at the beginning and end of life. They also constantly play a role during life itself. It is not only the embryo that dies, but the baby, the toddler, the schoolchild, the adolescent and so on, also die in us, and from these, new lives are born. During life, dying, letting go, and saying farewell are constantly necessary for the birth of new forms of life. For example, the adolescent in us has to die so that the adult in us can be born. If the adolescent continues to exist, the rest of his life becomes a caricature.

During the first part of life, the euphoria of the moment of birth often predominates, even if there may be a quiet sadness for what has to die in us. A boy may secretly shave the hairs growing on his legs because he does not want to be a man yet. A fifteen-year-old girl may hide her cuddly toys and dolls in her room when her friends come to visit.

After the middle years of life, the sense of loss and having to bid farewell often predominates. At these 'moments of death' people often feel exhausted and depressed for inexplicable reasons. Feelings of loneliness and fear, sometimes of their own physical death, can play an important role at these moments.

Whenever a person comes up against his boundaries during his life, this can be seen as a moment of death.

A production manager in the food industry has a strong identification with the product and the central processes in his factory. He is better informed than all the others in the factory. He constantly works on improving the production process and may successfully encourage his superiors to make repeated investments in new computer equipment. When there are production problems, everyone goes to him and he finds the solutions; sometimes they have a technical nature and sometimes they concern actual processes. In this way, he can manage the factory for many years. Then, more and more serious errors are made and the clients start to complain. The production manager works even harder, introduces rules to prevent errors but they continue to occur. Gradually, he starts to realize that his approach is no longer productive and that he can no longer go on like this. He becomes aware that people stop talking when he walks by, and he is avoided because they are afraid to confront him with the painful truth, just as a terminally ill patient is sometimes avoided so that he does not have to be confronted with his approaching death.

The production manager himself knows that he will not survive. He also has a sense of how things should be different, because he has been told about this in meetings, but he knows that he will not be able to do it. What should he do? What can he do? What is there left for him if he gives up this job or is thrown out? At this point, the production manager comes up to a boundary: something which is an essential part of him is coming to an end. He does not know what is beyond this boundary and this frightens him.

Sometimes people experience these sorts of boundary situations several times during the course of their life. They are moments of death which are part of life.*

As we described above, people in ancient cultures had a natural relationship to life and death. Modern man will have to find a relationship to this by himself, consciously and with his own resources. The present rational way of thinking is not very helpful in doing this. In order to gain access to the inner aspect, it is necessary to adopt an enquiring, intuitive, reflective approach, for example, by imagining the moment of your own death.

Most people are afraid of thinking or talking about their own death, and yet there are people who have long imagined what that moment will be like, where it will take place, who will be present, what sort of atmosphere there will be, at what age, and in what season. Imagining these things can help to achieve a more conscious relationship to the end of your own life.

---

* (See Part II, *Backgrounds: Crisis and transition during the course of life*)

You may wonder why it is necessary to consciously focus on your own death. What is the point of such a conscious attitude? We believe that it is a useful thing to do, because death is just as inextricably linked to life as birth; to such an extent that we would even say that someone's attitude to death has a great influence on the quality of their life.

Loss, ending, letting go and dying are all an integral part of human life. Sometimes, you can feel it coming. Sometimes it can happen unexpectedly. It can fill you with terrible fear and uncertainty. It can give rise to a need to hold on to what lies behind you, while it has no viability for the future. But no matter how difficult it is to allow the old to die before you can see the new, it is often necessary.

If you succeed in developing a conscious attitude with regard to death, your trust in that other process which also belongs to life, the process of birth, will also grow. You become aware that the processes of death allow for the possibility of new life. This insight can result in a basic sense of trust in steering a course through life itself, a fundamental feeling of surrendering to life, with less fear and less tension.

Surrender does not mean waiting passively, because this means that you sleep through the moments of birth. Learning to observe the seeds which contain the future of life is just as important as reflecting on the moment of death. A seed is small and easy to miss. Looking back at the moments of birth in the past can help you to identify them in the future and to take care of them in a more conscious way.

Seen in this way, the two gateways which mark our life on earth are not really borders, but true gateways through which the forces of birth and the forces of death flow into our lives. An awareness of these forces and learning to use them consciously, increases our independence and freedom in life.

Exercise tip

Think of a moment in your life when you had to say goodbye to something that was very dear to you. Examine what happened to you and in your environment. What died and what was born?

Support exercise:
Observation

For yourself

Find a pot plant which you find attractive or interesting, with different shades of colour. Place it in front of you on a table at a distance where you can see it clearly and draw it.

Take a sheet of A3 drawing paper and get a box of coloured pencils. Sit down comfortably and try to relax, breathing steadily. Make sure you breathe out properly as well.

Look at the plant and ask yourself what exactly you see. Take plenty of time to do this. Then choose what you want to draw of what you see, and the colours you want to start with. Look at the plant regularly and try to copy what you see as accurately as possible.

Practical instructions

Let go of the feeling that you have to create a work of art. It is not important whether you can draw or not.

Perhaps you have made drawings in the past in which the accuracy of your observation was subordinate to your draughtsmanship or your need for expression. Let go of this and follow the task.

It is a matter of observation. Drawing what you see is a way of helping you to do this. It encourages you to look, and at the same time produces tangible material for the discussion.

In dialogue

Everyone takes turns to show their work and the others characterize it.

If this exercise was done in the presence of others, they can start by saying to what extent the person who drew the plant was successful in drawing it accurately. When you do this, take a careful look at the position from which the plant was observed.

The exercise is then discussed in terms of the following points:

- How did you find observing the plant? Were you able to stay with it? What distracted you – external or internal stimuli?

- What inabilities, thresholds or barriers did you come up against when you drew the plant? What did you do about these?

- How did you set about following the task? Were you able to keep to the instructions?

– Do these things tell you anything about the observation of your own biography?

– What does this tell you in relation to your question?

The following abilities (inner skills) are involved in this exercise:

– being moved by a task;

– factual observation;

– relating observation to activity;

– maintaining an interest;

– respecting what you see.

Rounding off

Finally, write down what you wish to remember.

Examples of this exercise: Ill. 5 (after p. 280)

Task 13: Events in my life

The events people experience characterize their lives. The experience of a small girl peering at her father who is playing the great organ in the church, through a hole in a dark green velvet curtain of a large cupboard, is an experience which no other person has had in the same way. The course of your life is reflected in the series of events which you have experienced. That is why it is important to remember these events, to line them up in front of you like a tableau and to look at them.

For yourself

1 Look at the events in your life which meant a lot to you in a negative or positive sense, or which were a turning point in your life. When did they take place? What age were you then?

2 Describe these events briefly in your Logbook. Ask yourself questions such as:

– What happened?

– Where, and in what surroundings did the event take place?

– Who was present and what role did these people play?

– What did you do and what did you fail to do?

– What were your thoughts, feelings, desires or intentions?

3 Make a distinction between the events in terms of three areas of your life: your work, your private life and your personal development. Give every area its own colour or symbol.

4 Take a page from your Logbook and draw a horizontal line to form the age axis and add the vertical line on the left to indicate the value of the experience, positive above, negative below the line. Arrange the events on this graph in order.

Practical instructions

On a piece of rough paper, make a note of the most important events which occur to you, in an arbitrary order. Do not work systematically, for example, by going through your life chronologically.

In the first instance, it is a matter of thinking of the events which you consider important. These could be events with a strong emotional content, or those which mark a turning point in your life, or which proved to affect your life in the longer term. If you become stuck with particular events which constantly recur, try to find different ones.

Do this particularly for the events which are generally considered to be important, such as your final exams, marriage, 25th anniversary at the business, and so on. The two questions given below are suggestions. You can supplement them yourself, with aspects that are important to you.

In dialogue

Everyone takes turns to show their graphs, and picks a few events by way of example to say more about them. The others ask questions to clarify the image for the speaker himself and then characterize this image. Finally, they also try to feel the significance of the events for the speaker and ask him whether he recognizes it.

Practical instructions

For the speaker:
It is impossible to relate everything. We suggest that you make a conscious choice. For example, you could choose to tell the others about an emotional event, because just talking about it has a liberating effect, or you could choose an event of which the significance is not quite clear, in the expectation that the others will be able to help you.

For the listener:
Characterization can be aimed at one or several events, at a period, or at the whole thing. This also applies with regard to 'feeling the significance'.

The attention is often attracted by emotional or sensitive events. However, try to consider other events too, as well as the speaker's life as a whole.

It is important for the speaker to have an opportunity to recount a particular event in detail; it might be the first time that he has told this story. On the other hand, it may also be important to help the speaker to look at his own life from a distance. The others will feel in what direction the speaker has to be encouraged and will evaluate this on the basis of the situation. It is good if both 'directions' can come up in the course of time.

Rounding off

Finally, writes down what you wish to remember.

Explanation: Study of the past (p. 104)

Study of the past

At every point in her life, a person is between the past and future. The past affects the future: the meeting which you planned last week will take place tomorrow. The future affects the past: last week, you drew up a plan to deal with the expected decline in the economy next year. On the one hand, there are results and consequences; on the other hand, there are expectations, seeing what happens.

Past and future are the two poles between which our life takes place. We were formed by the past; it determines who we are now to a large extent. It lies behind us and can no longer be changed.

The future lies before us, and to some extent it remains open. You can still do something about it, though it sometimes seems there is very little you can do. The events and choices from the past seem to greatly reduce your freedom for the future. You *are* married, you *have* children, you are stuck with a lifestyle, your mortgage, your responsibilities, your training and choice of profession, your specific experience, and sometimes also the wounds which life has inflicted on you, the pain and the impotence. For some people the future is full of promise; for others, it is a dark hole, for yet others, it is an endless repetition of the same thing.

Both the past and future exist in the present. My question belongs to the present and I feel the tension which is brought about by my question, or the dissatisfaction of my working situation and my current life *now*. This can be illustrated as shown below:

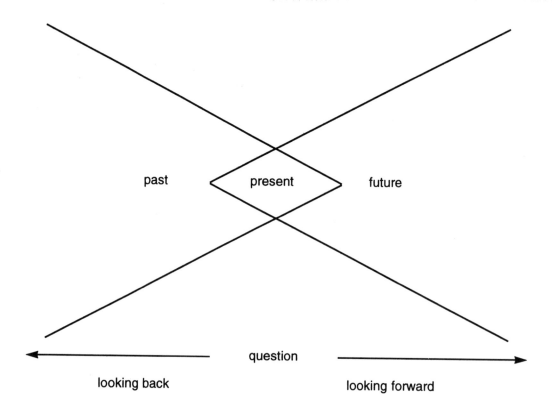

The point of examining the past

Even if your question relates to the future, you cannot ignore the past. Choices and decisions from the past determine your situation now, both your inner life and in external terms. You are not a tabula rasa. What you have become up to now goes into the future with you. This does not mean that you cannot change anything, and that everything is predetermined. On the contrary, your chances of steering a course for the future are increased if you are conscious of the influences in the environment which have had an effect on you, and of the way in which you dealt with these. By gaining an insight into the conscious or unconscious choices with which you determined the direction of your life, you can prevent unconscious steering mechanisms from having an effect in the future, possibly turning your plans into an illusion. Therefore, examining the past can give you greater freedom in relation to the future.

To do this, you need a certain basic attitude towards the past. In daily life, some people have a basic attitude which is unproductive with regard to learning anything from the past. We will mention some of these below, and then outline the basic attitudes which we consider desirable for examining the past. What is your attitude with regard to your experiences up to now?

As a victim?
People with this attitude consider themselves victims of people and circumstances which played a role in their lives in the past. Their own failures, mistakes and disappointment are attributed to parents, education, the church, the boss, the organization and so on. Sometimes people have certainly suffered terrible things in the past; nevertheless the attitude of a victim is unproductive, because it stops you from taking your fate into your own hands, and taking responsibility for your own life.

As a guilty party?
'I made a mess of it.'
'When I think of what I did to the children...'
'I was so stupid. I let all sorts of chances slip by.'

People who look at the past with feelings of guilt do take responsibility for what they did, but arrive at a negative judgement about the way in which they fulfilled that responsibility. Guilt plays a role in everyone's life, but a person can be taken over by feelings of guilt to such an extent that it constantly gnaws at her and she has no courage or freedom to face the future.

The opposite tendency, to look back with pride, is equally unproductive. Obviously, we have achieved things in the past which we can look back at with satisfaction or pride, but without examining these further (objectively), these feelings do not provide anything useful for determining the future.

There is a great tendency to judge the life behind us in a moral sense. You wonder what you have done wrong and what you have done right in your life. This philosophy is deeply rooted in our culture, and is difficult to shed. However, for this biographical study, you must let go of this attitude. Judging things to be right or wrong is of little value for this task. It can seriously obscure your view of yourself and increase your feeling of impotence towards the future.

As a product of coincidence?

People may say: 'My whole life is the way it is because of coincidence. It could equally have been very different.' In this case you see life like tossing a coin. All sorts of situations arise where the coin enters, and this could be story in itself.

With this attitude, we can examine which influences in the past have had an effect in our lives. You look for external explanations for the situation of your life now, for example, for your insecurity or fear, for your choice of school or studies, or for your career. What you discover in this way is not incorrect, but it is one-sided. If you see life as a series of coincidences, and yourself as a product of these, you do not acquire an insight into the direction in which you have steered your own life up to that point.

As the author of your own life story?

For the biographical study, it is useful to see the life behind you as a piece of work which you created yourself. From this viewpoint – which is our own viewpoint – it is not a coincidence that your life has been as it was. You yourself, consciously or unconsciously, helped to steer it. Obviously, you came across many things that you did not ask for, let alone that you chose yourself. But you can consider this as the material with which you wrote your own composition.

Some people find it difficult to see life in this way, particularly when their lives have been full of pain and disappointment up to that time. They will argue: 'Surely it is inconceivable that I would have steered this course myself? Doesn't this suggest that all this misery is ultimately my own fault?'

This brings us to a profound question which requires a separate examination. We do not have room to examine this in the context of this workbook. However, if you are able to see yourself as the unknown pilot of your life – if necessary, as a working hypothesis – without becoming bogged down in this question of fault, it is useful to ask yourself, 'What course have I steered in my life so far? What did I want as a pilot, even in these difficult situations?'

It may become clear that the lack of understanding you have encountered has made you more flexible, that your unjust dismissal has resulted in a situation where you were really able to grow, or that your difficult child helped you to learn to love. The study of the past can lead to the discovery of meaningful links, a sort of wisdom in the way the course of your life has been steered. It can lead to the discovery of a red thread through your life, which feels like part of you, events and circumstances are no longer coincidences which could equally have been different, but appear connected to you. You start to see them as the external reflection of your inner essence. By examining these external reflections, you gradually gain a better insight into your inner self, i.e., into yourself. Your self is expressed in your biography.

How do you examine the past?

The art of examining the past is to step back from it and see it through the eyes of an outsider.

It is as though you are standing on the top of a high mountain, looking back at the landscape you have just passed through. You see the places which you passed on your way up from a greater distance in relation to the rest of the landscape. You see the farm where you rested, and how it fits into the landscape, how the stream after the waterfall flows into other streams; how the mountain torrent disappears and then reappears again further on. There are some places which you recognize, and which you want to look at in more detail, as well as places which you did not really notice on the journey. You pick up your binoculars and focus on these places to have a better look.

You can also look at life as though you are looking at a panorama in front of you. As in the landscape, you see the facts and events from a greater distance, but they are more closely interconnected. You can also choose separate parts of the past to focus on in more detail.

It is important to keep a distance from your own past, in other words, to look at it without judging it, without disapproving or approving of it, without sympathy or antipathy, and without becoming involved in experiencing that moment again. It is a matter of building up these pieces of the past in images so that you can look at them as an outsider.

In this workshop, the study of the past is dealt with in such a way that step by step, you reach a deeper level. First, you express your feelings and moods about your life, then you collect the facts and events, and thirdly, you impose a structure by dividing your life into stages. Then you look for the themes of your life, and finally, you try to isolate the essence. These steps all have a very different quality; they all use very different skills. The steps are taken one after the other, but it is also possible to repeat every step at a later stage. For example, by going back to the events after finding the themes of your life, and so on. It is important to adopt an enquiring approach to life at every stage: searching, asking yourself questions, feeling, trying out, testing, carefully coming to conclusions and verifying them.

1 Feelings and moods about the course of your life

Every person has a feeling about her own past, and this often differs from period to period within her life. For example, it is possible to experience the years of your childhood and youth as warm and protected, to experience adolescence as liberating and light, to experience the first years of adulthood as a challenge and exciting, or tedious and boring. There are high and low points. It is a good idea to become aware of these feelings in relation to your life, and to see what they have to tell you. All sorts of means of expression can be used for this, such as mood images in colour, or a line with high and low points.

When you do this, you should not think too much, but approach the task spontaneously in terms of your feelings, and trust in what you do impulsively. When others look at the result and characterize it, you may be surprised by the things which strike them, and which you had never seen in that light.

2 Important events

Collecting important events from your life is a very different activity. You are dependent on your memory to recall the events and place them in time. It requires precision and accuracy to clearly visualize things which happened years ago. By focusing your attention as precisely as possible on the external circumstances of the time, such as the place, the furniture, the light, sounds, smells, appearance of people, their words and conduct etc., you can recreate the situation, while at the same time it is possible to look at it through the eyes of an outsider.

When you do this, you can lose the thread in two ways, so that the value of the exercise is greatly reduced. On the one hand, there is a risk that you end up by simply drawing up a cold list of the facts, as is usual in a CV. In this case, the image is totally lacking in vitality and you have an abstract indication without further detail, which is of little use for the biographical study.

The other risk is that you will evoke only the emotional experiences of the past; the sadness, the joy, the loneliness, the confusion, the sense of satisfaction, and so on. As a result, what was actually happening around you can become obscured. Sometimes it is inevitable that you become overcome by emotion. Allow this to happen for a while, but then try to go back to the facts and circumstances which pertained at the time.

Another difficulty is the problem of choice. So many things happen in a lifetime. Which events are the important ones?

The danger here is to list only those events which are seen a 'life events' in your culture, such as marriage, birth, children, retirement, the death of your parents, etc. However, we are concerned here with the events you consider important yourself – even if these do not seem to have much importance outside – such as a strong personal experience or a meaningful encounter. In this context, the turning points in your life are particularly important. These are the moments or episodes which are followed by a difference in your life – your inner life – but also your outer life.

The choice of events can also be determined by your specific biographical question. Even if your question relates to your working life, it is a good idea to look at the important events in your personal life which have an effect on your working life. For example, a divorce in your private life may result in a troubled period in your working biography, and a philosophical reorientation can lead to a different attitude in your profession.

3 The stages of life

The next step is to divide your life into periods or stages. These are the 'chapters' of your life story. You arrange the many different events in a particular order. Creating order is a way for you to come to grips with your life. It gives you an insight into your life as a whole.

The stages in which your life is divided reflect different qualities of moods, tasks or interests. This is not an abstract matter. It is important that the stages 'are filled with life'. You can achieve this by finding one or several characteristic situations for every stage, and then building these up to form a concrete image. For example, a Sunday afternoon from your childhood, a Christmas party, a holiday or a schoolday. How did you sit around the table at home when you were young, and what happened during meal times? What did you talk about to your first boyfriend or girlfriend? What was your working day like in your first job? Do you remember your first evaluation discussion?

In addition, it is worth examining the various stages of your life against the background of wider social development. What was society like during your childhood years and when you had your first or second job? How did you relate to it? In your life you are always influenced by the spirit of the age. It is important to be aware of this influence.

Finally, it is extremely important for this part of the study to look at the people who were important to you during a particular stage of your life. As a rule, a stage is affected by particular people. Ask yourself what you owe these people, or in other words, what they have contributed to your development.

If you do this seriously, it can liberate you from the egocentric illusion which we all tend to foster – the illusion that we formed ourselves to be what we are. As you start to see through this illusion, you acquire a very different view of your own life and of the role which others have played in it.

4 The themes of life

Your study will attain an even deeper level if you try to gain an insight into the themes of your life. These themes are subjects, problems, interests or tasks with which you have been involved for a long time, or even throughout your life. They form a sort of 'red thread' through your life, like the themes in a piece of music. Sometimes they disappear for a while to re-emerge later, possibly in a different guise. A theme such as a love for nature, can express itself in many different forms, as can themes like 'fighting fear' or 'pushing back the boundaries' .

The themes of your life are related to your life as a whole. You can find them only by looking at your life as a whole, to see whether you can find which lines emerge. You discover these themes when you are struck by particular relationships. For example, one person discovered that the theme of 'shutting himself up and then becoming free at the last moment' played a role in his life in different ways. As a child, he shut himself up in his bedroom, but just at the last moment, before he knew that his father would force the door, he would turn the key. Almost twenty years later, he was 'trapped' in a relationship with a woman, from which he could not escape. It made him ill. But just before the world around him forced the end of this relationship, he found the strength to break it off himself. Another situation with a similar nature occurred a number of years later in his working life. When he had become aware of this thread, he saw that this theme also emerged at other times in his life, even in very simple situations at work and at home.

The themes of your life are very close to you. When you discover one, it can be very exciting. You become aware that you have found an essential aspect of yourself, something fundamental that belongs to you even if you cannot yet give it a name.

It can also happen that you discover 'red threads' which do not please you at all. For example, that you have systematically walked away from responsibilities, that you have made people depend on you, or have even abused them, that you have constantly avoided taking any risks, etc. Such discoveries can be very depressing because they affect your self-image. This may be an inevitable consequence of the biographical study which you are undertaking. You have to cope with this and it can require courage; courage not to escape, not to become stuck in feelings of guilt as described above, but to recognize this theme and do something about it in the future. You can find this courage in the realization that you had the strength to discover these things and this will also help you to come to terms with them. Others can encourage you in this and support you. This is the most important reason why we insist that you should do this biographical study together with others.

5 Essence

This is the last step in your study of the past. Some of the questions of the study which are relevant here are the following:

– What do the things I have discovered up to now tell me?

– What have I been aiming for up to now in my life?

– What did I clearly want from my life?

– Who am I really?

You will probably never find a complete and satisfactory answer to these questions, particularly to the two last questions. What we want and who we are remains hidden behind many veils. At best, a corner of the veil may be lifted, because every person has infinite aspects. Sometimes you can have a glimpse of the immeasurable depths, both in yourself and in others; the depths of the secret of who you are and who the other person is. The infinity of the human spirit is as great as the infinity of the cosmos.

Exercise tip

In the evening, look back at an event that occurred during the day and that involved your emotions. Describe this event as precisely as possible, as though you are looking through the eyes of an outsider. Then identify what was the essence of the event for you.

Task 14: Stages in my life

The life of a person is not a linear event. It develops through very different periods. Every period – that of the child, the adolescent, the woman of thirty or someone over fifty – has its colour, music or story. In addition to this general classification into different periods, we can all recognize our own stages. These stages are marked by specific moments of transition. They too, have their own mood or theme. You can enrich and increase the panorama of your life by reflecting on these in a conscious way.

For yourself

1 Look at your life and try to distinguish different stages, your own stages. By this, we mean the periods between particular moments of transition in your life.
Look at what happened in every period, what was characteristic of that period, and what was your attitude at that time, your mood and so on. Give every period a name.
Now place the periods on a horizontal age axis. To do this, do not use the table in Task 13.

2 For every stage of your life, find one photograph of yourself which you consider characteristic of that stage. Look at yourself in these photographs as an outsider and at the characteristics of the stage of your life you were in at the time. How did other people, for example, the photographer, see you at that time? Bring these photographs with you to the discussion.

Practical instructions

When you are trying to determine the stages of your life, you may in the first instance, use the usual distinctions such as childhood, school years, university, etc., or you may use a more historically-oriented division, such as the war years, the post-war period of reconstruction, political involvement, democratization, no-nonsense era, and so on. Try to get away from these and find your own stages. Also try to get away from the well-known scientific classifications. Which classification is important for you? For example: left home at fourteen, *wandering around* from fourteen to twenty-five; *own home* at twenty-five, *period of calm* from twenty-five to thirty. Or: early years, *light and warm,* up to twelve, when my mother died; *failure* at school up to fourteen, father remarried, I went to boarding school; this was *successful,* university up to twenty-two, finished my studies; etc.

The moments of transition can coincide with important events. This may include one crucial event, of which you say: 'Since then, everything has been different.' In that case, there was a turning point. What was it about that turning point which caused everything to change? What was the basis of this turning point, what were the events taking place? What preceded that turning point, and what followed it?

Place the images of your life which were produced by the three previous tasks (11, 12 and 13) next to each other, all together. By looking at your life through different glasses and not linking the images you discovered together, you will eventually gain a clearer insight into your life. Furthermore, you will increase your inner flexibility when you are able to relate to your experiences.

In dialogue

Everyone talks about their stages with the help of the schedules they have made and finally show their photographs. The others characterize the image as a whole and/or parts of it.

Rounding off

Finally, write down what you wish to remember.

Task 15: The spirit of the age

The way in which people act is partly determined by the age in which they live. The way they look at life is also historically determined. Norms, values, views and behaviour – all aspects of culture are influenced by the spirit of the age. This is the basis for people's actions and individuals' choices. A greater awareness of the time in which you live can lead to a different evaluation of your own life.

For yourself

1 You begin with the stages of your life which you have identified. Again, place these on a horizontal time axis. Write down the names of the stages underneath this line. Above the ages which mark the stages, write down the relevant year. Now go back in your memory stage by stage, and above that line, write down what was happening in society at that time. Use only your own memory.

2 Now extend this to a small study, separate from your personal experience. What were the themes which characterized that period? What was happening in society? Choose your own sources to answer these questions.

Practical instructions

Start with your memory, and then go on to study the facts.
You don't have to be a historian. This is just a small study. For example, choose one source, such as films, newspaper articles, books or photographs.
Do not do it as a systematic study, but see what strikes you, when you casually see, for example, what films were popular in successive periods. Or go to the library and look at some of the newspapers from that time, or have a look at some books of photographs, and so on.

In dialogue

If you discuss this task together, show the schedule in turn, and say what you have found. The others characterize the spirit of the period which emerges from this. When everyone has had a turn, you discuss the spirit of that time and any possible developments which took place. Then summarize this in a joint time schedule.

Practical instructions

In this task, it is not a matter of looking at the subjective choice of every speaker, or the personal experience of the spirit of the period concerned. The individual material serves only to help to understand the spirit developing at that time, which has a supra-personal character.

Rounding off

Finally, write down what you wish to remember.

Explanation: The stages of your life and work (p. 117)

The stages of your life and work

The schedule shown below is a summary of the corresponding chapter in *Part II: Backgrounds*. It provides a classification of the phases or stages of life, which follows on from normal language usage: the twenty-year-old, the thirty-year-old and so on. For every stage of life, a short description is given of:

1 the relationship to work;

2 the dangers and one-sided aspects;

3 what is necessary to continue to develop.

RELATIONSHIP TO WORK	DANGERS	WHAT IS NECESSARY
The twenty-year old		
'Work is a way of testing yourself'	Fanaticism	Variety and a broad orientation in work experience
Temporary working relationships, do not enter into a permanent obligation	Happy-go-lucky attitude	Extending yourself to your limit
	Looking for security too soon in a single talent or type of work	
Seeing short-term results		Evaluating results in the short term
A great deal of enthusiasm, little experience, 'shallow' views		Positive working atmosphere, open communication, direct feedback
A need for positive contacts and being 'seen'		

RELATIONSHIP TO WORK	DANGERS	WHAT IS NECESSARY

The thirty-year old

Work goes before the partner	Rationality becomes feelingless and hard	Finding a balance between work and private life
Seeks career and development	Personal interest becomes a quest for power with no respect for anything	Greater professional experience, responsibility
Can cope with many things at once		Networks, making connections with people
Works in an organized way: with objectives, making plans weighing up priorities	A sense of order becomes small-mindedness	Real interest in other people's feelings
Can think in the long-term	Superficiality, taking advantage of the expectations of others	

The forty-year old

Afraid of tackling tasks, inner dissatisfaction, doing too much	Locks himself away in hard work	Personal discussions in which a sense of restlessness can be expressed
Work is a support and a burden	Impulsive change in way of life	Painful existential questions should be seen as development
Does not reveal weaknesses, insecure with regard to own capacities	Escapes in drink, relationships, financial expenditure	A recognition of an over-familiar working and living situation, inner emptiness and chaos, and dealing with this
Looking for the meaning of the work		Discovery of new meanings
Unexpected emotions and behaviour		

The fifty-year old

Is either a support or a weight at work	Holding on to the old way of doing things	Should be asked to do what he can at the age of 50
Experience, broad insights, ability to stand back and develop policies	Competing for position with younger people	Working on the basis that a person is never too old to learn
True leader, ability to inspire	Negativism and cynicism	To acquire real, positive feedback
Ability to take difficult decisions in relation to people, based on objective necessity	Idealization of own past when talking to younger people	To discover ideal or cultural sources of inspiration
Not so much at home in a dynamic environment, may see younger people as a potential threat	Wants to stay young, join in, in a dynamic way	Preparing for the end of working life

RELATIONSHIP TO WORK	DANGERS	WHAT IS NECESSARY

The sixty-year old

RELATIONSHIP TO WORK	DANGERS	WHAT IS NECESSARY
The end of working life is in sight	Inability to let go and to say farewell	Individual approach in terms of working times, workload and conditions of work
Working at one's own pace	One's identity may be lost together with the job (sometimes resulting in death)	To be given tasks which are 'close to the heart'
Giving support based on experience		Finishing things
Separating from the organization	Letting go too quickly, not seeing one's own worth to the organization	Preparing to find a content for the next stage
Continuing on one's own two feet		

Exercise tip

For every stage choose one to three people from your immediate environment. Look at them for a month, observe them, talk to them, listen to what others say about them. Concentrate on their relationship to the work they do and characterize the image which emerges.

Letting go and starting again. This might well be the most important task you have in your lifetime. It is the heart beat of our life.

Steps

As each blossom fades, and all youth
concedes to age, so each stage in life
will blossom, and wisdom too and every virtue
at its time, they may not last for ever.
The heart must be ready at each call from life
for partings and new beginnings,
to give itself with courage but not with grief to new connections.
In each beginning dwells an enchantment
which protects us and helps us live.
Through space, room we should pass brightly through,
clinging to none as if to home.
The spirit of the world would not chain and hem us,
it seeks to raise us step by step, to widen.
We scarcely indwell a space in life,
when slackness threatens, there are familiar ways.
Only he who can rise and be gone
can break free from numbing habit.
It may be that the death knell will send us, yet young,
to new dimensions.
Life's call on us will never end...
Well then, heart, take leave which yet is wholesome!

Herman Hesse

Task 16: Results and learning so far

You learn by doing things. To some extent, this happens automatically. However, if you wish to learn from what you are doing in a conscious and directed way, it is a good idea to stand still and reflect at regular intervals on what you have gained from the activities so far.

For yourself

Look at the material that you have acquired in this workshop up to now, and ask yourself what it has done for you so far. What are the results of your study? Focus particularly on the following aspects.

Discovery
You have heard or experienced new things which are important to remember. These may be thoughts, feelings, habits or working methods.

Awareness
You have become (more) aware of something that was present in you for a long time. You were already vaguely aware of it, or working on it unconsciously. Now you are better able to formulate it, or to admit or apply it.

Confirmation
What you already knew or felt or were able to do has been confirmed. This makes you feel more certain about your opinions, more confident about your feelings or particular skills.

Questions
You have started asking different or new questions. Your study starts with a question and ends with an answer. These may be questions for knowledge and insight, or related to skills. They may also be questions about your philosophy or your attitude to life.

Practical instructions

Read the above as suggestions to encourage your search for results. It is not the intention that you suppress findings which well up spontaneously.

Collect your results without focusing specifically on your questions from Tasks 1 and 9 too literally. It is inevitable that you will remember this question, but try to keep it in the back of you mind, semi-consciously. If you reproduce your question too exactly in advance, the results are more selective and therefore not as rich.

This is mainly an activity for yourself, but in order to involve the others in the process of your study effectively, it is important that they are informed of the results of your search.

In dialogue

Exchange your discoveries amongst yourselves. The listeners can add to the speaker's account on the basis of their experiences during previous discussions.

Rounding off

Write down what you want to remember.

Task 17: My question again

The question you are struggling with may become pale in the course of time. You are swept along by life, and other things come up. New questions arise, or the old question shifts, revealing a more profound theme. Therefore it is a good idea to take a new look at your questions from time to time, or to formulate them again.

For yourself

1 When you have collected your results from Task 16, formulate your question again with regard to your life and working situation. Ask yourself why you wish to go on with your study, and what results you expect from it now. Formulate this in a single question. In the formulation, again use the following criteria:

– a short sentence

– containing the word 'I'

– ending with a question mark

– aimed at what you want in the future

2 Compare the question you have formulated now, with the question you formulated earlier (Tasks 1 and 9). What has changed? What led to the new question?

In dialogue

One person speaks, the others listen and characterize. The listeners can help the speaker to give concrete examples in which the question is relevant.

Rounding off

Write down what you want to remember and if necessary adapt your question again.

Who am I?

An increased insight into your life and into the forces which have influenced it can result in reflecting on the question of who you are. What is characteristic in all these experiences? What really belongs to you? What sort of person is it that has experienced all these things? A deeper contact with yourself is an important condition of meeting the future in a more conscious and secure way.

Tasks

18 Mood about myself
19 Themes in my life
20 My working life again
21 My source of inspiration
22 Basic values

Explanations

Conversation
Your image of mankind?
Who am I?
Inspiration in daily life

Support exercise

Turning point

Task 18: Mood about myself

What feelings do you have when you look at yourself? Do you have a reasonably satisfied feeling? Or do you feel shame, sadness, and so on? Or do you hesitate to look at yourself? The way in which you experience yourself subconsciously influences everything you do.

Explanation: Working with colour (p. 42)

For yourself

Express the mood which you feel when you think about yourself. Do this on paper, using colour and movement.

Practical instructions

Take your Logbook or a separate sheet of drawing paper, the soft crayons and the stick of charcoal.

Before you start, concentrate on the feeling that comes to you when you think about yourself. Don't be in too much of a hurry. Concentrate on focusing your attention on yourself. When you do the task, don't think about it too much. Trust in your hands and the spontaneous choice of colours. Allow what there is to come out and avoid specific representations.

In dialogue

If you discuss this task together, everyone should show their mood image in turn, without indicating how it was created, what they think about it, what it means and so on. The others look at it and characterize it. When the person who made the image has responded to these characteristics, there is a discussion about the question of what in the mood image relates to the mood of this particular moment or the present situation, and what is related more to the basic attitude of that person. What effect does this have on the life of this person?

Rounding off

Finally, write down what you wish to remember.

Task 19: Themes in my life

Task 19: Themes in my life

You can see the life behind you as a piece of music composed by yourself and by other people. There are different themes to be heard in this piece in all sorts of variations, and played by different instruments. Sometimes a particular theme seems to have disappeared, but then it will reappear again in another part of the music. By listening attentively and involving yourself in this composition, you may be able to discover a central theme which can be heard through everything else.

For yourself

Look back at the results of the last tasks and see whether there are any particular themes in your life up to now. Do you recognize any themes which predominated during a particular period or which disappeared for a while to re-emerge later on? Or can you find themes which constantly play a role in your life?

Make a note of these themes in your Logbook and examine them in the light of questions such as:

– In what form did the theme first emerge?

– During which period(s) did it play a part?

– Which people were involved in it?

– How did you relate to this theme?

Practical instructions

The questions given above are suggestions. In your examination, use your own emphasis.

We have not defined the term 'theme'. This is something you must determine for yourself. All sorts of matters can emerge as a theme, for example:

– building bridges between people;

– acting as a leader for people;

– looking for the most rational solution;

– coping with insecurity or fear;

– experiencing your own boundaries;

– confronting suffering or death;

– the experience and enjoyment of your own body.

The themes can be small or large, with a practical or highly moral value. They can also be related to hobbies, such as music, technology, travelling. However, the more central themes are the recurring or permanent themes which have an existential character. The meaning of your life lies in these themes. This certainly applies for the theme of your life. To some extent, you could describe this as your 'destiny'.

Everyone's destiny is a mystery. When we refer to the theme of your life, it is not a matter of capturing that mystery with a few key words, but looking for the single unique theme of your life will help you to get closer to this mystery. Often the result is two or three key themes. If you discover more, you are probably still finding the central themes of your life. Try to go a step further towards discovering the essence.

In dialogue

Everyone takes turns to discuss their themes. The aim of this discussion is:

- to gain a better or deeper insight into one's own themes and particularly the central theme of life;

- to examine which themes are closed (for the time being) and which need to be worked on or require further attention in the future.

The theme of life is often so central, and interwoven as a red thread in your life to such an extent, that it never closes down. It constantly reappears in a new and often unexpected way. Gradually, you learn to recognize more quickly and clearly when it plays a part, and you also find new ways of relating to it.

Practical instructions

The speaker is given the chance to identify his themes and illustrate them briefly with the help of the following questions:

- When did the theme play a part and where?

- How did he relate to it?

- How closely is he or was he connected to this theme?

The others look at :

- other themes which can be identified amongst the themes that are mentioned;

- the theme of his life (which can be different from the theme discovered by the speaker himself);

- the characteristic feature of his connection with the themes;

- the significance of the theme for the speaker in the light of the future.

When the others have responded to the speaker on these matters, he chooses one or two of the responses which surprised him or moved him, and which he wishes to discuss further.

Explanation: Conversation (p. 136)

Rounding off

Finally, summarize your conclusions with the help of the following questions:

- What are the most important themes in the present period of my life?

- Which themes do I consciously wish to pursue?

- What do I see as the theme of my life?

Tell the others about the conclusions you have reached and make a note of them in your Logbook.

Conversation

'What is more wonderful than gold?' asked the king.
'Light,' answered the snake.
'What is more vital than light?' asked the king.
'Conversation,' said the snake.

J.W. Goethe, The Green Snake and the Beautiful Lily

In the above quotation, conversation is described as giving more life than light. However, many of the conversations we have in daily life are by no means life-giving; they exhaust us and require an unbelievable amount of energy. How should you discuss things in order for them to be life-giving? The Austrian/English psycho-therapist, Hans Schauder (see Lefébure, 1995), sees conversing, and particularly 'helping conversations', as a creative process closely related to the creative process in art. Whether this quality is achieved in a conversation depends, amongst other things, on:

- how you use empathy and confrontation as a helper;

- the degree of your authenticity;

- a few technical conversation conditions.

These are matters which play a role in any discussion designed to help. They are discussed in further detail below in the context of conversations about the themes of life.

Empathy and confrontation

In a discussion on themes, it is possible to make a distinction between two different attitudes on the part of the discussion partners towards the person contributing the themes, which can both be fruitful and helpful for her: the attitudes of empathy and confrontation.

Empathy is a question of feeling, living, and being moved by the owner of the themes. It is an attitude of warmth, understanding and acceptance. It is like connecting yourself to the speaker and reflecting her feelings and intentions. In this way she can be supported and encouraged to express herself further, even where there are emotional blocks. If people have a theme which is painful, or has sad consequences, an approach based on this attitude can be very helpful. An example of a response that reveals empathy is:

'At the point where you talked about the theme "taking responsibility", and said that you rejected the plant manager's offer, I could see that you felt restless and I heard you hesitate as you were speaking. I had the feeling that you were frightened of the offer and of your refusal. Is that right?'

134

An attitude of confrontation is one in which you are critical of the speaker, but involved with her. Instead of finding understanding and acceptance, the person who talked about her themes encounters resistance, which throws her back on herself and challenges her to become clearer, to explore the theme with more depth, or to adopt a clearer point of view. A confrontation is like shaking someone awake. A confrontation can be particularly helpful when people are constantly talking in riddles or give evasive answers, remaining vague and saying nothing or nothing real. For example:

'I detect a lack of concern when you talk about your themes, as though it doesn't interest you at all. Why are you actually joining us here?'

Many people find that empathy is much more sympathetic than confrontation. Nevertheless, many people say that they benefit most from strong confrontation.

Authenticity

You are authentic when your behaviour accords with your inner experience. Both the attitudes described above require the conversation partner to listen and speak on the basis of a truly helpful attitude.

A confrontation should never result in telling someone off, or scoring points off the other person by seeing through them in some way. To be helpful in a discussion, confrontation works only if it is based on an involvement with the other person.

However, it is also possible to go wrong with empathy. This happens when you project your own feelings and emotions on the speaker. For example, if you recognize something which you have experienced yourself, or if you think of how you would react in that situation.

There are two anchors which can help to secure your authenticity. The first anchor is the material which the speaker observed and contributed herself. The other is being yourself, a connection with your own inner self, using this consciously in the discussion to help others.

Some technical conversation conditions

Listening to another person's themes above all requires inner peace. You should consciously put aside your own cares for a while so that you can be truly open to the other person. If you find this impossible, but want to join in anyway, it is a good idea to tell the others about this, so that the group can bear it in mind, taking into account the common goal and time available.

When you are listening, it is a matter of trying to identify with the other person. This works better if the listener doesn't listen only to the content of the story, but also to the feelings and intentions which are revealed in it. To do this, you should listen not only with your ears, but also with your eyes, your whole self, and above all, with your heart. In this case, you will perceive the joy or sorrow, sense of belonging or detachment, doubts or determination, through the speaker's words.

When the story has been told and the speaker becomes the listener, it is her turn to take in the responses and comments of the others and assimilate them with a sense of inner peace. This can be difficult, because of the feelings and emotions evoked by the contributions of the others, and also because of your own critical attitude, which can prevent you from listening in an open way.

If you feel misunderstood or attacked, it is a good idea to express these feelings to the others. You should not be on the defensive or dispute their contributions, because that is pointless. It is more important to be open to surprises. These will come between what you know already and what you deny. In this case a surprise is something which affects you in a positive or negative way and which you immediately sense as being right, although you may not have wanted to or been able to think of looking at it in that way.

In view of this difficult inner process for the person who contributed the themes, it is important that the various contributions of the others follow each other calmly. Avoid an atmosphere in which everyone is impatiently waiting to have their say. Furthermore, wherever possible, it is best if the contributions follow on, one from the other. When one point has been covered sufficiently, the next points can be raised. In addition, the contributions, comments, suggestions, questions, will be more forceful if they are brief and clear. The people participating in these discussions often dilute their valuable contributions by adding all sorts of explanations, additional details or carefully wrapping it up in unnecessary information. Everyone becomes trapped in this, so be brief, clear and to the point.

Another important condition for inner peace is to clearly arrange the time available. Before starting the discussion, everyone should be clear when their themes will be dealt with, and how much time is available per person. In our experience, the discussion of one person's themes can be covered in half an hour to three-quarters of an hour. However, it is necessary to keep a careful eye on the arranged time, because discussions on themes can easily run over the time allotted. It is also good to have a short break between two people contributing themes so that you can step back from the preceding theme and prepare yourself for the next one.

Exercise tip

In the next few weeks, choose some of the discussions in which you were asked for advice or suggestions, or in which the other person wanted to confide in you. In these discussions, practise the attitudes of both empathy and confrontation. However, in your choice of one attitude or the other, be guided by the speaker's contribution. Make a note of what happens to you and to the other person.

Task 20: My working life again

You are connected to the world through your work. The aim of your work is outside you: in objective terms, you always work for others, for 'clients'. In your work and in co-operating with others, you also develop yourself, you become more skilled in certain areas, sadder but wiser in others. What is the significance of the various experiences at work?

For yourself

1 Look back at some of the most important events and stages in your working life, focusing particularly on changes of direction, i.e., the changes in your career up to now. Answer questions such as:

– What sort of change was it?

– What happened exactly?

– How did the change come about? For example: own initiative, asked by others, attractive advertisement?

– What were the reasons for your change of direction?

– How did you leave the previous job?

– How did you start the new job?

Look at the answers to these questions with detachment and ask yourself what this says about your relationship to your working life.

2 Look back at the successive stages of your working life and ask yourself what every stage resulted in for you. Ask yourself questions such as:

– What went well for me in this period, and what did I find difficult?

– With which people was I involved during this period and what did they mean to me?

– What skills have I developed during the different stages of my working life?

3 What were the specific themes in your working life? Briefly describe these in more detail, as in Task 19.

4 Examine whether, and to what extent your themes and the theme of your life have influenced your work and your working life.

Practical instructions

For 1: Examples of a change of direction or another change include:
- from employee to manager;
- moving from a job in personnel to a management job;
- moving from industry to health care;
- moving from computer work to personnel work;
- moving from the centre to the periphery, i.e., from strong links in the organization in the centre of activities to a more distant connection.

For 2: Include people who made life difficult for you – even those with whom you came into conflict can be very meaningful in your life. They may have developed skills in you which you might not otherwise have.

For 3: Themes in your working life can be questions or tasks with which you have been involved in your work for a long time. For example: the introduction of management training, monitoring the introduction of computerization, the care of terminal patients.

You could explore this in more depth by asking yourself what was essential in this for you, what was it really about?

You can also ask yourself what you found difficult when you were working on this task or problem, and whether you encountered these difficulties again in other places and in other ways.

It may be that the themes you discover are more like an ideal or a guideline, e.g., involving people more in the creation of their living and working environment, working for a cleaner environment, or for integrated nursing care. Try to relate these ideals more closely to yourself as a person, by asking yourself what it was really about, and how this theme plays a role in the rest of your life.

For 4: The way in which the themes from Task 19 are interconnected with your working life differs from person to person. Your themes may be in no way related to your working life, they may be only incidentally related, or they may actually be the main focus of your working life.

In dialogue

If you discuss this task together, everyone takes turns to say what they have found. Try to be as specific as possible. Focus as much as possible on your working life (inevitably there will be some overlap with Task 19), and answer the following questions:
- When and where did the theme play a part in your working life?
- How did you relate to it and how do you relate to it now?
- How (firmly) were you – and are you – connected to your theme?
- What role did – and does – the theme play in your life and work?

The others concentrate on:

- other themes which can be heard through the themes that were described;

- the central theme in the speaker's working life;

- the characteristic of her connection with the theme;

- the meaning which the (central) theme has for the speaker with a view to her future.

When they have responded to the speaker in this way, she chooses one or two of the responses which surprised her or moved her, and which she wishes to discuss in further detail.

Rounding off

Finally, summarize your conclusions on the basis of the questions:

- What are the most important themes in my working life at the moment?

- Which themes do I consciously wish to pursue?

- What do I see as the central theme in my working life?

Share your conclusions with the others and note them in your Logbook.

Support exercise:
Turning point

For yourself

Take an A3 sheet of drawing paper and make it into a square by cutting off a strip from one side. You can use this strip as rough paper. Make sure you have a stick of charcoal and three soft crayons (dark red, ultramarine blue and pale yellow). Sit down comfortably and try to relax. Breathe calmly, making sure you breathe out fully.

1 Make the paper dark from the edges, leaving a light area in the centre. Work from the outside inwards, i.e., from the whole periphery to the centre of the paper. Work in layers, so that the intensity gradually increases, and working from the outside inwards, try to make the transition from dark to light as gradual as possible. The more intense the darkness on the outside (make sure there is no white edge), the more powerful the area of light will be that you try to retain in the centre. Try to go as far as possible in pushing back the light. Start with blue, then add black, and work alternately with black and blue.

2 Now reverse the direction: working from the centre outwards. Make the same sheet of paper brighter or more fiery, in such a way that the area in the centre is more powerful than the outside edge. Do this gradually, always working from the inside outwards and around. The more intense the light and fire are in the centre, the weaker the dark will be on the outside that you try to retain. Try to go as far as possible in intensifying and distributing the light and fire. Start with yellow, then add red, and then work alternately with red and yellow.

Practical instructions

You are using soft crayons or pastels which can easily be pulverized, particularly the blue crayon. If you remove the paper from the crayon and place it flat, you can use it for larger areas, though the stick will become less strong.

Get away from the feeling that you have to make something attractive; that is not important. This exercise is about the inner process that you experience as you are working. The working method described here is important for this.

It may be that there comes a point when you feel a resistance to go further into the dark or into the light and fire. Listen to this feeling in yourself; do not give in to it too quickly, but do not force yourself either.

In dialogue

Everyone takes turns to show their work and the others characterize it. Then you discuss your working processes, taking into account the following points:

- What was required of you to make the dark areas, and then to reverse the process and make it light?

- How do you relate to light and darkness?

- Does this say anything about the way in which you have dealt with difficult situations up to now?

- Did you complete the task? How did you work?

- What does this contribute to your question?

This exercise makes use of the following abilities or inner skills:
- 'being moved' by a task

- persevering with a task, irrespective of inner reactions and other distractions;

- allowing anything to arise, and responding to it;

- observing and distinguishing what is happening outside you (on the paper) and inside you.

Rounding off

Finally, writes down what you want to remember.

Examples of this exercise, Ill. 6 (after p. 280)

Your image of humankind?

Sören Aabye Kierkegaard, the nineteenth-century philosopher from Copenhagen, said: 'Life should be understood backwards and lived forwards.' Understanding life backwards means looking back at the life behind you – with all its events, periods, and recurrent themes – and seeing what is characteristic of your life, what is right for you, and what will probably remain with you in the next few years, such as the theme of your life.

Looking back in this way, the following questions may arise; What is the significance of all the things which formed you? What do you do with them? Is that what you are now? Behind this, there is a question about freedom. How much freedom of choice do you have? Can you choose the direction for the rest of your life?

That depends on the way in which you look at people, and on your image of humankind.

We think that it is useful to be aware of your assumptions about human beings, of how you look at people – and to look at the image of humankind which others use around you. You can also ask some critical questions about your own image of humankind, and where necessary change it and develop it further. It is characteristic of this age, where there is no generally accepted image of humankind, that everyone must find their own image and possibly, constantly rediscover it.

We outline a number of the images we have discovered below. Usually they do not occur in such a simple form. Most people's image of humankind is complex and composed of different views.

The human being is essentially good.

The human being is essentially bad.

The human being is like a machine (the heart is a pump, the head is a computer).

The human being is a subtle balance of physical, chemical processes, hormones, temperature.

The human being is a biological being, the result of DNA codes, heredity, and so on.

The human being is a composition of values, norms, patterns of habits, resulting from education and environment.

The human being is *who she or he is,* s/he exists.

The human being is a spiritual being and is part of a world which is not visible to the naked eye.

The human being is predetermined and his freedom of action is prescribed within narrow limits.

Man has a free will able to choose where she or he wishes to go and the direction in which she or he wishes to develop.

In our view of humankind, the human being is a *traveller on the border,* a being which lives between polar forces which he or she can connect within himself or herself.

– He travels across the borders of time, living between yesterday and tomorrow in the alternation of day and night, light and dark.

– He travels across borders in the space of this world, with his head in the air and his feet on the earth, or in his space capsule between the sun and the earth. He also lives between castles in the air and physical practicality, between ideals and reality, between what he thinks he can do and what he really does.

– He travels across borders in his relationships with people and everything around him, living between what he observes and feels in the outside world, and what he experiences in terms of thoughts, feelings and emotions, and his will.

A person who travels across borders is a navigator or pilot who is looking for the path in these different dimensions or areas so that he can develop there.

But what is your own image of humankind?

Exercise tip

For a week, make a note of things people say about people, on TV, on the radio, in the newspaper. Write them down and characterise the image of mankind that is expressed.

Who am I?

There are times in your life when you are thrown back on yourself and questions arise such as: 'Who am I?', 'What do I want with my life?', 'What is the meaning of my existence?' These questions may also arise if you consciously consider the questions of life when you are working on this book.

At the same time that you ask these questions, you know that they will remain largely unanswered, because they go beyond the limits of ordinary consciousness. These questions have been asked for thousands of years. All sorts of religions and philosophies have tried to provide answers, but in Gabriel Marcel's words, 'Man remains a question to himself'.

Part 2 of this book includes a chapter entitled 'Who am I?' in which we try to reveal our own vision, inspired by anthroposophy, but also by writers such as Carl Rogers, Viktor Frankl, and Harry Mulisch. A summary of that chapter is given below.

The human being in three parts

Human beings live at different levels or in different dimensions at the same time. We describe the human being here as seen from three different perspectives.

I am a physical creature

Our bodies all have something in common, at the same time as having an extremely individual quality. This individuality is most visible in the face, but it is also expressed in fingerprints, in the teeth, in our organs and so on. The way in which different individuals move is also very characteristic.

For the most part, I know my body only from the outside. There are all sorts of processes which I know about because of biology or medical science, but not through an inner knowledge.

By linking this outside knowledge with my own inner experiences, I can know my own body better.

I am a being with a soul

I have an inner life. I have thoughts, feelings, imagination, judgements, desires, passions, and so on. The life of my soul is formed and coloured by the interaction with the outside world to a much greater extent than my body is formed by these things. When this is no longer the case, we should watch out. When our thoughts, feelings and intentions are no longer linked to the outside world, we can become unreal or insubstantial. In the specialist literature, this is known as 'cocooning': it is as though the person has become enclosed in his own inner world, in a 'cocoon'.

When people ask themselves, 'Who am I?', they are interested in the first instance in the soul. You ask yourself: 'How do I work? Why do I react in this way? What impression do I make on other people?' These questions are usually the result of experiencing many contradictions in the soul; wanting to belong somewhere, but also wanting to do your own thing, joy linked to sorrow, freedom which always requires a sense of obligation.

Knowing yourself in terms of the soul is only really possible through talking, through interaction with others, although individual reflection and assimilation are also essential.

I am a spiritual being

I have experienced that there is a deeper dimension to me than my body and my own inner world. Although my feelings come very close to the core of my personality, my real core has a different nature. This is the small inviolable 'place' in you which remains itself even when life is extremely difficult: when your thoughts appear to be in complete chaos and you think you will be overwhelmed by your feelings, and you have a sense of apathy and impotence. We call this the 'Self'. I become aware of my Self when I am rowing upstream against the current of life. For example, when I feel that I have to do something, even though no one expects this of me and it might be easier and more advantageous to do nothing. And yet I do it without hesitation. At that moment, I am quite alone and quietly myself. Then I have a sense: 'This is my Self speaking.'

This Self is unique. It is my most individual aspect. It is the essence of who I am. And it is this essence which ultimately guides my life. In fact the Self is a guide.

By studying the past, as we have in this book, we become more aware of this Self. Because of this Self, we are able to take our own lives in hand, we can educate ourselves and are less dependent on the forces in our bodies or the influences of the environment.

The Self has a different nature from the two dimensions described above. It cannot be derived from them or explained by them. It is a third, separate dimension of our being with a spiritual nature, i.e., it cannot be directly perceived by our ordinary senses and cannot be proved through rational thought. The Self is connected with and forms part of the spiritual world, which is concealed behind the ordinary visible world.

We are connected to the earth through our body. When we die and the soul and the Self have departed from the body, it remains on the earth and turns to dust.

Our Self is part of the spiritual world where we return after death.

The central area between the physical body and the spiritual self is the soul. Both the forces of the body and the forces of the Self have an effect on this, as do the forces of the environment, particularly those exerted by other people. The soul develops during a person's lifetime, surrounded by all these forces. After death, the result of this development is taken to the spiritual world by the Self.

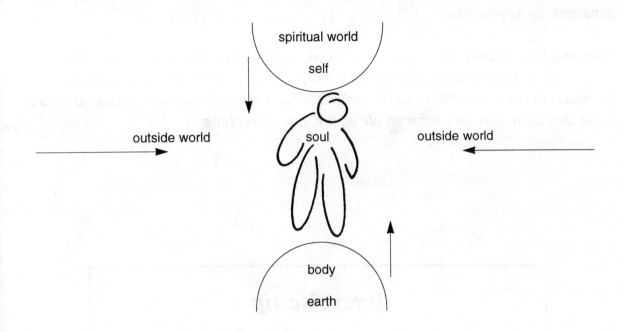

Reincarnation and karma

For us, death is not a definite end, but a gateway to another form of life – life in the spiritual world. This is where the results of life on earth are processed. As Rudolf Steiner and others described, we are then confronted with the effect of our behaviour on others during our life on earth. Then we may experience, for example, the joy and the sorrow which others experienced as a result of our actions. This period of assimilation is followed by a period when we prepare for another life on earth.

Every life on earth is one-sided, because you cannot be everything at the same time when you are alive: Chinese and American, dentist and politician, man and woman, beggar and millionaire. In every life, you develop certain aspects and leave others aside.

When you start preparing for a new incarnation in the spiritual world, you prepare a sort of design for the next life, aimed at the sort of development which you want yourself. At the same time, you balance the consequences of previous lives, such as your 'unfinished business' with other people, but also the patterns of thinking which you developed in previous lives and your basic attitudes, matters which you neglected or ignored. From this karma, you choose what to include in your plan for your next life.

You make an enormous effort, as do other (human and superhuman) spiritual beings, to make sure that, in addition, you can lead the life you choose. And that you can play your role in the lives of others. The cosmic wisdom and organization required to achieve this is quite unimaginable.

At the moment we are born on earth, we forget all this. We live our lives without being aware of our plans before birth, our time in the spiritual world and our previous earthly lives. In the study of your biography, you may come across some indications of this unconscious direction in your 'life plans', and gain an idea of the meaning of what is happening in your life.

The intention of this explanation is not to encourage you to start fantasizing about your previous lives on earth. By explaining our views, we want to emphasize how profound the question: 'Who am I?' really is. Moreover, this view can at least give us a sense that no matter how difficult life is, it is not for nothing.

Exercise tip

Choose someone close to you and follow this person for three weeks. Try to observe that person at three levels: in terms of the body, the soul and the spirit (or direction). Make a note of what you discover.

Task 21: My source of inspiration

If you are inspired by your work, you work with your heart and soul. You have more energy, and your enthusiasm spreads to others. But you can also lose your inspiration because of all sorts of circumstances. Your well runs dry and you don't know how to get it working again. Finding new sources of inspiration (or rediscovering the old ones) will support your work on a new future.

For yourself

Prepare yourself to give a presentation lasting at most seven minutes, on the theme: 'What inspires me?'. Do this in your own words without borrowing clever sentences from books or using other people's statements. Do not make your account too abstract, and relate it to yourself. Tell it from your heart, though you may use notes to remind you of certain points.

Practical instructions

The following four questions can help you to discover what inspires you.

What 'heroes', 'heroines' or role models were there, and are there in my life?
These are people you have known and who did something you admire and would like to do yourself. It may be a former teacher, a member of your family, an artist, a sportsman or sportswoman that you know, and so on. Choose one person and describe in one or two concrete examples what you admire(d) in him or her.

Where is my 'no'?
What are the things that you have said a strong 'no' to recently, certainly in the last year. Describe one or two situations in which this happened, in terms of images. The 'no' may have been expressed, or may just have been experienced internally. Sometimes it is an immediate response to a situation; sometimes it occurs later. Try to formulate your attitude in these situations. By becoming aware of what you certainly didn't want, you may become clearer about what you did want.

What affects me?
Go back in your memory to moments when you were truly affected by something. Being affected means that something is awoken in you. This may be accompanied by emotion, but also by tremendous enthusiasm which you would like to shout out to the rest of world.

   Describe some of these moments in images, as clearly as possible, showing what it was that was affecting you. It may be something that struck you when you read a book, saw a film, listened to music; it may be an event, something someone said, or something you did. (One person described the effect of hanging in the air when he abseiled from a grain elevator forty metres high; someone else was very affected by hearing a passage from Mozart's *Requiem* while stuck in a traffic jam.)

When you come across moments which are generally 'emotive moments' in life, such as the birth of a child, or the death of a parent or partner, try to be very specific about what exactly affected you in this.

What is my 'dream'?
Leaving aside any concrete circumstances and possibilities, what would you like to be most of all? Would you like to be a pop singer or a conductor, to sail across the ocean alone, or to be a mountaineer crossing the Himalayas? Or a teacher, a doctor, a cabinet-maker?

Do not just mention a profession or job, but describe the specific situation you dream of, for example, for a conductor:

'I am standing there with the whole orchestra in front of me and a packed hall behind me. It is absolutely quiet. I lift my baton and feel the intense tension. Then the first bars of the violins can be heard very quietly and tenderly.'

Or 'The concert has finished and the applause thunders in the hall. I turn around and see the packed hall, full of enthusiastic people.'

Ask yourself about the answers to these four questions, and then ask yourself, 'What inspires me?'. Finally, prepare a presentation in which you incorporate the answers. Again, it is not the intention that you should read an account that you have written in advance for this occasion, or that you know it off by heart. Just make a note of some key words and with the help of these, try to express what inspires you again.

Explanation: Inspiration in daily life (p. 155)

In dialogue

Everyone takes turns to give his account in a maximum of seven minutes. The others listen at two levels:

–   At what moment was I affected by this account, and what caused this?

–   What inspires the speaker?

When the speaker has finished, the listeners relate, as accurately and specifically as possible, the moments at which they were affected.

Then there is a discussion about the things that inspire the speaker. The speaker starts by listening without contributing. It is only when the listeners have more or less finished looking for the source of his or her inspiration that the speaker joins in. In this way it is possible to achieve a more profound and precise result.

Rounding off

The speaker concludes this part of the discussion by responding with his or her experiences and/or results from the discussion. Write down what you want to remember.

Inspiration in daily life

If someone asks you: 'What inspires you in your work or in your life?' you may not always have an immediate answer. 'Inspiration,' you might think, 'is for artists or inventors, not for me.' When you think of inspiration, you tend to think of a sort of spiritual flash of lightning, a spark which enables people to do very special things. This has never happened to you, and therefore it seems as though inspiration doesn't play a role in your life.

However, if you don't make it into such a big thing and stay closer to home, it may look rather different. For example, you may hear yourself say, after an interview on TV or a lecture which you have attended, that it was an inspiring event. By this, you mean that it appealed to you; that the story or the person who was telling it touched something in you.

Modern management literature often indicates that managers have to be inspiring to stimulate their employees. This means that these managers shouldn't be boring, impersonal and cool, but should be genuine, able to transmit enthusiasm and be personally involved in the vision they are promoting. Unfortunately, it does not always tell you how to become an inspiring person. For most readers, and perhaps for the writers of this literature, it seems to be the sort of talent which you either have or don't have.

We believe that anyone can be inspired, though it does require care and some practice to learn to use inspiration and to allow it to play a role in your work and in your life. Inspiration can be removed from the ivory tower of the artist and brought back to earth, to become something that we can simply learn, study and practise. When inspiration is demystified, it becomes worthwhile for everyone. It can provide a meaning and direction in our life. It can help you to find a purpose and direction for yourself, to develop a vision and fill your activities with spiritual strength. It can make you a more powerful and visible person, so that your actions and words become linked to your inner self. In other words, inspiration is spiritual nourishment.

However... this nourishment is not presented to you on a plate. It requires concentration, practice and effort. We will explain this in further detail below by focusing attention on three questions:

- Where does inspiration come from, what are the sources of inspiration?

- How do you develop and look after inspiration?

- How do you use inspiration in daily (working) life?

Where does inspiration come from?

In the first instance, inspiration comes from the outside world. There is something in the world around us or an event which touches our inner Self. These can be very different things for different individuals, or at different moments during the course of one individual's life. It may be a book or a film, a landscape or a work of art, a pop singer or a starry sky. In principle, anything in the outside world can inspire us, even negative experiences or events. At the same time, inspiration is connected to our inner world, because these phenomena and events from the external world touch our inner Self. They stimulate our inner Self to move. The dictionary defines inspiration as 'the act of blowing on or into, the action of inhaling, drawing in the breath, the action of inspiring.' Thus this also refers to an element from outside which 'moves' our inner Self. This is an essential part of it. We are also inwardly affected when we are angry or sad, but not every emotion is inspiration. This applies only if the experience of being affected leads to a feeling that you want to do something about it. It results in a desire to bring to life an aspect of ourselves.

The things which have this effect on our inner world can come from different areas in the external world.

Ideas

We can be inwardly moved by ideas, for example, by a vision of mankind, a view of life, education or patient care, of organizations, management and of leadership, for example.

Although ideas generally appeal, above all, to the thought processes, inspiring ideas also have a strong effect on feelings. It is a tremendous experience when an idea or thought sets fire to you inwardly. It can produce great warmth and light in your inner world. Examples which spring to mind are the ideas of the non-violent resistance movements of Gandhi and Martin Luther King, Carl Rogers' non-directive therapy, and Rudolf Steiner's views on world development. But the marketing concepts of Pim Hasper or Peter Senge's vision of the learning organization can also have this effect.

Sometimes you can be so taken over by an idea that comes from outside that you wish you had thought of it yourself; it may also be that it leads you to your own new ideas. This happens particularly when we are affected in a negative way by fascist or reactionary ideas. We reject these with a powerful 'No!' and this can lead to a counterview to which we feel strongly attracted, such as the fundamental equality of human beings.

People

We can be deeply affected by the 'existence' of people, i.e., irrespective of their ideas. In this case, the existence of a person represents something which is specially valuable for us. People can represent values such as sincerity, courage, loyalty, simplicity, perseverance and so on. It can touch you in such a way that you feel: 'That is what I would like to be like', and you feel encouraged to develop courage, loyalty, and so on, in your own way. Most people have come across such examples once or twice in their lives. Often, we have unconsciously assimilated certain aspects of these examples.

Apart from being affected by what people are, we can also be affected by what they do. For example, climbing a mountain, being skilled in a craft or achievements in sport.

Nature

Many people have experienced being moved by natural phenomena and events. This may be by a landscape or a sunset, a foaming sea or crashing storm, it may be a jungle full of life and noise, or the vast desolation of the desert. These may also be processes such as birth, the emergence of spring or processes of death and decay, such as autumn.

Many people find that the inspiration of nature is like a sort of liberation – a liberation from the smallness and confines of everyday existence and a longing to turn to essential elements. A person's own body also counts as nature, and the experience of the body can be a source of inspiration. For example, one person said: 'My ideals are not in my head, but in my legs'. He was a plant manager at a testing factory for a large multinational company where exciting things often happened. He said that he often went surfing in the sea at night when there was a good wind. The wind, the water, the night sky with the stunning clouds and, above all, his experience of his own body, standing up surrounded by these elementary forces, gave him an enormous kick, unleashed creative forces in him and gave him the energy to keep going in his daily work.

Things

We can be affected by things made by people. Again, there are many different possibilities, varying from ingeniously manufactured cars to a simple washing peg, from a painting to a fashionable garment, from a medieval cathedral to a modern computer, and so on.

We are often touched by a mixture of beauty and perfection. This can manifest itself in an almost physical way. We often have a tendency to touch things. Touching something can lead to a desire to possess the product that is admired, either in a real way, or symbolically. We can purchase it, collect models, e.g., trains or dinky toys, buy reproductions or make our own photographs. It can even lead to a sort of collection mania; in this case there is little left of inspiration. For this actually requires us to resist the urge to possess, so that the enthusiasm for the idea on which the work is based, for its beauty or the skill with which it was made, is kept alive.

These are some of the areas in the outside world where our inspiration stemmed from in the first place. Events and phenomena awaken something in us and bring it to life. It is no coincidence that one particular phenomenon has this effect rather than another. Of course, there are things that affect almost all of us, such as the birth of a child, or the death of a loved one. However, amongst these things as well as apart from them, there are things which touch only you. It is possible that many people witnessed the same event but passed it by without noticing, while it actually had a profound effect on you. These moments are very personal. They are related to you. There is a connection between inspiration and the theme of your life. You experience something in the outside world that is related to the reason why you are here on earth.

How do you develop and look after your inspiration?

It is a characteristic feature of our time that the things which appeal to us also quickly evaporate. Things which move us today are forgotten tomorrow because something else comes up. For example, in the past few years all sorts of new and enthusiastic visions and ideas have been put forward at conferences and symposiums on management and organization. People are enthused by these, but soon one inspired view makes way for the next. In other fields there is also so much happening these days that we are in danger of being anaesthetized so that we will no longer be affected by anything, or we become enthusiastic again and again, without any real depth.

If something from the outside world is to have any permanent value, so that it can act as a source of inspiration, we have to assimilate it.

The ways in which you can do this are very different, depending on what sort of person you are and on what comes to you from the outside world. Nevertheless, there are some general tips that you can follow.

The first step is often to hold on to the moment when you were affected, and not allow it to escape. The outside world quickly distracts us from our most intimate experiences. Some people use a small notebook to record these moments. They always have it with them, at home and at work, on holiday, etc. Sometimes they may not use it for weeks on end, but as soon as something happens, they always make sure to make a note of it. Underlining a passage in a book, or placing a piece of paper in a particular page, can also help you to hold on to what you have recognized.

The next step is to really start working on it. In this respect, it is a matter of blowing the inner spark with your own breath. The initial enthusiasm was granted by the outside world. Now you must try to keep the flame going.

One person told us: 'I am reading a book and suddenly I come across a passage which appeals to me enormously. It says something which makes me think: That's it, it couldn't be said more clearly. I put a piece of paper by this passage and a few days later, I think: Oh yes! I was so enthusiastic about that piece in that book, what did it say again? I have forgotten and look it up. Often I then find myself thinking: Goodness, was that all? Why was I so enthusiastic about that a few days ago? But then I start to work on it and try to bring it to life myself. If that works, then it really becomes something. But often it doesn't work and then I let it go.'

One way of bringing it to life is to put it into words in your own way, or to write it down. Some people do this in the form of a sort of diary in which they write down their inspirations. Another way is to write letters to a reader who really exists, or to an imaginary reader who is interested in you. Some people are able to publish their inspirations in an article or in a book.

But you can also work on it in a very different way. Somebody said to me, 'Inspiration means wasting time.' He meant that for him, working on this inner task involved being busy with all sorts of apparently useless things. Tidying up the office, making coffee, sitting down and writing something down, doing an errand, etc. But at a deeper level, he was constantly working on the theme that fascinated him.

Some people do this by going for a walk, or sitting down in a special spot in the countryside. Others feel that they want to work with colour or clay, and in this way come to grips with the inspirations.

Another way of extending and developing an inspiration is to talk about it with other people. You can ask them to respond to your views. By exploring their questions, you are forced to clarify matters. You can also ask them to indicate which parts of your vision you could develop further. You do not have to follow up all the tips which this question might produce. You can choose those which appeal to you most.

In the past, faith and religion were a source of inspiration for many people. They can also be so in our own time. But faith, religion and philosophy require a conscious choice nowadays, and it is necessary to develop your own personal relationship to these matters if they are to be a true source of inspiration.

How do you use your inspirations in your daily working life?

It is not usually very productive to impose all sorts of models, ideas and views on reality. This can be seen as 'introducing' a vision into day-to-day practice and this often fails. Nothing happens, the situation remains unchanged, or all sorts of unintentional side-effects occur. Many ideals, models, systems and concepts founder as a result. Lots of managers and employers know all about this. In this situation it is easy to blame others for failing to co-operate or for being unwilling to help – sometimes with good reason – but you may not be aware that you are insufficiently realistic yourself, and are too much stuck with your own ideas. This means that you are blind to what is happening in the real world, the forces which are present there, and what next step would be possible.

It is very important to make a distinction, on the one hand, between developing and nurturing your sources of inspiration, and on the other hand, being active in the real world. Nurturing inspirations, as we described above, is a separate field, and you should more or less forget about this when you start to act in the real world.

In order to do this in a fruitful way, it is necessary to concentrate on reality, to connect with it by observing specific phenomena and specific people, and characterizing them. In other words, you are not focused on your own inner world, but on the external world.

However, if you cannot introduce your inspirations directly into the real world, what are they good for? Is there any point in carefully nurturing these inspirations?

There most certainly is! By developing and nurturing your inspirations, on the one hand, and forming a connection with the real world, on the other hand, the real world evokes inspirations in you. In other words: the real world itself awakens them in you and brings them to life. You recognize your vision, concept or idea in the reality of daily life.

Then it starts to flow in you. You become enthusiastic, but at the same time, you remain connected to the real world that you are in, and do not become imprisoned in the thoughts and ideas which you developed somewhere else, outside this concrete situation. As a result, your actions become infinitely more productive than if you try to control reality on the basis of your own ideas.

This can be explained in the following illustration:

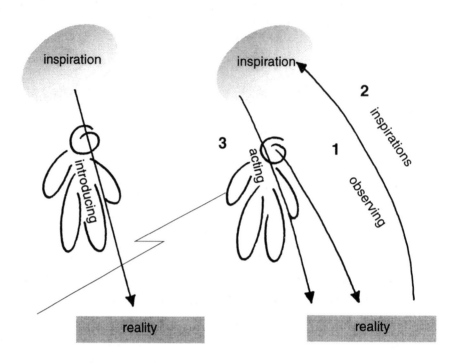

Many of us know this from our own experience. For example, if you have to make an introductory speech or give a lecture, you prepare it thoroughly, but when you are standing in front of the group and start to say exactly what you have prepared, with or without the help of an overhead projector, what you say is often lifeless and puts the listeners to sleep. This means that you are so fixated on the content that you no longer see the group. If you are able to forget the preparation entirely for a moment and focus on the people sitting in front of you by listening to their questions and feeling their concerns, something starts to flow. All sorts of things that you prepared come to you, and you are able to put them across in an inspired way, in words created at that moment. Thorough preparation is absolutely essential for this. If you have not prepared yourself sufficiently, or nurtured the sources of your inspiration insufficiently, you might lose this inspiration entirely in the real world, and become a plaything of the forces in the situation.

In this light, focusing on the reality of the client can help us to become inspired in daily life and stay inspired. Just as it is essential to prepare a speech, it is also essential to constantly develop and extend this field, but in our contacts with the client, we must concentrate on her. If we are able to do this, we can expect the inspiration to do what is necessary to be automatic.

Exercise tip

*Choose two or three people from your work
whom you see as emanating a special quality.
Without asking them directly, but simply by
observing them and listening to them closely,
try to discover what inspires them.*

Task 22: Basic values

Values play an important role in life. They often unconsciously direct your thoughts, feelings and actions. At critical moments, you may be overcome with the force with which they colour and determine the content of your reactions. 'But that was an agreement', you may exclaim if someone has not phoned up a quarter of an hour after the agreed time. Another person might say that you could have phoned. Or you might respond: 'That's no way to treat people!', when someone is shouted down in an authoritarian way. If you are conscious of your values, you have a firmer grasp on life.

For yourself

This part of the task consists of four steps:

1 Make a list of values in order of importance. What are the important things in life ? What is essential or valuable to you?

2 Try to look at what is happening in the world, in the news in newspapers, on TV, and so on, with unprejudiced, fresh eyes. Make a note of when you are affected, both in a positive and in a negative sense. Perhaps you are shocked or incensed by a particular item of news, or perhaps you are intensely saddened by it. Try to discover in very specific terms what actually causes this. Then put the essence of your response into words.

3 Look at the events of your life, both in your private life and at work, which were of existential importance to you. What was happening? What did you feel this was about? What made you enthusiastic?

4 Now write a short story, no longer than a half a sheet of A4, in which you write down the most essential things for the future. Prepare to tell this story afterwards, without using the paper, and without learning it off by heart.

Finally make a list of, at most, ten important values, using key words.

Practical instructions

The first three steps are three entrances which could lead to the same result. Try to do them independently from each other; this will lead to the greatest surprises.

For step 1: Write down the values as they occur to you spontaneously and then list them in order of importance.

For step 2: Obviously there are other sources of information than the newspapers and TV. Choose a source which suits you.

For step 4: You can choose your own future, that of the place where you live, your children, etc.

In dialogue

Everyone takes turns to tell their stories and then show their lists of key words. The others help the speaker to specify the essence of what she said.

Then there is a discussion about the role which the basic values play in the speaker's current working life. She describes some specific events. The others help her to describe these in images as clearly as possible.

Rounding off

You may wish to change your list with your most important values after the discussion. Make a note of this new list in your Logbook, using key words, together with anything else you wish to remember from the discussion.

What do I want?

Increased assurance about what is appropriate for you is a good stepping stone for exploring aims and paths to the future. By creating pictures of the future, or whole scenarios, you can discover the things which you are really enthusiastic about.

Tasks

23 My mood about my future
24 Results up to now
25 Scenarios
26 Questions from the world around me
27 More scenarios
28 Results and learning so far
29 My question again

Explanations

My central question for the future
Studying the future
Discussion on the scenarios

Support exercise

Movement and imagination

Task 23: My mood about my future

When you look at the future of your working life, what mood does this put you in? Does it make you feel curious and enthusiastic? Do you feel challenged? Are you neutral about it ('I'll see what happens')? Do you feel unsure, possibly sombre? Or are you afraid; do you hesitate to imagine your future? In other words, what are the feelings which colour your attitude to the future?

For yourself

Express the mood which you feel when you think of your working life in the future. Do this on paper with colour and movement.

Practical instructions

Take a piece of drawing paper (or work in your Logbook), the soft crayons and the stick of charcoal.
Before you start, concentrate on the feeling you have when you think of your future. Do not let yourself be hurried, and do not ignore unpleasant feelings.
Don't think too much when you are carrying out this task. Trust in your hands and the spontaneous choice of colours. Allow whatever comes to come.
Do not work towards a preconceived result, and avoid representations.

In dialogue

Everyone takes turns to show their mood image without indicating how it was created, what they think of it, what it means, and so on. The others look at it and characterize it. When the person who made the image has responded to the characteristics, there is a discussion about the question of what in the mood image refers to the mood at this particular moment or the mood of the present situation, and what relates more to the basic mood of the person who made the image, with regard to the future.

Explanation: Working with colour (p. 42)

Rounding off

Finally, write down what you wish to remember.

Task 24: Results and learning so far

An enterprising life involves taking initiatives to achieve things in the world. An enterprising life also involves setting yourself goals for learning. In both cases it is necessary to reflect on the results obtained. Then you can set yourself the next challenges.

For yourself

Collect the most important results of your study with the help of Table 1 over the page in the Logbook. Copy the completed table for your discussion partners.

Practical instructions

Most points in the table are self-evident. For some, we will add a short explanation.

Skills can be in three fields: in the field of knowledge and ideas, in the interpersonal field and in the physical or practical field.

Needs:
With regard to needs at the *spiritual* level, you could think of your interests. Examples of interests related to work: the development of interactive computer systems, co-operation between nursing staff and doctors, the consequences of redevelopment projects for people and organizations, etc. Examples from private life: the history of the Celts, repairing and building old wooden sailing ships, living together with people with different religions, the migration of birds through the Netherlands, gardening, etc.

Explanation: My central question for the future (p. 172)

My central question for the future:
As for the study of the past, you need a starting question when you study the future. This is your central question with regard to the future.

In dialogue

Everyone takes turns to explain their tables. On the basis of what the speaker says, the others can make notes and ask questions. The speaker weighs up their contributions, and if necessary, makes additions to her table.

Rounding off

Finally, write down what you wish to remember.

Table 1: Results up to now

	at work	in my private life
What have I got? Experience		
Skills		
What do I need? Spiritual		
Human		
Physical		
Material		
What challenges am I looking for?		

Date _____

The *theme of my life* is:

The three most important *themes at work* are:

The *sources of my inspiration* are:

My *basic values* are:

The *central question* for my future is:

My central question for the future

In *Living with questions* *(p. 23)*, we raised the question of the motor of personal development. We were referring to real questions which can constantly arise and make you restless. These questions originate when you experience the gap between what you basically want and how you live and work in reality. By becoming aware of this sense of dissatisfaction and of the questions resulting from this, you can start looking at your work and life in a meaningful way. But this awareness does not happen all at once. Searching for the backgrounds and causes of your feelings, you will discover that you have to reformulate your question from time to time. In this way, you will be able to distinguish the essential from the incidental aspects in your work and life with increasing accuracy, and it will slowly become clear to you what your central question is for the future. We deliberately refer to this as the central question. By looking for one central question, you force yourself to find the most existential question, or at least, the question on which you wish to work consciously now.

Examples of such central questions are:
- How can I learn to distinguish between personal matters and work?
- How do I avoid repeatedly getting into situations which I don't want?
- How do I learn to cope with my own fears and those of others?
- What aspects of myself should I work on in order to achieve development in the organization?
- How can I respond more calmly to the official hierarchy?
- How can I use my strength constructively without killing the initiative of others?

Remember that you will feel the full weight of such central questions only if they are your own questions. You can feel the importance of these questions when you closely observe the person who is asking them.

In order to explore your personal possibilities for the future, it is important to choose this central question well and formulate it clearly. But how can you find it? There are three ways that will lead you there: as an archaeologist, a historian, or as a Parsifal.

The archaeologist's path

This is like the exploration of Troy, the city of the famous horse, and of Hector and Priam. The archaeologist exposes one city after another, digging deeper and deeper. Finally she concludes: I have found ancient Troy. Then another archaeologist comes along and digs deeper until she has found the true Troy. But every archaeologist/digger decides for herself: *This* is Troy.

Looking for your central question is like digging for the real question which concerns you. It is a matter of going deeper and deeper down to the essence of what really matters. You can start with the question closest to the surface: 'What should the next step be in my career?' Then you dig on and get to deeper questions such as :

– 'What are my strong and weak points?'

– 'Do I want to go on with this work, or are there other possibilities?'

– 'What is the point of this work? What do I consider meaningful work?'

– 'What is my life really about, what is the central theme that I come across, again and again?'

The question which is the real issue is anchored in a deeper layer of your existence than the question of what you can or cannot do. Looking for the question of what it is all about can involve a struggle in which you encounter yourself. You may slide into a depression about your weak points or you may be too jubilant about the possibilities which you see. Or you encounter rage, sadness and despair about the pointlessness of your job – which you are unable to give up, because you have to work to eat. Or you can come across indomitable optimism which tells you that everything will be OK. As an archaeologist, you are digging into your soul and only you yourself can say, 'This is my central question.'

The historian's path

You can also follow the historian's path, moving through the past, looking for the way in which trade used to be conducted. What were the trading routes? How was transport arranged? What products were fetched and where, and where were they taken throughout the world? Did they barter goods or did they use money, or other forms of payment? What was this like, for example, during the time of the Phoenicians, or Marco Polo, the United East India Company, in the age of steamships, supertankers or the present transport of freight by air? How did people communicate, arrange finance, etc.? What were the problems facing entrepreneurs, traders and transporters? Were these always the same problems throughout the centuries? Or is there a single central recurring question which applies throughout history to those concerned, constantly reappearing in a different guise? Have some problems fundamentally changed in character during the course of time?

You can try to discover your own central question in the same way, exploring the history of your own life. Which things were important to me yesterday, last year, or when I just started work? For example, now that I am fifty, I wonder about the point of the work I have been doing for about twenty years. What does it actually mean? Did I ask myself that question at the beginning of my career? Or was I more concerned then with my potential for development or growth? There were all sorts of possibilities in the late 1960's, early 1970's. It is different nowadays. At the time, it was an existential question as to what work I could do, and yet, it was different. When I was twenty-eight, my life was still before me. Now at the age of fifty, I wonder what I will 'still' do. Then I asked myself above all whether there was any point in it for me, so really I wondered whether I wanted to do this or that. Now I also ask myself what the point of my work is for the organization where I am working or for the society where I live. Ten years ago, what was I thinking of? My partner, our children, their school, our house, both our careers. Everything went round and round in that small circle, and I felt a need to break out of that drudgery. Was there nothing new that would be really meaningful?

The questions which you ask are related to your age, but also to the age in which you live. Take early retirement, and the question of retirement in general, for example. It seems a growing trend for some people in view of the current recession, to work into the seventies to earn a living. About ten years ago, this was only an idea, an intuitive feeling that people of fifty then would not be able to stop when they were sixty-five. Every age and every period in history has its own questions. But what is my central question through the years? How does this emerge in different forms, and how does it emerge now?

Parsifal's path

The third path that can take you to your central question is like that of Parsifal (*par ce val* – through the valley). It is certainly not an easy path. Parsifal was a hero in a medieval epic who joined the famous circle of knights around King Arthur, as a young, inexperienced and daring knight. Later on, he entered the fortress of the Holy Grail, full of knowledge about how to do this, but still rather naive with regard to the deeper layers of life. He took part in the holy mystery of the Grail and witnessed the suffering of Amfortas, the lord of the castle. However, he failed to ask a single question. When he left the fortress the following day, without seeing a living soul, a young shield bearer called out: 'Silly goose, you could have opened your mouth and asked the lord of the castle a question.' His cousin Sigune, whom he told the story of his adventure, reproached him and did not want anything more to do with him. He also had to leave his friends, the band of knights around King Arthur, when they heard about his shame in the fortress of the Grail. He had failed to do what was expected of him and what was implicitly asked of him. From that time, he wandered through the world in a daze, and abandoned by God. At the deepest point of his life, he opened his heart on Good Friday to the hermit Trevrizent. As a result, he became open to others again, and when he returned to the fortress of the Grail, he was able to ask the question it was all about: 'Uncle, what is the matter?' In this way he liberated Amfortas, and became the keeper of the Grail himself.

The path followed by Parsifal is not an unknown path. It is the path of action. Parsifal was a young man who set out without experience, acting on his own impulses and colliding with the world because he did not see what was needed. Then he turned away in despair, and only achieved true reflection when he was in the depths. He did not 'look before he leapt'. Reflection often requires the help of another person, who is prepared to listen and able to reflect back what he has heard, without judging. By reflecting in this way, it is possible to arrive at an opinion based on the matter at hand. This means that you are better able to approach the world in a more conscious and sensitive way with an eye for the needs and questions of others.

It is often your disappointments, clashes and reprimands which have made you painfully aware of what you are unable to do or what you have omitted to do. This sort of crisis can occur in all sorts of ways. It can happen as the result of an appraisal, when you are passed over for promotion, or when you apply for a new job. It may be when you fail in a task, when you are abandoned by your partner, and so on. Without self-knowledge, you will suffer, rebel against it and attribute your failures to everything and everyone except yourself. But these painful experiences in your contact with others can put you on the right track of what really matters, what you have to learn.

To summarize, there are three paths which you can follow to find your central question:

- by digging into the deeper layers of yourself;

- by looking back at your life and seeing what constantly mattered to you;

- by experiencing where your feet will tell you to go, what you come up against, and by discovering your deeper impulses in your confrontation with the world.

Exercise tip

From the last three months, choose three moments when you came into collision with someone or something in your working situation. Describe these moments in terms of images, characterise them and find the question which is essential for you.

Support exercise
Movement and imagination

For yourself

Take a lump of clay (about one sixth of a lump of clay) and a hardboard sheet approximately 40 x 50cm to work on. Put this in front of you and read these instructions.

In this exercise you will be asked to express three different things consecutively, and every time, you should imagine what the result should be like in advance. When you are working you must use all the clay in front of you. Follow this procedure.

1 Leave the clay in front of you and imagine an open sphere. Visualize this as concretely as possible, taking into account the amount of clay in front of you. A sphere is a sphere, but an open sphere can be expressed in very different ways. Choose one way. Keep your mental image in mind (do not sketch it on paper) and work with the clay until you have made your image. Do this as precisely as possible.

2 Destroy the piece of work so that you have another rough lump of clay. This time, imagine an open cube, in which the open quality is achieved by taking a smaller cube out of the larger cube as a hole or hollow. Imagine this as concretely as possible, and again use all the clay you have. This task can also be carried out in many different ways. Keep your image in mind and work with the clay until you have made the image as exactly as possible.

3 Again destroy the work so that you have a rough lump of clay. This time, visualize a pair of beating wings. There are many sorts of wings: a swallow, a swan, a butterfly, a ladybird, and so on. Decide whether you want to represent the wings in a stylized way or more realistically. Make your representation as concrete as possible. Keep your image in mind, and work with the clay until you have formed it as exactly as possible.

Practical instruction

It is best to knead the clay thoroughly before you start on the first task. If the clay is too dry, it is difficult to work with. It becomes more flexible if you knead it with some water. However, if you make it too moist, it will lose its strength. Often it is enough just to wet your hands.

Make sure that your work is not too delicate or the walls too thin, or the whole thing will collapse.

In dialogue

Take turns to describe the process you used. You can do this with the help of photographs of the interim result: the sphere and the cube. Take the end result of your work in clay to the discussion. The process of the work is then characterized by the others.

Practical instructions

Of course, you can also do this exercise together. This has the advantage that you can also see each other's earlier results and can tell each other more easily about the process you used.

In describing the process he used, the speaker talks about the following points:

– How did you cope with making a representation of your desired image? Were you able to monitor this process?

– What happened to this representation when you were making it in clay? Were you able to hold on to it in a lively way?

– How did you find working with clay? Were you able to form the clay as you wanted?

– How did you react to destroying the results of your work?

– Does the above say anything about your performance in your situation at work?

– Did you fulfil the task? Did you follow the process outlined above?

– What are the results of all this for your question relating to the future?

The following abilities or inner skills are involved:

– making a concrete representation;

– retaining a representation you have made and creating this in clay;

– linking yourself to a representation and letting go;

– being moved by a task.

Rounding off

Finally, write down what you want to remember

N.B. In the following support exercise, you will again need clay. Keep the clay that is left in a sealed plastic bag after sprinkling it with some water.

Examples of this exercise: Illustrations 1a and 1b (on the following pages)

Support exercise: Movement and imagination

Illustration 1a

Illustration 1b

Task 25: Scenarios

It is a human quality to dream about the future, to dwell on it, and have fantasies based on fear and desire. By actively creating concrete images or representations of your future (scenarios), you can explore what suits you, what appeals to you, what you want or what you want to connect yourself with.

For yourself

Starting with the question which you formulated in the last task, list the different possibilities you see for your future. Try to write down five to ten possibilities. Choose three of these which you consider are worth exploring in more detail. Work on these to form an image of the future or a 'scenario'.

Scenario 1
Choose one of the possibilities you see before you, and work on it to form an image of your work and life in three years' time that is as specific as possible:

- form an image of a working day and a working week;

- describe the situation in your private life (social and material);

- indicate which themes you will be working on for your own development.

You can add to this scenario as you think fit.

Explanation: Studying the future (p. 185)

Scenario 2
Erase Scenario 1 from your mind and choose one of the other options for the future. Follow the same procedure as you did to create Scenario 1.
Concentrate on this possibility and make sure that as few elements as possible of Scenario 1 are automatically included in this new scenario.

Scenario 3
Now erase Scenario 2 from your mind and choose another possibility from the future which is clearly distinct from the previous two. Again follow the process for Scenario 1. Describe this future situation as accurately as the previous scenarios. Finally, erase this scenario from your thoughts as well.

Practical instructions

In this exercise, you create your future with the help of your imagination. This is a creative activity, working with your imagination. You form an image of the future in your mind. It is also an exercise in flexible thinking. You erase a scenario from your mind and then create another one. This involves inner activity. By forcing yourself to be as specific as possible, you stimulate your will. You will notice that all sorts of temptations arise not to fulfil this task. Some of the pitfalls are thoughts such as:

- 'I can't achieve that anyway.'

- 'Scenario 1 is the most fun, or the most realistic, or..., so why should I bother with the other two?'

- 'What's the point? The future is shrouded in mist anyway.'

- 'You shouldn't dwell on the future.'

The scenarios are not intended to be realized, but are a means of exploring the future. In reality, the future is always different. However, by creating scenarios you will discover what is valuable and important to you and this will give you a direction to your actions.

It is a good idea to carry out this whole task first without making any notes. Then try to remember the most important elements from each scenario, and make a note of them in your Logbook.

In dialogue

For every participant, the discussion takes place as follows:

- The speaker describes his first scenario in images as clearly as possible; the others listen and may make short notes.

- When the scenario has been described, there is an opportunity to ask some questions to clarify the image. The listener can also ask the speaker to describe a different aspect which he feels could be important for the speaker.

- This is followed by a brief silence when the listeners make a note of their characteristics of the scenario that was described, and of any other ideas. At this point, they do not yet exchange ideas or characteristics.

- This process is repeated for the following two scenarios.

- Finally, everyone characterizes the scenarios together and decides what is important to exchange or discuss.

- Then the most important characteristics are given, followed by a discussion.

Explanation: Discussion of the scenarios (p. 194)

Rounding off

Finally, write down what you consider important to remember.

Studying the future

Working with scenarios

The questions about work and life which concern people are related to the past and the future. With regard to the past, these are questions about insight, about backgrounds and the interrelationship of certain events in their lives. With regard to the future, they are questions about making conscious choices, for example, the choice about whether to continue to specialize, or to do more general work.

The past is a piece of your life that is behind you. You can call on facts, events and experiences in your memory. They provide the material for you to study.

The future gives much less support. Apart from the laws which govern the physical world, the so-called laws of nature, there are very few 'hard facts'. We can count on the sun rising again next week, and on the laws of physics continuing to apply. This sort of certainty does not exist with regard to arrangements between people. We try to reduce the uncertainties of the future as much as possible by means of agreements, contracts and rules. But many people have recently found, to their cost, that even the agreements enshrined in social legislation cannot provide permanent security. The sun cannot be stopped, but the old age pension can certainly be significantly changed, or early retirement schemes can be abolished.

The future is an uncertain area. Throughout history, people have made attempts to get a grip on the future. It has been predicted on the basis of dreams which were analyzed by dream specialists. It has also been read from natural phenomena; the flight of birds, the rushing of the wind, the flow of water. And there were certain places, springs or trees where initiates have been inspired by images of the future in the form of visions inspired by the gods. The future which was prophesied was often seen as being inevitable, as the Greek saga about Oedipus shows: by trying to escape his destiny, he actually completed it.

Nowadays, people tend to shrug their shoulders about these ancient practices, assigning them to the realm of fables. Predicting the future has become fairground entertainment. This does not mean that the future leaves us cold. These days, serious attempts are made to explore the future, using rational methods and techniques, such as the charting of trends, the calculation of future effects, making strategic plans and so on.

At the same time, there is growing scepticism towards this rational approach, and the possibility of controlling the future is increasingly regarded as an illusion. The great revolutions which took place in the world in the late 1980's – which were unexpected even for most leaders in politics and industry – as well as the chaotic conditions in the years before this, have led to a breakdown of the belief in a predictable, and therefore controllable world.

It is not only at the social level, or at the level of the organization, but also at the micro-level of personal life that it is difficult to find a satisfactory approach to the future. And yet it is important to do so for anyone who wishes to pursue a more conscious direction in his or her life.

How do people relate to their own future?

Waiting

There are people who think that you should simply wait to see what the future will bring. For generations before us this was the self-evident approach. Expressions such as 'You should take life as it comes' and 'Man proposes, God disposes' reflect this attitude. People regarded their lives as being externally determined. In reality, their own contribution was very slight, although there have always been people throughout history who achieved some form of self-determination.

In our own time there are also people who adopt an attitude of waiting. They believe there is little point in making lots of plans, because life is always different from what you had thought in advance. For example, you can go to work in the morning intending to do all sorts of things that day, but from the very start your plans are thwarted by unexpected events. When you go home in the evening, you become aware that you have been incredibly busy all day, but that you haven't achieved anything you set out to do. This applies even more often to resolutions about your attitude or behaviour. Very soon, you are reacting as you used to.

These and other experiences, like the fate of many New Year's resolutions, cause people to adopt a waiting attitude towards the future. They do not want the feelings of guilt and frustration about plans and intentions that were not fulfilled. Of course, you can also be hesitant in the face of the responsibility entailed by making your own choices. There is no getting round the fact that choices have consequences both for yourself, and for those with whom you have connections in your work or private life.

A waiting attitude to the future also reveals a certain experience of life. It indicates a realization that there are forces in your life that cannot all be understood, let alone controlled. However, this attitude also has a negative aspect. There is a great danger that you will 'sleep through' the opportunities and possibilities concealed in the future, and that you will constantly have the feeling that you are too late.

For that matter, the attitude of waiting is not so self-evident for modern man, and it is going in the face of the spirit of the time to adopt this attitude. If you do so consciously, the waiting is less directionless. It becomes an alert way of waiting for life, which you allow to go its course and allow to inspire you in your choices and acts.

Plans

In this age when action, initiative and independence are popular themes, many people approach the future in almost the opposite way. They assume that you can plan, control and therefore guide the future. There are many variations of this attitude which all have their own elements, such as the analysis of trends in the environment and in your own life up to now, charting your own strengths and weaknesses, setting objectives, and drawing up plans in stages.

For example, Peter, a thirty-six-year-old controller and the head of an I.T. department in a multinational company, said:

'I don't worry about the future. If you keep your eyes open and look after things a bit, not much can happen. Look, I'm thirty-six years old now and I'm here.' (He points to a square in the organization schedule). 'In a year or two, perhaps three, I can have this promotion.' (He points to a higher square, near the board of directors.) 'I'll stay there until I am forty-four or five, and then I'll get a transfer to a management job in personnel and organization.' (He points to another square, slightly lower.) 'Because, you know, by that time, you can do with a bit less pressure. All around me, people between forty-five and fifty are cracking up: they are stressed, have heart attacks or worse. I don't want to be finished at forty-five. I'll probably earn less, but that doesn't matter. The mortgage will be paid, the children will have left home...'

Peter considers that you have to know what you want and should plan the future because you can control the future. Many people think the same way. Waiting to see what life brings is the last thing they want.

We also come across this attitude with regard to inner development. For example, a young manager recently told me:

'In an appraisal, it became clear to me that my interpersonal skills are poorly developed. Of course, that's no good in my job and I'd like to do something about it. Anyway, I've also noticed that it's necessary in my private life. I'm looking for a programme which will first analyze the causes of my failure in this respect, and then I want to follow a specific training course to deal with these failures. In a year's time, I want there to be clear improvements, noticeable to people around me.'

This attitude to the future has many positive aspects: taking responsibility for your own life, setting goals and making sure that you achieve them, being alert with regard to setbacks and deviations from your plan, taking the initiative, and so on. It is a common attitude in people who seem to be doing well. Many others feel jealous of the way in which they know what they want, and their ability to set themselves goals. However, although these successful people give the impression that they are directing their development themselves, with a great degree of determination, it is often the norms and expectations of the outside world which determine their goals and the paths they follow.

If you genuinely ask yourself whether the wishes and expectations of the outside world are really compatible with what you want from life yourself, it becomes much more difficult to formulate clear and specific goals and paths to follow. Moreover, by making too many plans, you can easily become fixated on your ideas about the future. You will no longer see all sorts of chances and opportunities which actually exist. If you consciously include moments of reflection and practise allowing surprises to happen, this attitude of planning becomes less forced and you will find that you can trust life more.

187

The future and the will

It is clear that in the planned approach to the future, thinking is a dominant factor. The future is designed with rational fittings and measurements, targets are set, strategies are formed and stages are planned. You think you know what you want, but it isn't as simple as that. In fact, there is also a strong unconscious will at work in your life. This unconscious will is more important for your future than thinking. In order to consciously direct your life, it is important to discover the direction of this unconscious will. This means you will be able to find the middle ground between waiting and planning.

You follow a path in life between, on the one hand, the people and circumstances which you encounter, and on the other hand, the inner effect of your unconscious will. Many people have lost their way, their own biographical track, because of the circumstances of modern life. They lead a life which is no longer compatible with what they really want while they are here on earth. This can express itself in a feeling of pointlessness, of no longer feeling connected with the world around you, feelings of depression, anger, irritation, constant restlessness and indecision. The complexity and highly dynamic nature of life nowadays are confusing and require a great deal of flexibility. A sense of being directionless is always close at hand. There is good reason why many training courses focus on 'finding yourself' or 'being or becoming yourself'. Studying the course of your own life is one of the ways in which you can stimulate your connection with yourself, the people around you, and with the circumstances in which you are living.

The scenario method

In order to explore your will with regard to the future, this workshop uses a method which we call 'the scenario method'. This follows a path midway between planning and waiting, and adds another element.

By a 'scenario' we mean a description in images of something which could occur in the future. This image of the future can relate to the situation in which you will be working or living at a particular time, or to the path leading to this, i.e., to everything you do in order to achieve this situation in a particular time.

In order to distinguish between these two aspects, we call the image of the future situation a 'scenario', and the image of the route leading there, the 'stepping stones,' or 'stages leading to the scenario'. These are both dealt with below.

Scenarios

You start by listing a number of possibilities for the future, based on your central question regarding the future. Then you choose the three most appealing possibilities. For example, one person arrived at the following choice:

– 'I am going to go on working in my present field and in the company where I am working now. However, I will ask for a transfer from the laboratory to a production unit so that I can work in a more practical, result-orientated way.'

– 'I will stop with my present work and finish my interrupted training at music college. Then I will become a music teacher.'

– 'I will start a small technical consultancy bureau in our specialist area, together with a friend'.

If you list these three possibilities for the future, they probably all have attractive aspects as well as threatening ones. There is a tendency to start weighing them up, to look at the advantages and disadvantages, the pros and cons, of every possibility. You can easily become trapped if you do this, and feel increasingly paralyzed. You can avoid this trap by creating scenarios.

Follow this procedure. You concentrate on the first possibility and try to create an image of the situation which arises if this possibility is realized. For example, you imagine that you are three years into the future. You are now working in the production unit and you describe the situation. What work will you be doing, for example, on a particular day (i.e., not an abstract job/task description)? What does the working area or working environment look like: tables, tools, walls, colours, smells, sounds, light, air, people? What are the problems you are concerned with? When do you see your boss? What does he look like? What does he talk to you about?

The above questions are examples. You have to create a scenario, or vivid mental image yourself. Others can help you to create this image by asking questions, but they should not determine the content. Their questions may reveal gaps, important aspects that you have forgotten because they are too unfamiliar or possibly too threatening to think about. Another person's question can act as an eye-opener. The end result is a lively image without abstraction, without an explanation of backgrounds or motives. It is a clear, concrete image, and someone else listening to a description should be able to say: 'Yes, I can see it in front of me.'

When you have created the first scenario in this way, erase it from your mind. Let it go consciously, to make way for the next scenario. Then you work on the scenario of the second possibility, taking as much care as the first time. Once again, erase it from your mind before you start on the third scenario. Finally, you erase that too.

This is the end of the first stage. The next stage depends on the results which the exercise has produced up to now. The possibilities are:

a) It has become clear to you which of the three scenarios you want to achieve. This usually happens intuitively, based on feelings, and not on rational arguments: 'Yes, it suddenly became quite clear to me that I had to do this.' In that case, the next action is to create vivid pictures of the route you will have to follow to get to the future scenario from the present: the so-called 'stepping stones leading to the scenario.'

b) When you are working on the three scenarios, you realize that there is a fourth that you had not thought of in the first instance, but of which you feel: 'That could really be it.' In that case, you create a fourth, or even a fifth scenario. This leads to a choice, and then you are ready to go on to the stepping stones on the route leading to the scenario (as for *a*).

c) If there is no particular scenario that appeals to you, you can at least try to isolate the essential elements from the three scenarios you have created. In the discussion about your scenarios, these are characterized both separately and together. In this way some characteristic features of all the scenarios may become apparent, for example:

- You are working alone. There are people around you, but they are doing something else, separately from you.

- There are people around you that confront you.

- You are looking at small-scale situations.

- You are constantly challenged by people.

- You stay yourself in the new situation.

These are then the aspects which you must remain alert about when you design your future. We refer to these as 'areas full of opportunity.'

The stepping stones on the routes leading to the scenarios
There are many roads leading to Rome. Similarly, there are always different ways to achieve a desirable situation in the future. The aim of creating stepping stones leading to the scenarios is to outline these different routes.

Of course, every new step is determined by the result of the preceding steps. Therefore when you create the stepping stones leading to the scenarios, it is not usually possible to go beyond the first three or four stepping stones. However, these should be worked on in detail and in a very concrete way, and they should not be kept open because they depend on the first stage. By imagining the second and the third step as well, you have more inner strength to continue, even if the results are disappointing.

It is a good idea not to begin by working out the stepping stones straightaway, but first to focus on the areas which are concerned. Looking at your goal or scenario, the desirable future situation, you ask yourself which areas these are. Examples which spring to mind are information, people, training, the right job, finance and so on.

Then you move back to your present situation and think of at least three different routes leading from there to the desired future scenario. You create a series of stepping stones for every route by indicating in a very concrete way what you will do at every step. As we said above, you restrict yourself to the first three stepping stones. As in the earlier scenarios, you erase every picture of each stepping stone from your mind when you have completed it. It is a good idea to make a fourth picture of the stepping stones on a route in case everything fails: what will you do if none of these routes are successful in taking you to your chosen scenario, when you come to carry them out?

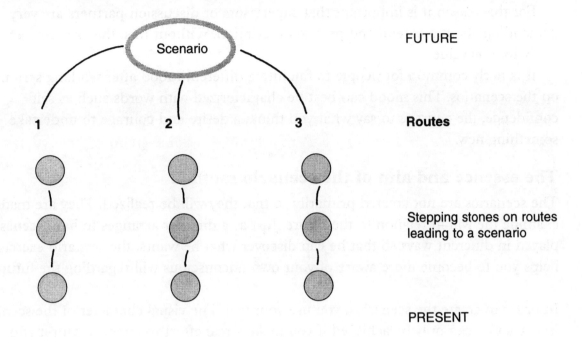

This part of the study concludes with a choice for one of the three routes of the different stepping stones. If it is not possible to make a choice, a discussion with the others may reveal the areas which are rich in opportunities that are concealed in the stepping stones of the different routes.

In any case, the result will be that these efforts stretch you so that you will not be stuck to a single possible route.

Experiences with the scenario method

It takes a while before people understand what is entailed in creating scenarios of the future. In the first instance, they easily interpret this task as listing a number of alternatives which then have to be explained or motivated. When it becomes clear that it is a matter of creating concrete images, they often feel a sense of resistance: 'What does it matter about the carpet in my office, or what clothes my boss is wearing?'

However, when they persevere and overcome their resistance, they often become quite enthusiastic, and although it is difficult, they enjoy doing it.

As soon as they have completed the first scenario, they feel a connection with it, so much so that some people say, 'I don't have to go on. This is what I'm going to do.' In a sense, they have fallen in love with it. We would still ask them to let go of this scenario and to create the second one. It is essential for the process to create different scenarios. Another striking experience is that some people work on this very quickly or untidily. They want to make eight or ten scenarios and flit from one to the next. In this way, they deny themselves the chance to reflect and try out the scenario. By constructing an image very carefully, you connect yourself with it, and this is necessary

191

to observe inwardly whether the image contains anything you really want, or perhaps which surprises you. The essential core requires more than a fleeting acquaintance. If you rush past, you feel only sympathy or antipathy, and you know about these already.

For this reason it is important that supervisors or discussion partners are very demanding about a careful and precise description. Without this, the exercise can easily lose its value.

It is fairly common for people to fall into a different mood after working seriously on the scenarios. This mood can best be characterized with words such as self-confidence, the courage to say what you think, a desire and courage to undertake something new.

The essence and aim of the scenario method

The scenarios are not created primarily so that they will be realized. They are made to examine the will in relation to the future. Just as a director arranges to have scenes played in different ways so that he can discover what he wants, the scenario exercise helps you to become more aware of your own unconscious will regarding the future.

In order to create the scenarios, you use your will. The visual character of the scenario in particular can only be achieved if you make a real effort to connect with it and work on it.

If you do not make this effort, you may produce a number of abstract ideas and representations, but you do not create an image for the listener. Making a scenario is a creative process, and without the will, it is not possible to create anything.

The resistance some people feel to describing things in images can be regarded as a problem of the will: a resistance to visualizing the consequences of choices.

It is possible to choose a favourite scenario, but you do not have to. You can also stop after creating the scenarios and not make a choice. In fact, this also applies to the stages leading to the scenario. When the will has been awoken, you have a better eye for the chances and opportunities which arise in concrete situations and what is demanded of you. By not choosing a particular view of the future but working on different scenarios, you become open to the reality in which you are living and for the 'opportunities' contained in this reality. You achieve a freer relationship with your past and a more open one with your future.

In this process the effect of the night should not be underestimated. It is a good idea to leave a few nights between making one scenario and the next ones – certainly before choosing a favourite one. The effect of the night is essential for self-confidence to develop and for finding the enthusiasm and courage to work on this exercise. Sleep on it for a night.

Rounding off

How does this sort of study of the future relate to the attitudes described above of waiting patiently and planning in a particular direction? Some people say that it is in between the two, and in a certain sense it is. The method links your own actions, initiative and responsibility with being open to the questions, inspirations and possibilities directed at you from the world around you. To this extent it is in between the two.

However, the method also adds another element, viz., the appeal to the Self made by the will. When you make the scenarios, the Self does the work. This does not happen automatically and others do not do it for you. In this way, the method is also a school for life.

Exercise tip

Create three scenarios for a celebration in your honour. Use the same occasion every time (birthday, anniversary, etc.).

Discussion of the scenarios

'What can you see?' said the Director.
'The park,' was the answer.
'But you can't see the whole park all at once. You must restrict yourself to one particular spot. What can you see straight ahead of you? '
'A gate.'
'What sort of a gate?'
Leo didn't answer, so the Director went on,
'What's the gate made of?'
'What sort of material? Cast iron.'
'Describe it. What does it look like? '

Konstantin Stanislavski

The director places his actors in an imaginary situation and helps them to describe it in a concrete way. The situation doesn't exist, it has to be created by means of what we call 'concrete imagination'. The director tries to place the actor in the situation he is imagining by asking him questions. 'What can you "see"?' He asks for observations. Later he also asks him to act things out. In this way, he brings the situation to life for the actor in such a real way that he has real, strong inner experiences.

When you study the future with the help of scenarios, imaginary situations in the future, it is not so much a matter of the experiences themselves, but of the way in which your will explores these experiences.

Explanation: Studying the future (p. 185)

The scenarios should have the same quality of concrete images as that required by the director above.

See the explanation: Describing in images (p. 28)

Below, we include some instructions for the discussion on scenarios.

Speaking

It is important for the speaker to describe her scenarios in *images* that are as clear as possible. If the scenarios are described in concrete terms, the speaker's resistance or desire is evoked more realistically. Moreover, abstractions, reflections, summaries, backgrounds, and so on, lead to all sorts of questions and therefore take a great deal of time. The art of describing the scenario consists in leaving out these things and sketching it in a few characteristic images. This does not usually work without thorough preparation.

In addition, it is important not to read out the scenarios or to know them by heart, but to *tell them again in a fresh way,* if necessary, with the help of a note of some of the key words. Often this can have a surprising result: you hear yourself saying new things, or the context in which they are said suddenly makes them sound different. This makes the scenario more lively and therefore gives a better chance of good feedback from the others.

Listening

The task of the listeners is to explore the connection of the speaker with the scenarios, to taste and feel it. Does she really want this scenario? What parts of this scenario does she want and doesn't she want? In addition to what we said before in the *Conversation (p. 136),* there are two important questions:

- To what extent are the scenarios described in concrete terms? Some people do not succeed in this, despite their greatest efforts. Others find it easy, but do not take it seriously. The inability or unwillingness to present things in concrete terms can be related to a fear of the consequences of a scenario or of the bare details. Even a delicious longing can be seen in a more sober light when it is viewed in more concrete terms.

- How involved is the speaker in her scenarios? Where is she in the spectrum between 'flitting' and 'fixating'?

By flitting, we mean the ease with which one scenario is created after another. This reveals a high degree of flexibility, and the speaker seems to create different possibilities quite effortlessly, but this approach gives the impression that she is not altogether part of these scenarios. It seems to be a game played for its own sake, or to avoid the serious aspect, or can be like toying with all sorts of desires. In any case, the speaker's will is left out of the picture.

Fixating is the opposite tendency. The future has been mapped out in painstaking detail. The speaker knows what she wants and is at most prepared to change a few, small, insignificant details. But there is an aspect of desperation in this precision, and it leaves little room for surprises. And yet the future cannot be predicted, planned or carried out according to plan. Another form of fixation is to become fixated on the details. Everything is described in such minute concrete detail that there is no room for manoeuvre.

Helping

After every scenario, questions can be asked before the characteristics are presented. It is a matter of creating the scenario by asking questions which reinforce the images used in the scenario. For example:

- 'What do you do when you co-ordinate those projects? '

- 'Describe some of the customers in your consultancy.'

- 'When you look at yourself in this scenario, what do you see? '

Questions which ask only for information are pointless. These are questions which are not aimed at clarifying the image which has been described, but at pointless digressions. For example:

– 'What will the organization's structure be like then?'

– 'How do you think the finances will be arranged?'

In general, it is a good idea to keep your questions as close as possible to the speaker's material.

Helpful questions come from an interest in the speaker and not from a critical view. Critical questions could be:

– 'Do you think that in your position it is realistic to start working for yourself? '

– 'Are you aware of what you are giving up if you start to do this? '

When the questions aimed at clarifying the image have been answered, it is important to have a little break before the speaker goes on to describe the next scenario. During this moment of silence, every listener can reflect on the scenario and the way in which it was described. You should not be too rational and analytical about all this, but simply wait to see what this scenario has to tell you. As you let the description pass through you again, try to be aware of your responses. These do not have to be profound thoughts; seemingly insignificant impressions can turn out to be very valuable later on. When you have made a note of a few key words, you will be ready for the speaker's next scenario. The discussion takes place after the third scenario.

Obviously the speaker is central in the discussion about the scenarios. This does not mean that the other participants shouldn't discuss them amongst themselves. On the contrary, this can make the discussion all the more lively and fascinating. You can ask each other questions about a characterization or comment ('Why did you say that?'), or encourage each other to explore a particular aspect ('Will you say a little more about that?'). The only danger is that these discussions amongst the listeners start to live a life of their own, separate from the speaker. She should always be involved and interested.

Rounding off

It isn't possible to describe in general terms what the discussion about the scenarios should produce. Obviously this will differ from person to person. One person will come away from the discussion with a question that seems to have an essential character, or with specific advice from one of the participants. Another will decide to create one or two more scenarios following the discussion. The discussion can also clarify where your own preferences lie or what your general attitude to the future is.

The listener/helper can gain something from the discussion as well as the speaker. By becoming involved in the questions of other people's lives, you can also learn to know yourself better.

Exercise tip

*Ask someone in your environment to imagine a
future situation, for example, a holiday or a
party. By asking questions, help her to describe
what she sees and what she does in concrete
terms as clearly as possible.*

Task 26: Questions from the world around me

The seeds of your future are already present in your life, on the one hand, in your 'leitmotif'. This works in your inner self as a personal inspiration, your basic values, and so on. On the other hand, the future works as a guiding star in what comes towards you from outside and in the possibilities and opportunities given to you by others. The possibilities which are given to you also include the questions you are asked. Often you can pass over these quite carelessly.

For yourself

1 Reflect on the questions which you have been asked recently – requests to do something, both in your work and in your private life – which you did not respond to. What have you ignored which you were explicitly or implicitly asked to do? If you cannot find anything – or very little – in this respect, ask the people in your immediate environment. Perhaps they have seen that you were asked such questions, or asked them themselves. Make a note of what you found in this way in your Logbook.

2 Try to imagine as specifically as possible what sort of situation would have come about if you had responded to these questions.

3 For the next three weeks, take some time every evening to look back at your day. Were there moments when other people asked you to do something which you ignored? Make notes of this in your Logbook.

Practical instructions

By consciously asking yourself which questions you ignored, you become more aware of these stimuli in the environment. Many questions are asked directly or indirectly, such as: 'Isn't that your sort of thing?' or 'Something should be done here, really. Don't you agree?' There are also non-verbal questions such as that of a colleague who raises his eyebrow in your direction at a meeting after the chairman's question, 'Who's going to do this?' Finally, questions can be implicit, because a situation clearly shows that something has to happen. For example, you are in a meeting, and see that a matter has been dealt with inadequately. Once again, the essence of the matter has not been tackled. The person who is responsible for it has let it go, and you have the feeling: 'Things can't go on like this. Shouldn't I really do something myself?'

In dialogue

Everyone talks about what they have discovered in images as clearly as possible.
Describe both the *question* and the *situation* in which the question was asked. *Who*
asked the question and *how,* are also important. The others listen and characterize.
In the following discussion, the opportunities raised by the questions are discussed, as
well as their significance for the speaker.

Rounding off

Write down what you wish to remember. Also see whether you have had any ideas for
new scenarios. (These can be worked out in the next task.)

Task 27: More scenarios

You can go on creating scenarios until you have achieved some inner peace, and until you know in which direction you want to continue. This means that you have to weigh up how long you have to keep going, for example, by creating a scenario that is absolutely unsuitable, and when you should decide, 'That's enough.'

For yourself

If you do this task, make a new list of possibilities, taking into account what you discovered in Tasks 25 and 26, and other people's suggestions. In any case, choose a scenario that isn't particularly obvious. Work on one or more new scenarios.

In dialogue

Everyone takes turns to describe their scenarios.
Follow the same procedure as for Task 25. Extra attention is paid to whether the speaker has done anything with the contributions in the discussion of that task. For example, did this encourage him to start moving or was there an increase in his involvement in his scenarios, etc.?

Rounding off

Indicate which scenario you now prefer and which aspects still have to be elaborated or explored. If necessary, this can be briefly discussed. Finally, write down what you want to remember.

Sleep on your decision overnight and see if it remains firm.

Task 28: Results and learning so far

You learn by doing things. By reflecting at regular intervals on what your activities have produced up to now, you can speed up this learning process.

For yourself

Look at the material you have collected since Task 25 and ask yourself what it has resulted in. What has your study produced? Focus on these aspects.

Discovery
You have had a new experience which is important to remember.

Awareness
You have become (more) aware of something that was already present in you.

Confirmation
What you already knew, felt, or were able to do, has been confirmed.

Questions
You have different or new questions.

In dialogue

If you discuss this task together, take turns to say what you have discovered. The others contribute their own comments.

Rounding off

Write down what you wish to remember.

Task 29: My question again

The question you are struggling with can change in the course of time. It is good if this does not happen unnoticed, but to reformulate and reassess your question in good time.

For yourself

1 After collecting your findings from Task 28, reformulate your question with regard to your life and your situation at work. Ask yourself why you wish to continue with this study and what results you expect from it now. Formulate this in a single question, again using the following criteria:
- one short sentence
- containing the word 'I'
- ending with a question mark
- aimed at what you want in the future.

2 Now compare the new question you have formulated with the original question. What has changed? What led to the new question?

In dialogue

One person speaks, the others listen and characterize. The listeners can help the speaker to give concrete examples in which the question is relevant.

Rounding off

Write down what you want to remember and re-formulate your question if necessary.

What am I going to do?

After exploring your future and what you wish to achieve, it is now a matter of, 'How are you going to do this?' In order to see this choice in concrete terms, you work on a definitive scenario. This serves as a signpost to start moving. At the end of this stage you have a plan consisting of a number of steps: agreements with yourself about specific actions.

Tasks

30 Definitive scenario
31 Looking back at choices
32 Stepping stones on the route leading to a scenario
33 My mood about my first step
34 Steps of the plan

Explanations

Taking initiatives and being enterprising in your life
Giving and receiving tips

Support exercise

Designs

Task 30: Definitive scenario

When you are creating scenarios, certain aspects can evoke the feeling, 'Yes, that's it. That's the direction I want to take.' These aspects of a scenario are called 'areas full of opportunities' or rich in potential. Your mood about this can often be ambivalent. At the same time, you can be happy and frightened, or know what you want at the same time as being unsure whether you really know, and yet you will have to find a connection with these areas full of opportunities.

For yourself

Look back at the scenarios you have created up to now and make a list of the aspects you came across that were full of opportunities. Weigh these up and create a final scenario of the situation where you want to be in three years' time.

Practical instructions

Areas which are full of opportunities are those parts of the scenarios you created which make you feel, after discussing it with the others: 'This appeals to me', 'I have become aware that this is important to me', or 'I am enthusiastic about this.'
For example, it could be that there is something in all your scenarios which has become explicit and which is very important to you. Or you have spoken about part of a scenario so clearly and powerfully that the others tell you: 'That's where your heart and strength lie.'
Therefore those aspects which have a real chance of being achieved are the areas which are full of opportunities. On the basis of these areas which are full of opportunities, create a new (definitive) scenario.

In dialogue

It is best not to discuss this task with the others until you have done Task 31, *Looking back at choices.* It is possible that you will want to modify your definitive scenario, following the completion of Task 31. In Task 32, you can tell the others what it is like.

Explanation: Taking initiatives and being enterprising in your life (p. 215)

Rounding off

Write down what parts of yourself you encountered in this task. For example, how did you arrive at the decision to create the definitive scenario?

Task 31: Looking back at choices

Working on your future means making choices. But how do you make choices? How have you done this up to now in your life? What is characteristic about your way of doing this, and do you want to do this in the same way, or differently, in the future?

For yourself

Look back at a number of important choices you have made in the past. Describe how you ended up in your present *occupation or profession,* with your present *private* life, and your present *developmental theme.*
When was it? What was happening at the time: in yourself, with yourself, around you? What guided you in this? Describe this, using images. Then look at these images, and ask yourself what is characteristic about the way in which this happened.

If you wish, you can extend this by looking for a number of important times of choice in each of the three areas mentioned. Again, describe these in the way mentioned above and characterize them.

Finally, look at what you have collected and draw conclusions about the way in which you clearly arrive at choices.

Practical instructions

We are concerned here with three important stages in a person's life: work, private life, and development.
– *Profession or work:* By your present profession, we mean what you are doing now, not what you are trained for. It is possible that you have always been in the same occupation or profession (possibly in different jobs and organizations), or that you have changed profession once or several times. Therefore the situation in which you made the choice of your present profession may be a long time ago, or quite recently.
– *Private life:* In the first instance, this concerns your present situation in life: family, partner, home, and so on. You can extend this as you wish with friendships, membership of clubs, and so on.
– *Development:* It is possible that in the first instance you will not find anything here, because you associate this word with all sorts of profound matters. But this field also covers certain leisure activities, hobbies, and so on, in so far as they do not serve only as entertainment, but you are also interested in developing yourself further. Examples which spring to mind include music, sport, gardening, photography, telling stories, Russian language and literature, and so on.

There may also be more serious themes of a more personal nature, such as coping with insecurity, allowing others to come into their own, improving communication or co-operation. Usually developmental themes are not separate from work and private life. If there are several themes, choose the most recent or most up to date. If there are two very different themes, look at both.

We assume that by now you will have mastered the core skills of describing things in images and characterizing them. If necessary, read the relevant chapters again *(p. 28 and p. 44)*.

In this task, it is a matter of discovering what it was that determined your decision. Which views or thoughts and which events or themes guided you in the process of making choices? Examples of the above-mentioned three areas respectively are:

- 'Jan was an authority figure for me. I did what he said.'

- 'My mother never really thought much of my previous boyfriends, but she was very fond of Michael.'

- 'I was fascinated by working with light and dark in photography.'

In dialogue

Every speaker describes in images how he has ended up in his present profession and private life, and with his developmental theme. He can add another important moment of choice for one or each of the three areas. The others listen to and characterize these descriptions. The speaker compares their characteristics with his own, and this is followed by a short discussion. The speaker concludes the discussion by sharing his conclusions and the others can respond to these if they wish.

Rounding off

Finally, write down what you consider important to remember.

Taking initiatives and being enterprising in your life

Reflect before you do things, and when you do them continue to reflect.

Guido Gezelle

In the concluding stage of this workshop it is necessary to leave the sheltered atmosphere of reflection and take the step to adopt an enterprising approach towards your own life. You cannot simply continue to look backwards and forwards in a spirit of reflection forever. It is important to bring out what you discovered in that chamber of reflection. This reflection and study are now linked to concrete action: 'You reflect while you do things.'

Living means making choices and taking action, i.e., taking risks, because it is impossible to foresee everything. We call this *enterprise* or *taking initiatives*. In this, you are supported by a number of *life skills* which have been regularly dealt with in the tasks and exercises in this book. Finally, an essential source of nourishment for taking initiatives in life is provided by constant inner schooling or training. We will discuss all these three aspects below.

Undertaking things

When we refer to 'undertaking things' or 'being enterprising', we do not mean enterprise in an economic sense. We are concerned with people who have an enterprising attitude in their work and in their life. What characterizes them?

Taking initiatives

Enterprising people are active in themselves and determine the form of what they take on. One person can do this steadily and almost unnoticed, another impulsively, forcefully, and very obviously. Everyone has their own style. People who cannot sit still for any length of time are easy to spot. As soon as they have finished one thing, they have thought of the next and have started on it. They are real go-getters. People around them sometimes sigh in despair, 'Can't you ever calm down and take it easy?' 'Yes,' say the go-getters, 'as long as something happens!' People who resolutely develop an initiative step by step over a longer timespan are not as noticeable. Others often do not realize this, and sigh, 'I wish you would do something.' 'Yes,' say the steady sort, 'but it has to be at the right moment.' Even for them, a time comes when they have had enough and undertake something new.

These different styles can be recognized even in a young child. This personal style of undertaking things can be reinforced by nutrition, education and experiences, but it can also be inhibited. Whatever these influences in your environment amount to, in general you are carried on and propelled by youthful vitality and physical energy until you are about forty years old. This vitality helps you as a healthy person to develop through the changes demanded of you by every transition to a new stage of your life.

spiritual energy obtained
through the conscious effort
of the Self

vital energy from the body

the course of your life

innate developments   acquired new developments

During the second half of your life, a change takes place sooner or later. Your physical vitality declines and is replaced by a spiritual vitality, an energy which is nourished by spiritual activity. This does not happen automatically. It requires a conscious effort of the Self. The sooner the flow of physical energy declines, the earlier the Self is called upon to make this effort. The longer the physical energy remains active, the longer it is possible to postpone consciously involving the Self. However, in general, it can be said that from the age of thirty-five, new developments have to be increasingly *acquired*. This means consciously taking initiatives and being enterprising.

Exercise tip

Regularly check what initiatives you have taken, for example, once a month.

216

Taking risks

Being enterprising involves taking risks. If you want to be absolutely sure you are taking the right step, nine times out of ten you won't take it. What we know and think is related to the past. If you trust only in the past, then you drag it into the future. It isn't possible to determine the future by thinking. You can never think in advance exactly what is going to happen. There are always unforeseen circumstances. This means that going on is a gamble. But an enterprising person doesn't gamble, she trusts her feelings and intuition. The future is expressed in these; they are the signals of her will. If you are not used to this, it requires courage to trust your initiative, to be guided by the feeling 'that's probably the right thing'. Acting for the future means that you must trust your will.

Whether you are constructing a railway line or taking the next essential step in your life, it is obviously sensible to think about things and create scenarios. But in the transition to action, there comes a time when you must rely on your intuition, no matter how insecure you feel about it. This means that you do what you feel is right, and that you see what is happening. How is the step you have taken seen by others? Do you have practical support, such as the right information sources, the names of people who can help you, ideas, resources? These will give you the encouragement to go on. Life will always tell you when you are going in the right direction. The most important thing is to start moving and to be open to signals. Do not focus only on the disappointments, but do not be satisfied in a one-sided way either, when you have the wind in your sails. Be enterprising, steer a steady course, and allow yourself to be guided by the signals you receive.

Exercise tip

Listen to what you want and, with this in mind, take a step that is unusual for you. Then try to see, in an unprejudiced way, how this step is regarded by others.

Being open to the questions of others

The questions which other people ask you are some of the signals from your environment. Being enterprising means that you are conscious of your own valuable assets, of what you have to offer, and also that you have an eye for what is required, what others are asking for and need. In your work, you are not working for yourself, but for others. You work by focusing on the outside world, on the implicit and explicit demands imposed on you.

The way in which people ask things of you can be very subtle. For example, they could outline a problem for you, but refrain from asking you to do something directly, to see if you will be affected by the problem. It is matter of observing and listening to the questions which arise around you and which concern you. Then you have the choice whether to respond to these questions or not.

You can also be moved by other people, trust in them, and see where that takes you. This is also part of being enterprising. In this way, you are working at the same time on building up, developing, and looking after your network.

Exercise tip

For a particular period, keep a note of the questions which are explicitly and implicitly directed to you, in which situations and in what form they are asked, and looking back, how you responded.

The ability to relate to tasks

You do not have to respond to every question. A conscious person has the freedom to choose. An enterprising person does not connect in this way simply because it is the thing to do, or because it is expected. She chooses to form this connection from a profound personal feeling. This connection has nothing to do with surrender, and is not slavish or impotent, but comes from the will to actively use what you have discovered. During the second half of your life, your own development consists of being available for something outside yourself, with which you form a connection from your own free will. It is an exercise in 'not my will' – my demanding will, the fact that I desperately have to do something – 'but your will be done', i.e., what is needed in the situation. You can experience this as something that comes to you from outside. Listening to this does not mean ignoring your own needs, because what comes towards you is related to you. Listening to this means being of service to that for which you are on earth. You discover why you are on earth by directing yourself to another person or other people.

It is necessary to make choices in life. Being in a situation and at the same time not wanting to be in it, because the organizational chaos, the boss, the relationships, the income and all that stuff doesn't appeal to you, wears you down. Not wanting to be there and not wanting to go because it's probably the same everywhere, makes you ill. It is better to ask yourself what is still keeping you there, even if it's just the money, and making a conscious choice for that 'rubbish' situation on the basis of that fact. This means you are connected with it, no matter how difficult the situation. Perhaps this is the most important characteristic of an enterprising approach to life. At the same time, it requires looking after the sources of your inspiration. (See *'Inspiration in daily life'*, *p. 155)*.

```
┌─────────────────────────────────────────────────────────────┐
│                                                             │
│                    Exercise tip                             │
│                                                             │
│   For a week try to be aware of people and situations to    │
│   which you initially react in a rejecting way. In all these │
│   cases, try to consciously suppress your rejection, and    │
│   try to take an interest in these people or situations.    │
│                                                             │
└─────────────────────────────────────────────────────────────┘
```

Skills for life

It is possible to learn the above-mentioned characteristic skills of an enterprising person. The exercise tips will help you to do this, but it is even better if you can find your own exercises. There are many skills, and for every skill there are many different possible exercises. This means you have to make a choice. In addition to the above-mentioned skills, this book also describes a number of general skills for dealing with life, and for continuing to learn from it – *life skills* (Barrie Hopson). We mention the following skills.

Living with questions

Living with a question starts by taking a feeling of dissatisfaction about your work or life seriously, as a signal that 'something is not right'. Then try to translate this dissatisfaction into a question with regard to your attitude and the approach you would adopt in the future. When you have written down the question, think of a concrete situation in which this question has played a part recently. Describe it in images, and characterize the situation and the way in which you acted in it. This can be described as anchoring your question in the world outside you. Then try to imagine what your situation will look like after a while if you do nothing with your dissatisfaction. Describe this situation in images, characterize it, and observe what this does to you, and your mood which results from this.

The art of looking ahead

You start with your question. On the basis of this question, you imagine a number of future situations in your life and work, i.e., you create different scenarios in your imagination. The more this scenario is like an image, the more realistically you will respond to it. Connect all the possible scenarios as though they are reality, and listen, feel, and inwardly explore how your will responds, what you essentially want and do

219

not want. Creating scenarios means that you must constantly connect with them, becoming inwardly creative and open to your inner response.

The art of looking back

Again, you start with your question. On the basis of this question, look at your life up to now. Describe what you have experienced in images as clearly as possible. Despite the responses, feelings and emotions which well up inside you, try to describe the situations as though you are looking at them through the eyes of an outsider. Try to characterize them, looking for the essence, and try to look at your life as though you are seeing it for the first time. For example, you could get into the habit of looking back at the day that's just passed.

Observing the effects of your own actions

A different aspect in looking back is looking at your own actions and their effects on other people. What are the consequences of your acts? To a large extent they remain unknown, although it sometimes becomes clear to you after a while. It is easier to be conscious of what you are thinking or feeling than of the consequences brought about by your acts. Nevertheless, you can increase your consciousness of the consequences of your acts by asking the question: 'What am I actually bringing about? ' This should not be asked from a sense of guilt or from a need to feel self-important, but on the basis of a businesslike interest. When you have taken a sober look at the consequences of your actions, you can decide whether this is what you want, or whether you will modify your actions. The best thing is to foresee the consequences of your acts as you are doing things, but this is also the most difficult. Reflecting on your acts retrospectively is a way of helping you to increase your awareness during your actions.

The dialogue with your biography

You can have a dialogue with your life, the biography you have written and are writing yourself, by asking questions, looking forward, looking back and observing the situation. It is a dialogue in which you learn from your experiences and expectations.

When you do this, try not to create a division between the past, the present and the future, or between the stages of your life, for example, by thinking: 'Older people don't change' or 'Young people do what they think is right, but they don't really understand anything about life.' Playing is not just for children, and old people do not have a monopoly on wisdom.

The distinction between working, learning and living should not result in a division of these three areas of life. Experiences and skills acquired in one area can become productive in the other areas. Moreover, you live in your work, and your private life can often be hard work too. You also learn in both other areas.

Using other people

You can do many things on your own. Ultimately, you have to do it on your own. But use other people to help you in your 'dialogue with your biography'. Pour out your heart to a friend, cry on his shoulder, but above all, ask him to help you to learn from your experiences. This is asking for a sober response, and sometimes to reflect truths you do not like to hear or see. Give him concrete tasks such as getting him to ask questions in images, to characterize aspects of your descriptions or to listen to what you really want.

Inner training

The above-mentioned skills of the enterprising person are life skills. But how do you achieve these? Intending to do something does not mean that you actually do it. You can be distracted by all sorts of things. It requires inner strength to start on this and to persevere. How do you develop this?

The following basic exercises support what was described above. They have a slightly different character. For example, they are aimed at working in your inner world without other people asking you to do so. They are basic exercises with the aim of reinforcing your will and your way of thinking and feeling. These exercises bear fruit only if you do them for a certain length of time. The results are not immediately visible, not for yourself either, but after a while, you will start to experience their effect. They are subtle inner changes.

Some exercises for this inner training are described below:

Training your will

Decide to carry out a completely pointless act every day at exactly the same time, an act which no one asks you to do and which is without any consequences for the world around you. Examples could be to tie a knot in your handkerchief at noon, to turn round your ring three times, to take the pen top off your pen and put it back. Clearly determine the end of the exercise as well as the beginning, for example: 'I will do this, starting tomorrow, for three weeks,' and then renew the agreement you have made with yourself.

Practice has shown that you will not be able to carry out your plan exactly. You forget, you are distracted, and so on. In fact, the point of this exercise is not the result. When you succeed, you should stop immediately, regardless of the period which you have agreed with yourself. Make the task more difficult, for example, by choosing a more inconvenient time.

Training your thoughts

How can you master your thoughts? Normally, 'you' don't think, but 'it' thinks in you. Thoughts sent to your mind flutter around and drag you along. How can you make sure that you think what you want?

Take a simple object such as a paper-clip, a coin or a pencil, and think about it for five minutes in a meaningful way that you choose yourself. For example, concentrate on the shape of the object, its use, where it comes from, its history, etc. Make sure that you do not become distracted and that everything you think, imagine and wonder about this object is determined by you. Think step by step.

You will notice that at first, you will not even be able to do this for one minute. Very quickly your thoughts start to wander in completely different directions. Another obstacle arises if you think about the same object several times, a routine creeps into your thoughts, and you become aware that you are mechanically repeating earlier thoughts. Of course, the intention is that every time you are all there.

Again, what is important is not the result, but the activity. By doing this exercise regularly, you discipline your thoughts and stimulate the force of interest in yourself.

The intensification of feelings

The above-mentioned inner force of interest increases if you intensify your feelings without expressing them directly. This doesn't mean that it isn't important to express your feelings. Sometimes it is necessary to become aware of them or to avoid being overwhelmed by their vehemence. It gives a sense of relief, but the result is that they are gone, and that's a pity, because feelings are valuable signals about yourself and about the world outside you. Take your feelings seriously. Observe them and listen to them. Often they are very volatile. At other times, they can be so violent that it is difficult to discover the core of the feeling in the storm. Experience them and repress the urge to express them. Finally, try to put them into words for yourself. Give them a name.

In this way, you can intensify your feelings and they become an organ of perception which can pass signals. Just as a gull can land on the crest of a wave without being engulfed, you can learn to experience and live through your feelings without being overwhelmed.

Finding the positive

Look for a single positive aspect when you have a difficult experience, so that you are not entirely taken up with negative feelings. For example, if you feel like shooting someone in a conflict, look for just one positive thing about him or her. No person is all bad. It is not a matter of seeing only the good – on the contrary, that would be equally unrealistic. If you have a tendency to think that everything is wonderful, look for things which are not so good, for the negative aspects. However, this is much easier than the other way round. That is why we have included this exercise in positive thinking. Again, what is important is not the result, but the repeated effort.

Support exercise:
Designs

For yourself

Take a quarter of the lump of clay that you used in the previous support exercise, and place it in front of you on the hardboard. Also find a pencil, ruler and sheet of paper. Roll up your sleeves and read these instructions:

1 The amount of clay in front of you is probably still too large. Break off enough to make a sphere which you can almost hold in two hands when you put the palms of your hands around it. This is the amount of clay you need to work on. Mould this into a solid sphere as perfect as possible.

2 Place the sphere in front of you. Take a pencil and paper and design a three-dimensional figure with straight lines and planes which you can execute in the amount of clay there is in the sphere. When you make the design, take into account a period of twenty minutes for executing it.

3 Make your design in clay as exact as possible.

Practical instructions

Work without using any appliances, using only your hands.

Stage 1 is aimed in particular at becoming familiar with the material, the (im)possibilities of your hands, and the time it takes to achieve the desired result.

Stage 2: Produce a realistic design, taking into account the possibilities of the clay, your skills and the indicated time. When you execute the design, you should use all the clay in the sphere. Work on the hardboard base, using only your hands.

Examples of this exercise: Illustrations 2a and 2b (next pages)

In dialogue

Everyone takes turns to show their designs and the final result. The others characterize this. Then the process is discussed, bearing in mind the following points:

- What did you encounter in your design and in the execution of your design? You should examine the relationship between the design and the product, the character (soft, dry, etc.) and the amount of the material, your skills and the way in which you use the available time.

- Did you complete the task? How did you work?

- Do these things say anything about the way in which you perform in your working situation?

- What does this mean for your question with regard to the future?

This exercise involves the following abilities or inner skills:

- creating a realistic design, bearing in mind the material, your own skills, and the time available;

- keeping to a design while you are executing it;

- being moved by a task.

Rounding off

Finally, write down what you wish to remember.

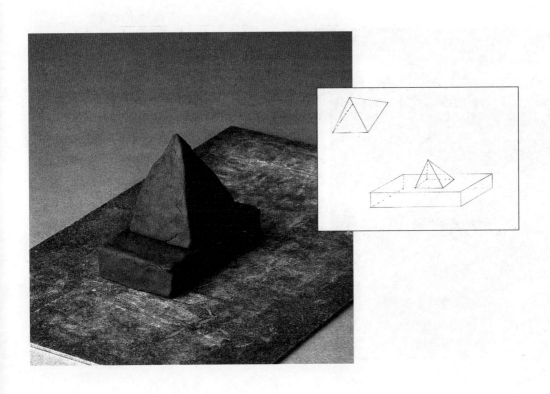

Illustration 2a

Illustration 2b

Task 32: Stepping stones on the route leading to a scenario

When you have a definite scenario, you make a decision so you can go on. If you leave everything open, you do not start moving. The definitive scenario indicated where you want to be in three years' time. But how do you get there? There are many roads to Rome which can pass through very different landscapes. Which route do you want to take? To make a choice, imagine different routes. We call these imagined paths the 'stepping stones leading to a scenario'.

For yourself

Focus on your definitive scenario. Imagine what has to be done between now and in three years' time to achieve this scenario. Do this in the following two ways, and make a note of your most important findings.

1 *Areas to concentrate on*
Put yourself into your situation in three years' time, and look back. What have you had to do in the past three years to get to where you have moved to?

Practical instructions

Suppose you had the following scenario: 'In three years' time when I'm 56, I'll no longer be in management or have any management responsibility. I will be working four days a week in the same company in the training department as a supervisor, so that I can use my experience of the existing production processes to help the company. In addition, I will work one day a week at the campsite which I run together with my wife. It is a permanent site for people with caravans.

When you have moved forward to that situation, look back. The areas to concentrate on were:

- to convince the new management of the loss of production quality caused by insufficient experience (because the company was taken over, first, by a Belgian, and soon afterwards by an American concern with the related reorganization and turnover of people, so that many unnecessary mistakes were made by the younger, more highly trained people;

- to convince management that your management job was becoming too difficult because of the higher level of training of the new employees and the more dynamic approach adopted from the top;

- in addition, that many new employees were coming to you for advice, and you would like to carry out this job, which is a new position in the company, for a number of years. Four days a week would be sufficient for this job;

- to discuss with your wife the financial consequences of the drop in salary;
- to arrange for all the licences and regulations related to the management of a campsite;
- to buy a campsite with your wife, as well as a large caravan to live in;
- to sell your house.

At a certain point your imagination will be exhausted. Then go on with part 2 of the task. When you are working on this, you will certainly encounter new possibilities. Add these to the list and see whether it entails a change in the following things.

2 *Steps leading to the scenarios*
Go back to the present. Create 'stepping stones' of three different routes which would achieve your future situation. Outline one route in general terms, and then describe very specifically and in chronological order, the first three stepping stones you will take in this direction.

Practical instructions

For example, you may see the following three possibilities in front of you:
a) 'First I will sound out different people in the company about the feasibility of my idea, and examine why I should be entitled to this new job with my record of employment.'
b) 'I will go straight to my boss and submit my proposal to her.'
c) 'First, I will discuss the matter at home to see whether I really want to fulfil our dream of having our own campsite.'

There is no point in thinking more than three stepping stones ahead when you work on these directions. Each time you take a step, the situation changes, and you will have to adapt your next steps. Describe your three stepping stones or steps in very specific terms with your diary at hand. Keep them 'small' and 'simple'.

For every step think of:
- what you are going to do;
- when, with whom and how;
- what you want to achieve with this;
- what will be the effects on yourself and on others: how will they – and how will you – react?

For example: 'My first three stepping stones on the second path *(b)* are:
i) Tomorrow I will go to my boss's secretary and ask her to ring me next week at a time when he has half an hour to spare and is feeling open-minded, because his moods are rather variable. She will respond positively and ask whether she has to prepare the boss. When we have got to this point, she will have to introduce me and say that I want a quiet discussion of no more than half an hour. She is a woman who always encourages me, and that makes me feel calm. Usually, I can stay and talk to her for a bit.

ii) Then I will go to my colleague on the second production line, who came with the boss from a previous company, and arrange a discussion with him to talk to him about my proposal. I will ask him to give me some tips about the best way to present this proposal to the boss. He always has time for new ideas, and he will tell me what he thinks of my proposal. I expect him to have a positive attitude. I will have to be convincing for him, but then I will have to be convincing for my boss as well.

iii) I have the discussion with the boss in which I put my proposal to him and ask him to think about it. At the same time, I will arrange another meeting in a week's time. He will start to respond immediately. I'm not sure that he will be positive. When he is too critical, I often withdraw. I don't want to do that this time. In any case, I will ask for another meeting'.

Being specific and detailed, outlining your plans with your diary at hand – these are the ingredients for evaluating what you really want in the future. That is the important thing. It will prevent you from falling into the trap of being too non-commital.

3 When you have noted the areas to concentrate on and the *stepping stones leading to the scenarios*, make notes of what you encountered when you carried out this task. For example: enthusiasm, or being afraid of things, problems which you started to explore, or which have been resolved, or other important ideas, feelings, intentions and so on which came to you.

In dialogue

Take turns to outline your definitive scenarios, the areas to concentrate on, the paths to take and the specific steps on these paths. Talk about these as factually as possible without reflections, judgements or conclusions.

The others listen and characterize what you have said. At this stage it is important for them to accept the definitive scenario that was made, and to focus particularly on the realistic content of the steps to be taken. Look at them in the light of what you know about the speaker and her situation. Try to be the devil's advocate with regard to the specific detailed nature of her ideas, her commitment, her self-knowledge, her insight into situations and so on. However, this contribution should come after characterizing what she said.

This results in a discussion where the speaker can contribute her own findings during her preparation. The others can now also give advice to do things very differently, i.e., choosing different stepping stones on the route leading to a scenario.

Rounding off

Finally, write down what you want to remember.

Task 33: My mood about my first step

Making plans is one thing; carrying them out is quite another. No matter how lifelike the scenarios you created are, they are created in your imagination. You do not have to get up from your chair to do this. In order to realize them, you have to get up and go for them. How does this feel? What mood are you in when you think about going into action?

For yourself

Express the mood which you feel in yourself when you think of the specific steps you will have to take to realize your scenario. Do this on paper with colour and movement.

Practical instructions

Take a sheet of drawing paper, or a sheet from your Logbook, the soft crayons and the stick of charcoal.

Before you begin, concentrate on the feeling which comes up in you when you think about having to take action. Do not hurry.

Do not think too much when you carry out this task. Trust in your hands and in your spontaneous choice of colours. Allow whatever there is to come and avoid concrete representations.

In dialogue

If you discuss this task together, take turns to show your mood image without saying how it was created, what you think about it, what it means, and so on. The others look at it and characterize it. When the person who made the image has responded to the characteristics, there is a discussion about whether their mood image is only about this particular moment, or whether it also reveals a basic mood with regard to taking action. How does this basic mood operate in his life?

Rounding off

Finally, write down what you want to remember.

Task 34: Steps of the plan

You start moving only when you start to take steps. As soon as you have taken one step, others respond to it, and your perspective changes. You are constantly confronted with the question: what is my next step?

For yourself

Make a definitive plan of the steps to take in order to reach the scenario you have chosen. Describe the areas you will concentrate on, outline the path you are following in general terms, and describe the first three steps as concretely as possible. Make sure that the first step follows on from the meeting in which you discuss this task. Make a note of the steps in your diary.

Practical instructions

Look at the stepping stones on the routes leading to your scenarios and choose one of them. You could also look for areas which are full of opportunities and make a new (definitive) scenario.

The smaller, more specific and realistic the steps are, the greater the chance that you will actually take them. This can give you the confidence to keep going. The most important thing is to start moving. After this, the path reveals itself.

In dialogue

Everyone says what agreements they have made with themselves. The others support this with practical tips wherever possible.

Rounding off

Finally, write down what you want to remember and what you decide to do. Then you make an agreement for the last meeting in this workshop, when you will look back at the actions/steps you have resolved to take. In our experience, it is best if this meeting takes place about a week after the third stepping stone is achieved.

Explanation: Giving and receiving tips (p. 236)

Giving and receiving tips

Like describing things in images and characterizing them, giving tips is an effective skill in discussion. It is slightly less unusual than describing things in images and characterizing them. For example, think of a waiter who will say when you are choosing a meal on the menu: 'I would recommend this...' or 'I have a fruity red wine which...' He attracts your attention to what is available and helps you to make a choice. A choice is always followed by action, in this case, eating and drinking. A tip is concerned with action, with something you could do. The art is to listen to the other person so well that your tip follows on from what he wants, and the tip is given in such a way that the other person feels free to accept or reject it. For example, if a waiter is too insistent about his recommendation, either from impatience or, for example, because he is very busy, you will be inclined to reject it, regardless of the content. On the other hand, if you have given in to him too easily, you will no longer eat and drink with the same enthusiasm.

One person gives the tip, the other receives it. How does the person come to give it and the other person receive the tip? What can you do to increase the effectiveness of giving a tip?

Finding a tip

'You ought to do some sport,' says a friend when he sees you running up the stairs, out of breath. From his tone, you will know whether he is joking, making a casual remark, or whether he is serious. Your friend sees you doing something and has an idea. Giving a tip starts with observation.

In the Tasks *Stepping stones on the route to a scenario* and *Steps of the plan,* you listen to what the other person says. From his description in images you see what he is going to do. At the same time, you look at him as he is talking. You form a picture which has three aspects:

- what the other person is planning to do in the near future;

- the way in which he is presenting it now; and

- the relationship between the two.

This is the first stage in finding a tip.

Then you explore whether this picture tallies with what you know about the other person up to now, and with your own experiences. You feel where it clicks and where it comes unstuck, and where it corresponds, and seems to be in harmony. You may experience some inner movement in the attempt to connect the image of the other person's plan with your own experience. In the first stage of forming images, you are mainly focused on the other person, but now you focus on your inner self. You listen to your feelings and ask yourself what is the cause of the fact that the image clicked or didn't click. When you do this, you may have an idea and it becomes clear what the other person should 'really' do. It can seem as though this idea comes from outside, as though it is actually given to you. Some people experience this as though something is whispered to them, and they hear a voice. Others experience a moment of insight.

We would like to mention two sorts of ideas here.

Listening to the person opposite you and exploring your own inner self, you may have ideas which are separate from the specific situation the speaker is describing. For example: 'He should really take up singing.' How does this sort of tip occur to you? It may be that you suddenly realize that the other person always has difficulty in expressing what is happening to him. You hear him saying how he intends to say more about what he thinks of his work. He also wants to do a course. Suddenly you think: 'Singing, in a small choir, in which he can't be drowned by the masses. When you sing, you have to express your feelings, and co-operation is very important. It's easy to be insecure, but even if you are insecure, you can't fall silent; you have to go on singing your own part. That's just what he needs.' All this can pass through you in a flash, and then you suddenly notice that he has a good voice.

This idea is not directly related to the situation to be changed, but does support what the other person wants to learn.

The other sort of insight is linked to the specific situation. For example, the speaker may have the question: 'How can I make myself more visible?' Her chosen scenario: 'In a year's time, people at the meetings will take more account of what I think.' The chosen path: 'To take a presentation course, to find colleagues who want to support me, and to practise this in meetings.'

When you listen to this, you remember what she has told you, how she went from one meeting to the next, often making telephone calls between, discussing, writing letters and dealing with administration. She experiences this busy life as a challenge, but at the same time misses moments of quiet. You think: 'Really, she should take fifteen minutes for herself before every meeting, to prepare herself.'

This insight is directly related to the situation that is to be changed. Whether it is a fruitful one depends on how the tip is given and how it will be received.

How to give a tip

When you give a tip, you are again focused on the person sitting next to you. Very often the process goes so quickly that you don't even realize that you start by focusing on that other person, listening to what she's saying, then turning in to yourself to have an insight, and then turning outwards again to voice this insight. It all goes so quickly that it is easy to give general advice, such as: 'You should take time to relax more in your life,' based on a feeling of what would be good for her. But these feelings can be deceptive. You may not be aware that it is your own need for restfulness that prompted your response, and that you feel uncomfortable imagining another person's life. If you are responding more from a personal need, the other person will be aware that you have not understood her when you gave this advice. It is too distant from her. But even if it is a good idea for her to have some relaxation, she will not be able to do much with this idea because it has such a general character. She's probably heard it lots of times and knows it all too well, but cannot imagine how to actually do it.

A tip must connect with the other person. You have to imagine the situation and have an inner experience of the other person to such an extent that you can feel her thresholds and possibilities. Then the general idea should be put into words in such a concrete way that the other person can follow up the suggestion immediately. A good tip is ready for use.

For example: 'My tip is that for three weeks before the meeting which takes place on Monday afternoon, you take a quarter of an hour for yourself and walk around the block on your own, without anyone else, alone, solo. During this time, you prepare for what you want to say regarding one point on the agenda.'

Another person may have the following idea: 'Make sure that next Thursday you are present earlier, and ask the chairman, who knows you well, to invite you to say something. You tell him what you want to practise.'

In this way the tip again has the character of an image. Anything which is felt intuitively and which is first of all formulated in a very general way can be translated into a concrete situation. It does not have to be a very big tip. In fact, the strength lies in being small and specific. If it fits like a piece in a jigsaw, it will be like a direct appeal to the other person. 'Do I want it, or don't I?'

Receiving a tip

The first thing which you do when you receive a tip is to imagine what it requires of you. The more specific it is, the simpler it will be to imagine what you have to do. Immediately, other questions arise. What is the intention behind it? How does this make you feel? Can you do anything with it? What are the consequences?

When you receive a tip, you have to have the opportunity to assimilate it and process it. That is why it is not a good idea to give too many tips in succession, for example, in the discussion relating to this workshop. It may help the person receiving the tips to write them down first and then go back to them later. In this case, the first emotional reactions – which are often feelings of resistance – may have subsided.

For example, the first reaction can be to feel insulted because the tip is too simple. It is as though the serious nature of the problem has not been recognized. Another reaction is that the tip is not accepted because the person is expected to do something he does not want to do. When you receive a tip, you must form an image of it, despite these emotional reactions.

Then you have to choose. Do you follow up the tip, or do certain tips give you ideas of your own? When you choose, you do not have to be polite or nice. The important thing is whether you are able or want to do anything with the tips that were given to you. In many cases, they are not taken on board literally, but stimulate someone to find their own variation which is more suitable. For example:

'Your idea of walking round the block appealed to me, but I have more opportunity to do this on Tuesdays, and in any case, that meeting is more important.'

'Being invited to say something can help, but not by the chairman. But I know a colleague in that meeting who I can ask. He sometimes asks other people in that meeting to say something. It won't be so noticeable.'

'Moreover, I think I'll cancel one of the meetings. It's too much. I don't really have to be there on Wednesday mornings and Friday afternoons. There are always two of us from the department. I'm going to discuss it with my colleague. Perhaps he would like to miss a meeting as well.'

It can happen that tips are brushed aside as being impractical or already tried. This is troubling. All the efforts of the person who gave the tip have come to nothing. But in some cases, it does help to place the problem of the person who received the tips squarely on the table.

However, if the person giving the tip manages to empathize successfully and give a useful tip, and if the person receiving this can really follow it up to change things, this will lead to enthusiasm on both sides.

I learn by doing

We conclude with a working method which you can use to continue on your own in an enquiring, enterprising and self-monitoring way.

Tasks

35 What did I want?
36 Experiences
37 What am I going to do?

Explanation

Learning by doing

Learning by doing

Sooner or later, you reach a point where you can continue the study of your biography only by taking actual steps in the reality of your working life. You have to start doing things!

For most people, this is a barrier. You may be hesitant to take action and follow new, unknown paths. Other people arrive at this point, full of enthusiasm, and are keen to start moving. In many cases the first results will determine whether you feel encouraged or discouraged, and whether you will be able to persevere with the course you have taken.

You can come up against yourself and get to know yourself in this active stage in a very different way from your earlier biography work. Apart from the tangible result which your concrete steps may produce, they can also provide important learning results. Something which appears to be a negative result can often have an extremely positive learning effect. This learning from experience, or learning by doing, is sometimes known as 'action learning'.

The learning process in 'action learning' is different from the learning processes we are used to. Normally we first learn something, then do it. In this case it is the other way round. First do, then learn. Try to learn something from the experience. This type of learning is more unusual and more demanding than traditional learning. In the case of courses and training sessions, the learning situations have been organized and structured by experts. In 'action learning', learning from your own experience, you have to do this yourself. If you fail to do so, you will have experience, but you will not learn anything from it.

Even in the 1960's, the American organizational consultant, Chris Argyris, was critical of the well-known adage, 'Experience is the best teacher'. He noticed that there are many people who continue to make the same mistakes, despite all sorts of experiences, and go on repeating the same things even though they know it won't work. According to Argyris, the adage should be changed into: 'Experience is the best teacher if the person is able to learn something from what he is experiencing.' (Argyris 1964) In this case, it is possible to establish a continuous process, as shown below.

If you want to learn from experience, you must devote attention to a number of points.

Choosing a situation
You must identify an experience as a situation from which you want to learn either beforehand or retrospectively.

You choose the situation in advance if you consciously want to try or investigate something, for example, a different style of management, recruiting people for an idea,

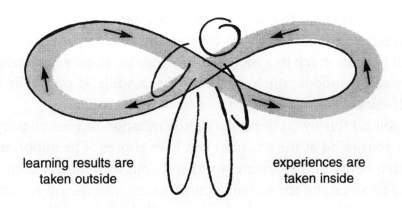

learning results are
taken outside

experiences are
taken inside

or acting in a more enterprising way. In this case, you create or find a situation where it is possible to experiment. This method is the most suitable for the last stage of the biographical study.

You make a choice retrospectively if something has happened in a situation which has given rise to questions: one of your proposals was chosen or was unexpectedly successful, a discussion was rather unsatisfactory, the results of a project were disappointing, etc.

If you do not consciously turn an experience into a learning situation, you will at most learn something unconsciously. You may be greatly moved by the experience, but it will not take you any further, it will simply take you from one experience into the next. If the experience is pleasant, you will act in the same way when the opportunity arises. If it is unpleasant, you will try to avoid such experiences in the future. Of course, this is also a type of learning. However, by deliberately making experiences into learning situations, you achieve greater learning results which can be more easily applied in other situations as well.

Formulating a question
We have already indicated the importance of living with questions. For 'learning by doing', it is also important to approach experiences with questions to examine them. This question can be posed either before or after the experience. For example:

– How should I coach my colleagues so that they co-operate better?

– Why did no one follow my proposal this afternoon?

Asking a question in this way gives inner support in examining the situation and a sense of direction in the seeking process. If the question is formulated in advance, like the question above about coaching, you choose situations: where, when and with

243

whom can I try this? Throughout the examination, the question is the guideline. Every time you ask: what does this tell me with regard to my question?

Standing back

Formulating a question is the first way in which you can step back. Stepping back is one of the most important preconditions for learning from experience. If you do not do this, you will become stuck in a mood and in your personal experience. You have all sorts of feelings and emotions which ebb away after a while. If you really want to learn from your experiences, it is necessary to step back.

First of all, you do this by (re)formulating the question of your enquiry and then looking back in your mind at the situation you have chosen. The important thing is to make a distinction between the outside world and your own inner world. By looking back at the specific situation, the actual circumstances, actions and statements of people, you concentrate on the world outside you. You ask yourself, amongst other things: 'What did I see? What happened exactly? What did the people involved say?' You can also look at yourself, your own conduct, attitude, what you said, etc., as though you are looking through the eyes of an outsider. 'Where was I? What did I say? What did I do?' In this way, you form an image of the situation, as we did before, for describing things in images.

However, your own inner world, with its thoughts, feelings and emotions, is also very important. Again, you must look at this from a certain distance. 'What did I feel, what did I think, what did I want from that situation?'

Usually you are concerned alternately with the outside world and with your own inner world. You must step back from both of them. Moreover, it is important that you are aware which of the two worlds you are examining. Sometimes it is so turbulent, or sad, or cold and chilly inside, that it is not possible to stand back. In that case, it may be helpful to stand back by first doing something else like going for a walk, or playing the piano or working in the garden. Then you can return to it later when you feel more peaceful inside.

Observing effects

When you learn from experience, you must devote special attention to observing effects. There are effects in the outside world and in our own inner world.

The effects in the outside world are a sort of mirror in which we can see ourselves. We see ourselves in the effect we have on the outside world. At the same time, the other person or persons also play a role. Therefore it is difficult to establish what part we play ourselves in these reactions. Very often, we tend to ascribe the negative reactions which we do not want to other people, without recognizing our own part in this. 'It's a shame that you see it in that way,' was the response of a manager to the reaction from one of his employees, not realizing that his own attitude and behaviour had led to that reaction.

In all sorts of situations, for example, in education and business, we often condemn the behaviour of other people which we evoke ourselves. By proceeding in this way, you obviously learn very little or nothing from these situations. The main remedy is to closely observe the reactions of other people and to ask yourself: 'What is it about my behaviour that evoked this reaction in the other person?'

In addition, learning from experience is also hampered because we have a tendency to shut our eyes to the undesirable effects of our attitude and our behaviour. We would rather adopt an ostrich-like policy than change ourselves.

Of course, there are also effects in our inner world in the form of emotions, feelings, moods, and so on. It is important to learn to observe these effects without being overwhelmed by them. Sometimes we do not wish to acknowledge these either. We simply suppress them, because to recognize them could have consequences that we cannot cope with, or do not want to recognize.

These are all ways of deluding yourself and it is clear that you learn very little as a result.

Discovering steering principles

Just as important as observing the effects of your behaviour is to discover the steering principles which lie behind it. When you have seen a particular situation pass and have looked at the characteristic elements in it, you can ask yourself the question: 'What directed me in this situation? What were the principles which guided me?'

A steering principle is different from an intention. An intention is part of your inner world, a steering principle can be found in the effect of your actions in the outside world. For example: when there are problems with regard to the co-operation between people in your project group, you do not intervene. Your steering principle may be the view that it is the project leader's task to deal with problems of co-operation. Your actions are guided by this view. Another view could be that these problems of co-operation will resolve themselves.

A very common steering principle amongst managers is: 'It will only really be done properly if I do it myself.' This often results in an overworked chief and demotivated employees.

Thus the steering principle is an idea, assumption or view that is often unconscious, but determines your actions in a specific situation to a large extent.

Using the night consciously

It is important to involve the effect of the night when you are learning by doing to achieve the best learning results.

We experience things during the day, evaluate them, discuss them with others, and so on. At night, while we are asleep, the learning process continues in a very different way. What we take with us into the night continues to be processed at other layers of consciousness. We all know that 'sleeping on it' can help to make things clearer, place them in a completely different perspective, or give us a sense of assurance about what we should do.

It is important to devote attention to the moment before falling asleep and the moment after waking up, if you want to use the effect of the night consciously. When you fall asleep it is important to think about the question of your study, and then look again at the facts of the situation in your mind's eye, before letting everything go consciously. Prevent all sorts of feelings and emotions from starting to play a part, because this will probably give you a sleepless night. When you wake up, it is important to be alert to your inner feelings. Take a moment to concentrate on these before the everyday world takes you over again. A shrill alarm clock can disrupt this sensitive moment and cause the learning results to escape your consciousness.

These are some of the points to devote attention to when you are learning by doing. Your own experience of work and life is the most important source of your development after the years of childhood and youth. It is much more important than books, courses, and all sorts of training. However, you must want to make use of this source yourself. If you do not want to, nothing will happen. If you can make your experience fruitful for your development, your life will achieve an extra dimension. It will become more adventurous and interesting.

To summarize, the following things are important for learning from experience:
- Choosing a situation
- Forming a question
- Standing back
- Observing effects
- Discovering steering principles
- Making use of others
- Using the night consciously

Task 35: What did I want?

You resolve to do something, and you make a start. At the same time, all sorts of other things are happening and you are dragged along by life. At the moment that you want to evaluate your acts, you become aware that your intention has slipped through your fingers. You ask yourself, what you were planning. Perhaps you still remember. But how was it exactly? In order to learn by doing and then monitor your acts, you need the memory of what you wanted in the first place.

For yourself

1 Fill in the table *Results of the study of the future* in pencil, in the Logbook. Try to answer the questions in your memory as precisely as possible, i.e., without consulting your notes.

2 Now take your notes and collect the most important results following Task 24 (i.e., after the previous summary, *Results up to now*). Compare the table you completed from memory with your notes and fill it in definitively.

Practical instructions

In Task 24, you formulated your *Central question for the future*. It is possible that you would like to modify your question in the light of your latest learning results. In this case, fill in the new question in the table.
Make another copy of the completed table and that of Task 24 for your discussion partners.

In dialogue

The discussion takes place after Task 37.

Rounding off

Make notes of what you discovered about yourself.

Table 2: Results of the study of the future

My *central question* for the future is:

My *vision* is

The *way in which I want to make decisions* is:

Date _____

My *scenario* is:

The *areas to be looked after* are:

The *path I want to take* is:

Task 36: Experiences

How often do you have an intention and then do something different? Why is this? Why were you distracted? What stopped you? In order to monitor your life more consciously, it is necessary to look at this very carefully, and at the effects of what you did. These may be things that you planned to do, but they may also be spontaneous acts.

For yourself

Complete Table 3, *Learning by doing,* in your Logbook. What steps had you decided upon? Did you carry them out? Did you do other things? What were the effects and experiences resulting from your acts?

Practical instructions

Write down the first three steps you decided upon. Then make a note of any other following activities which you undertook (in chronological order).
For the 'effects', make a distinction between the consequences for others and the consequences for yourself.
Copy the completed table for your discussion partners.

In dialogue

The discussion takes place after Task 37.

Explanation: Learning by doing (p. 242)

Rounding off

The things which distracted or prevented you from carrying out activities you had intended to do and the effects of your acts are particularly significant. Write down what you discovered about this in your Logbook.

Table 3: Learning by doing

(Planned) steps	If they were not carried out, what stopped you?
1	
2	
3	
4	
5	
6	
7	

Date _____

Effects of carrying these out on others	Effects on yourself or experiences

Task 37: What am I going to do?

Every step in the future results in new questions and moments of choice. Will I go in this direction, or that direction? Will I go on, or simply leave matters for a while? Will I keep to the scenario that I chose? Or will I adapt the stages of my plan to my new situation, leaving the scenario as it was? What am I going to do now? This is always the question which remains.

For yourself

Look at the tables which you copied for your discussion partners, and at your notes. Ask yourself which of your recent experiences you wish to discuss. Which question would you like to be the central question in the next discussion, the last one? How can the others help you in this process?

In dialogue

The tables of each contributor are discussed in the light of his central question for this discussion. He determines the direction which the discussion will take, and what contributions he wants from the others.
The others try to help in this.

Rounding off

Finally, present your next steps.

This is the last meeting in the context of this workshop. If this is really going to be the last time you are together, we suggest that you arrange a special form and content for this meeting. Make it a warm, friendly, significant occasion, and in any case make it special!

It was at least six months ago that you picked up this book, came together and started on the workshop. What were your expectations when you started, and what has happened in the meantime? What insights, skills, attitudes and other results has it produced? This workshop is now over, but the end of one thing is always the start of something new. Every moment is a moment of transition.

We wish you all the best.

PART II

BACKGROUNDS AND PERSPECTIVES ON LEADING AN ENTERPRISING LIFE

Contents

Introduction

In Part I of *Workways,* the *Workbook,* the central theme is the study of your life and making personal choices for the future. Therefore the core of the workbook consists of the tasks and exercises. The other texts, the 'explanations', are primarily aimed at facilitating these tasks.

The readings in this part of the book – the *Backgrounds* – are further removed from the tasks and thus from your personal study. In the following six chapters, we explore the more fundamental questions of life and work: questions relating to the course of life, crisis and development, and meaning.

We allow ourselves a great deal of freedom in the way in which we ask questions and search for the answers. You will find a general chapter on *The stages of life and work,* as well as a contribution in the form of an essay on the life and work of one person, the painter Paul Cézanne. You will come across reflections, as well as poetry, observations by other people, as well as personal experiences. The theme behind this arrangement – and the aim of the *Backgrounds* – is to stimulate the reader and inspire him to formulate his own questions and thoughts. Another advantage is that the reader who needs this can learn to know and get a 'taste' of the view of mankind which forms the basis of this workshop and the philosophy of the authors. However, we consider that the proof of the pudding is in the workshop itself.

My work and I

These days, unlike in the past, people live in three different, more or less divided worlds: the world in which they live, the world in which they work, and the world in which they learn.

The world of life or private life
In the world you live in, you are together with those who are closest to you in life: your partner, children, parents, friends and so on. It is the first world which a child knows. It is the 'social body' which is part of you from birth, just like your physical body. In the course of your life, this body may change profoundly, but the world in which you live always encloses you like a cocoon. Without it, you will catch cold, because it is the area in your life where you give and receive warmth and love, and where joy and sorrow are most powerfully experienced. This world is concerned particularly with elements such as meeting people, exchanging ideas and support: 'being there for each other'.

The world of work
The world of work has a different character. It requires a specific effort on your part, a contribution to satisfying the needs of others. It imposes demands on you and requires you to produce results, whether you are an entrepreneur, an employee, a therapist or a police inspector. In this world you are evaluated by what you can do. But you can also prove yourself. Even if you work together with others, you are not there primarily for each other. You are there to make a product or provide a service for third parties.

The world of learning
This world is not as obvious as the previous two, but can be clearly identified, following some self-reflection. It is the world in which you work on yourself and consciously take responsibility for your own development. Obviously you also develop in your private life and the world of work, but in the world of learning, your own development is the main aim. It is the world of training and study, interests and hobbies, in so far as these are not aimed only at relaxation, but also at the development and enhancement of your skills. An interest in art or religion, or the search for a view of mankind and society are all included in this world. In these things, you withdraw from the other worlds, and take time for yourself.

In a sense, the world of work is diametrically opposed to the world of learning. In fact, the former requires that you concentrate on the needs of others while in the world of learning you concentrate on yourself (and are therefore, in a certain sense, selfish). The world of your private life exists between these two. It is concerned with an interest in other people, in give and take and in personal encounters.

Of course, there are also aspects of encounters in the world of work, and the world of your private life sometimes has the characteristics of work. The same applies for the world of learning. Thus, in the above-mentioned classifications, it is a question of identifying the predominant characteristics.

Not so long ago, the lives of many people, especially men, were completely dominated by the world of work. Everything else was subordinated to this. Nowadays, people are more concerned with the quality of life as a whole. They try to achieve a proper balance between work, life and learning. Neglecting or placing too much weight on one of these areas is unhealthy in the long term.

The dominance of work

If you are always concerned only with work, your private life and development will eventually deteriorate. The things which matter to your partner or your children become more and more distant. You have no time for going out or for social contacts. And you put so much energy into work, that at home you are unable to do much more than sit and watch TV.

This can result in a vicious circle. If home life becomes a cold affair, you devote even more time and attention to your work. The recognition and value which you receive there compensate for the emptiness of your private life and your development. However, eventually you will also become stuck in your work, for example, you will no longer be able to let go at work. You are no longer able to delegate anything, or are unable to brook any intervention in the working methods you have introduced. You are under increasing pressure and become stressed.

The dominance of private life

For some people, their private life comes before everything. They see work as something which is outside life, and which simply serves to create the conditions (mainly income) to enable you to spend your free time as you wish. Work becomes an incidental aspect of your life and this will make it difficult for you to find a connection with your tasks and your colleagues.

It also happens that private life requires so much energy that there is nothing left for your work. Problems with growing children, problems in your relationship, with parents going into a retirement home and so on, may totally take you over for a while. Sooner or later, this will also result in problems at work. You forget things or neglect them, and at meetings your thoughts tend to wander. You are no longer all there when you communicate with other people. In the first instance, people at work probably have some sympathy for these situations if they have been informed, but after a while this stops, particularly if the others are at the receiving end of an inadequate performance, repeated absenteeism and the complaints of third parties.

The dominance of the world of learning

It is also possible that your development can start to dominate at the expense of the two other areas of life, although this is not so common. Sometimes people are so taken up with their own development that they start to ignore their work and private life. For example, their thirst for self-knowledge or for an insight into human relationships becomes so great that they have very little time left for anything other than conferences and workshops, both during working hours and in the weekend.

However, the most common aspect of this predominance is when people turn their work into a hobby. In this case, there is a danger that they lose sight of the client or the market, and that they do only those things which are interesting for their own development. However, the spirit of our age means that this is no longer so common because organisations nowadays keep a much closer eye on the added value of work for the client.

Rather than allowing it to dominate, most people neglect their own development. Their work and private life require nearly all their attention and energy. Moreover, development means taking time for yourself. Most people are afraid that this means they are neglecting others. 'When I do something for myself, I feel guilty' – this is something we hear again and again. However, it is necessary nowadays to consciously devote some time to your own development, because otherwise it will lose out.

Guiding your own career

Nowadays, it is very rare for people to spend fifteen years or more in the work for which they were originally trained, or to stay in the same organisation where they started work long ago. People not only change their jobs, but the jobs themselves change, or even disappear to some extent or entirely, and yet very few people take this into account. As long as everything is OK, you assume that you will be doing the same sort of work in the same organisation, unless you are actually looking for a specific job. Many people respond with complete surprise when we ask them to imagine, as an experiment, what sort of work they will be doing in three years' time, assuming that their present job will no longer exist. And yet this is by no means an imaginary situation, considering the increasing number of reorganisations, mergers, cutbacks and closures. However, most people are not prepared for this.

With regard to their own career, many people still have an approach which harks back to the past, though it is no longer appropriate in our own time. This is the attitude: I am good at my job, I do my best and therefore the organisation will reward me with promotion, career prospects and training opportunities. This attitude implies that you are waiting to see what the organisation will offer. In recent years, many people have felt deceived, and feel that their organisation has let them down. The attitude was appropriate at a time when organisations were growing and many qualified people were needed to support this growth and provide personnel in all the new functions such as marketing, logistics, and environmental management. The opposite is happening now: organisations are shedding jobs, they are becoming smaller and flatter, and instead of a shortage, there is a surplus of qualified personnel. Sometimes a single advertisement attracts hundreds of applications.

It is no longer sensible to adopt an attitude of waiting and seeing with regard to your own career. Nowadays, you must actively steer your career, looking not only at vertical upward mobility but above all at horizontal mobility, and sometimes even at downward mobility. You should ensure that you do not become stuck in the long term, for example, by over-specialising or concentrating your experience narrowly. Staying in the same job for years on end so that you have one-sided experiences means that you are particularly vulnerable. That is why there is so much emphasis these days on employability, which means making sure of your own employment in the future.

Making sure your work is meaningful

At a very different level it is also necessary to adopt an active approach nowadays, i.e., with regard to making sure your work has meaning. For many people, the point and meaning of their work has become lost. They have a sense of the uselessness of countless meetings, the paralysis resulting from bureaucratic procedures, the frustrations resulting from opposition and intervention from above. People despair and wonder, 'What on earth are we doing?' It is not only the 'weaker' people in organisations who think like this. Sometimes people with important jobs who seem to be doing very well feel a great inner emptiness when they look at the value and meaning of their work.

In the past, religion and ideologies defined and emphasised the meaning of work. Nowadays, hardly anyone feels this sort of connection. Moreover, the representatives of these philosophies are now themselves struggling with the same problems. Organisations are also less able to give their employees a sense of the meaning of the work. The managing director's speech, the 'mission statement' of a department or a business – they all sound so hollow and abstract that they do not touch the people working there.

Nowadays, the meaning of the work you do is no longer given to you from outside. It is up to you to find the meaning of your work, because no one else can do this for you. In the first place, it is a matter of finding something in your work or in the situation at work that is worthwhile for you – not a clever abstract formulation, but one or more very specific things.

Basic motivation

Traditionally, there have been three aspects which define the meaning and purpose of work: as a source of income, personal development and the provision of a service. Most people are motivated to work by a combination of these three elements.

Source of income

Work can provide you with an income so that you can look after yourself and those who are dependent on you, and so that you can be independent of others. This is the most obvious reason to work, but it is by no means the most important. An inconceivable amount of unpaid work is done in the world.

An income is important because it enables you to organise your life in the way you want. On the other hand, it can also take away your freedom, if it means you are caught in a working situation you do not want. This is sometimes known as the 'golden cage' problem.

A one-sided fixation on income means that you may lose your life path or 'biographical track', so that you eventually become alienated from yourself. The important thing is to choose what will make you 'rich'.

Personal development

Many people see the meaning of their work as a way of expressing and developing their skills. In your work you are faced with challenges which call on your latent skills, not only your professional skills, but also your skill in involving others to overcome resistance and to achieve results.

The opposite situation can also occur: people who never face any challenges in their work become frustrated, and lose a sharp edge. In this case experiences at work have an 'anti-developmental' character, and can even erode a person's sense of self-worth.

If the organisational conditions are present, one important precondition for developing in your work is to use the dynamics between a sense of connection and a sense of detachment. On the one hand, you should be able to feel a connection with tasks, challenges, and above all, your colleagues at work. If your attitude is too critical and your approach is constantly characterised by 'Yes, but', you will be too much of an outsider and you will not be able to become enthusiastic and wholly involved in your work. On the other hand, it is also a good idea to stand back from time to time and to look back critically at what you have done, asking yourself about what you are working on. If you become too involved in your work – which is easily done if you are successful and attract great recognition – you lack the critical distance which is necessary for your own development.

Other people are the main source of your development: colleagues, clients, superiors and so on. They will serve as a mirror for you whether asked, or unasked to do so. By being open to their contributions and taking them into account, you will be able to develop in your work much more successfully. Peter Senge's book on the learning organisation, *The Fifth Discipline,* is worth reading in this context.

Working for others

Many people see the meaning of their work in its importance and usefulness for others. This applies not only with regard to idealistic professions such as overseas development work or social work, but a business manager also wants to provide a useful contribution to the organisation, and a personnel manager will use his knowledge and skills to ensure that the 'human resources' are used as efficiently as possible.

Ultimately, it is possible to see the meaning of work as the satisfaction of other people's needs, i.e., the client's demands. However, as organisations become larger and more complex, the client is often lost from view. This means that people start to think that they are working for 'the boss'. However, this reveals a vertical orientation, while it is particularly important to have a horizontal view. Looking for the meaning of your work, you could for example, try to find a client and discuss with him what contribution he expects. In this way, you can experience the meaning of your work again.

Integration of work, learning and living

People who are looking for a new relationship to their work sometimes have high expectations. They look for work in which they can 'give something of themselves', in which they can 'use and develop their capacities', in which they 'mean something for other people', and so on. To some extent they are right to do so, but there is also another side.

A study of the development of the work done by man over a long period reveals that one of the most important characteristics is the division of work or specialisation. It is because of this that the products or results of work have become increasingly 'objective', i.e. more independent of the subjective preferences, desires and even abilities of individual workers. It was different in the past. Until far into the Middle Ages, the products of human labour, such as food, clothes, furniture and tools, bore the characteristics of the craftsman to such an extent that you could even recognise the individual maker from the product. This is because the maker expressed his identity in the product.

At the other extreme, we have the modern product straight off the assembly line; for example, a plastic beaker is devoid of any subjectivity and is mechanically manufactured on the basis of the client's or the market's objective quality criteria. The machine operators can no longer place their personal stamp on the product. When they are replaced, you cannot see this from the beaker.

What started with machine-based labour in industrial production has spread like an oil stain to the 'higher' levels of work, where more standard procedures and quality requirements, such as ISO norms and other criteria, are increasingly applied. This means that people can no longer express themselves in their work or profession as in the past, and increasingly have to adapt to the requirements imposed from outside. This puts pressure on values such as self-expression and self-development. There may be no demand at all in your work for the qualities which are present as latent skills in you. And you may not be very keen on those aspects which your work does want you to develop.

All this means that many people feel very dissatisfied in their work and have started to look for a more satisfactory working situation in which they can give more of themselves. Sometimes they are successful, because there are still great differences with regard to possibilities for self-realisation in work. But often it is an illusion and in their new work they are soon confronted with the same reality.

Employment in industry, dependent on machines, has resulted in enormous problems of motivation. Attempts have been made by all sorts of artificial means, such as performance-based rewards, work meetings, and independent working groups, to revive this motivation. Usually this is in vain. The same problems are now appearing at higher levels, where there is also a great deal of dissatisfaction, demotivation, powerlessness, frustration and absenteeism.

Is this an indication of a very negative view of the future in which work becomes a single huge machine or complex system devoid of all humanity? Will the only compensation be in leisure time when people can express themselves, relax, or become anaesthetized to it all? We believe that there is certainly a danger of this, with all the attendant negative consequences, both for the individual, and for the organisation. It is not possible to reduce man to a cog in a machine without paying a penalty. In fact, modern working situations do require personal involvement, an effort, an interest in the product, the client, co-operation with colleagues, and so on.

There seems to be a paradox. On the one hand, work is losing its human qualities because people can no longer express themselves in the results of their work; on the other hand, the working situation actually requires all sorts of human qualities to produce good products or services. You might say that because work has become spiritually deadening, people now have to contribute their own spirit. This means that they must motivate themselves, they must give meaning to their work themselves and discover the strength to show an interest in the product, the service and the client.

In the future, the human quality of work will increasingly have to come from ourselves. This is a considerable task, but it is one that can serve as a great leap forward in our own development. It is a task imposed by the spirit of our age and it is crucial both for our personal life and for the future of society that we succeed in this. First of all, it is necessary to recognise and accept the developments that have been described. In this way you will be freed of a number of illusions and your expectations with regard to your work and working situation will be more realistic. In addition, it is important to be actively responsible for your own development outside the working situation. You must develop strengths in the world of your personal life and in the world of learning so that you can operate at work in a way that has human dignity. It will serve as the source of nourishment to do what has to be done in your work with a personal effort.

This completes the circle. We have come back to the three aspects of our life on earth: the world of our personal life, the world of learning, and the world of work. They are closely interrelated, and must all three be cared for consciously for the sake of the quality of our personal and social existence.

The stages of life and work

Connecting and letting go: the heartbeat of life

Work

Compulsory education ends at the age of 16 and the obligation to work ends at the age of 65. These ages more or less demarcate the period in your life when work plays a dominating role (for some, as a burden; for others, as a delight). Work is linked to an income, and without that you cannot live, or at least not as you might like. Work also gives you a social status. The unemployed know all about that. And it gives a meaning to your life. You do something which others consider useful and in which you can give something of yourself. But the meaning of your work and how important it is for you depends on many factors. One of these factors is the stage which you have reached in life.

Young people of about sixteen do all sorts of jobs such as paper rounds, clerical work and packaging, serving food in old people's homes on Sundays, helping the florist on the Saturday market, babysitting, and so on. It has to be reasonably paid, not take up too much time and energy, and be fun to do for a while. This is a playful way of getting to know society. If the work becomes too serious, or the boss is too difficult, they easily pack up and leave.

Some of our colleagues who are older than sixty-five have not stopped working. They concentrate more on what is important for them or what they enjoy doing. The pressure to provide an income has diminished, or disappeared altogether. So have the demands imposed by belonging to a working community. People feel freer, more relaxed, and therefore more creative. Very often, they will do jobs for organizations in the Netherlands, Europe or the Third World which pay little. They enjoy life and are busier than ever.

These are impressions of what people do at either end of the 'compulsory' working period in life. In fact, these boundaries are constantly under pressure. First, the early retirement option was introduced, and then it was scrapped. There has even been some thought about raising the pensionable age. In view of the increasing number of elderly people in society, this seems unavoidable. There are many people who wish to continue to work as long as they are fit enough – after all, work keeps you fit. It allows you to maintain a connection with the world and it stimulates the mind.

If you do not work, you do not experience the substance of existence. How could you ever have an idea?

Andrei Platonov

267

The threshold at the start of the working period in life is also under pressure. Compulsory schooling and part-time education, in which working and learning are combined, is constantly being extended. The importance of education is undeniable. In 1989, I saw the words 'Learn, learn and learn!' painted in bright pink letters on a cream school wall in Chabarovsk (Eastern Siberia) next to the striking profile of Lenin, chin up, nose pointing forward, fierce gaze. 'Education permanente' or lifelong learning is with us today.

Stages of life

What are the stages of our lives, and how can they be characterized? In Ancient China, life was divided into three periods: a time to learn, a time to fight, and a time to grow wise. In those days, the Hindus distinguished the stages of being a student, a householder (the stage of social responsibility), a pilgrim (the stage in which a person can withdraw and seek himself and the true meaning of life), and sannyasin. As a sannyasin, a man or woman had no more hatred or love, lived with the eternal Self, and had no possessions. The Greeks and Romans also had views about the stages of life. In our own century the theme has come back to us in the work of Charlotte Bühler (as well as that of Rudolf Steiner, Martha Moers, Romano Guardini, and Bernard Lievegoed). Erik Erikson and Else Frenkel-Brunswijck, a pupil of Charlotte Bühler, left Europe to go to the United States before the Second World War, and stimulated research into the stages of life there (also see Levinson, Selles, Sheahy, and Washbourn). After this, developments in Europe and America followed fairly parallel paths more or less independently of each other. Since the 1970's there has been an increase in the number of publications on the course of life and about 'the mid-life crisis' on both sides of the Atlantic, and the study of the personal biography has become an essential part of careers advice.

How have you lived? What have you done? How did you make the choices? What are the work situations you have been in? What experience, skills and knowledge have you acquired? What are your strong and weak points? What do you want in the future in your work and in your life? Biography work is an individual approach, It is carried out against the background of general characteristic stages of life and the transitions between these, which are also referred to as crises. These crises are experienced as a threat, but actually provide the opportunity for a new step in your career. The study of the stages of life has increased our consciousness of life.

Every person is born and dies – this is the law of nature. Our life may be a short or a long one, a path of thorns or grassy meadows, passing by dangerous chasms or over challenging peaks. But each of us comes to earth and finds a place, achieving our desires to a greater or lesser extent, and then shrinking and eventually disappearing, unless the path is broken off prematurely.

When a baby's head appears from the womb, you see a wrinkled face, anticipating the face of an older person much later. But this soon disappears, and in the first few days the face is surrounded by a pure and beautiful glow. Then this disappears and she lies there, more closely linked to the earth, and starts to respond to her environment when she is not asleep. For large parts of the day she is still not here. Later on, the position is reversed. When a person becomes active in life, she can manage with a minimum of sleep for long periods.

Then, when this person has grown old, she may sit by the window or the fire , still fully present and impossible to ignore, with her own opinions or complaints, still arranging various matters. But increasingly you lose contact with her and she lives in her own world. Occasionally you see her mask of death. And when the time comes, it often happens that she lies there peacefully. It is possible to see the glow which was there at the beginning. But who can remember this? The people who were there at the beginning have already gone before her. And then the glow disappears again.

This applies to all of us. We grow, we bloom, and we wilt, just like the trees and plants. Our greatest physical vitality is between the ages of twenty and forty. You travel, you are enterprising. You build things and organize things. It is all about performance. People are traded for their performance (for example, professional footballers) and used (think of the planned career system for managers). You do all this yourself: a job, a partner, children, a house and garden, and even a second home, whether this is a tent, a holiday home, a boat or a caravan. Your actions are nourished by your vitality, until 'the man with the yellow jersey' comes (a cycling term). For some, he comes at the age of forty, for others at the age of fifty. The man hits hard or pushes gently, but you get to know your limits. His heart or back, stomach, intestines or head cry 'Take it easy,' and 'live sensibly.' In the course of your life, you reach the limit of your vitality. Is this the beginning of the end?

There are people who seem to be waiting for the end from the age of fifty. Life becomes more difficult, and all the fun has gone out of it. Minor problems become serious complaints and result in endless moaning. Other remain active up to their seventies, eighties or even nineties. They take their decline in physical vitality into account, but seem to be full of spiritual energy, and even achieve their best performances (there are many examples of this). They often look young, as though they are becoming more mature and younger at the same time.

> *You grow younger with maturity.*
>
> Hermann Hesse

But where do these people find this spiritual flexibility? Is it a question of education? To some extent it certainly is. You are always formed by your family, school, the organizations in which you worked, radio, television, and so on. Every person is a child of his time and is formed by the prevailing spirit of the age – in this age by the spirit of cutbacks, the breakdown of the welfare state from the cradle to the grave, the encouragement of initiative, the spirit of enterprise and commerce. If the physical and material aspects of these things are excessively emphasized throughout your life, it is much more likely that you will become spiritually weak at the end of your life.

Therefore there are favourable and unfavourable conditions for developing spiritual strength and flexibility. But there are also examples of people who survive in very difficult circumstances and continue to grow spiritually. The way in which people respond inwardly to conditions imposed from outside is extremely individual and varied. Someone adapts, another protests, the third person finds his own way, remaining himself. This reveals a central core in people, which can develop independently. Very often people with a physical handicap or in very difficult circumstances actually have great spiritual strength.

For example, when you ask people who were in Japanese concentration camps in Indonesia during the Second World War, what helped them to survive these difficult situations, they come up with the following things which reveal a spiritual orientation.

'I read the Bible and prayed regularly. You know that God has something in mind for you.'

'Deep inside me, I knew that there is a meaning hidden in everything in life. Even in those terrible circumstances, and even if I could not see the meaning myself in that moment.'

'I realized that this was the situation I was in, and that I had to make the best of it.'

'I held on to what had to be done now, today, right in front of me. Even with the most awful jobs – after all, someone had to do it.'

'I always tried to pay attention to other people, even – in one case – the enemy.'

'My mother repeatedly said: "My boy, it will pass. It is only temporary".'

People were also able to survive the situation by holding onto certain ordinary human values and norms, even if it was just one.

The stages of life and work

What are the factors which affect this individual core in life, apart from education, training and physical vitality? Everyone is a child for some time, then a teenager, a twenty-year-old, a thirty-year old, and so on. What are the typical characteristics of these stages, and what does this mean for a person's working life? We begin our description with a person in his twenties, as many people don't start work until then because the period of education and study has been extended. Bearing in mind the increasing number of older people, we have also included some characteristics of those in their seventies and eighties. A general description does not detract from the fact that every person passes through these phases of life at his own pace. The unique aspect of individual destiny is revealed in the differences between people, how they differ in the ways they live through the life phases.

The twenties

A twenty-year-old steps into life, often full of expectation. Life lies before him. It is exciting and adventurous, and he is open to it. He has little self-knowledge, and that is what is particularly important during this period, to acquire self-knowledge, to explore your own limits and possibilities, to discover what suits you, and what does not. By doing this, a young person builds up inner security, which contrasts with external security, such as a guaranteed income, social security, and so on.

Older people are sometimes surprised to see what they are prepared to do, but when you look back on your own life, you become aware that you entered upon these 'reckless' adventures without being aware of any dangers.

In these things, young people are mainly governed by the – still unconscious – will. 'You go where your legs take you.' There is no definite path to follow. 'I'll see,' is his favourite expression. The young person easily becomes enthusiastic about certain (new) ideas. He has only a limited capacity for forming judgements based on experience. That is why this age group, like teenagers, are easy prey for dictatorial regimes, terrorist groups, sects, and so on.

Work gives a twenty-year-old the possibility of testing himself in the same way that clubs, associations, friends and travel do. It often has a temporary character. A young person does not want any permanent commitment. If possible, he will seek change, rather than doing the same thing for a long time. Employment agencies give him an ideal opportunity to do this. Moreover, he wants to see the results of his work in the short term. He is not yet able to start on something if the product becomes visible only after one or two years, This leads to a lack of motivation. He still has a strong need for positive contacts with others in his work, people who think he's alright. He is not yet a soloist. Others have to show him who he is.

The thirty-year-old

In their late twenties or early thirties, most people start to evaluate their lives for the first time. This point may be postponed by years of study, but by this stage the young person is more or less familiar with his limits and possibilities, and would like to start making use of them. Guardini called this transition: 'the crisis of experience'. The mobility of the twenty-year-old disappears, but the vitality and speed remain.

Apart from the will, the intellect also starts to play a guiding role in life. The thought processes become more businesslike and serious. The thirty-year-old thinks that he can control life in a rational way. He has a planned approach to things, at home, in his hobbies or at work. He will attempt many things and organize them well, and in so doing he is constantly in discussion with others.

A serious element enters his life: 'I am thirty. My youth is behind me, the serious part of life has started.' Halfway through his thirties he may start to realize that life is finite. This is not a very profound awareness. It is more something that occasionally surfaces. Apart from this, the person in his thirties becomes more strongly connected to his work, his partner, the home, clubs, or other social responsibilities. Following the stage of exploration in his twenties which covered a broad spectrum of activities, he now seeks to specialize and explore things more profoundly. Many people are in the most materialist stage of life in their thirties. Just listen to their conversation at a party: houses, cars, boats, mortgage, and so on.

For many people, work becomes the place to develop, both in an external sense (making a career) and in an inner sense (developing as a person). It is reminiscent of the words of 'Loesje': 'Do you also have a full-time job and a part-time relationship?' Your work becomes your life.

In his thirties a person is able to cover a broad spectrum and have responsibilities which go beyond carrying out his own work. He starts to think in the longer term. He can cope with many things at the same time, and likes to use his intellectual capacity, setting goals, planning, organizing, establishing systems, weighing up priorities, and so on.

A person of about 35 is an ideal employee for many organizations, at least in our present culture: powerful, clear, businesslike, orderly, and full of vitality. This can take him into the external world with an emphasis on becoming 'visible', or 'scoring' to such an extent that he passes over his own inner need for development. It is quite a task to remember the importance of this need.

The forty-year-old

At about the age of forty, many people begin to ask themselves existential questions. This often starts with vague feelings of restlessness and dissatisfaction, and sometimes even with a sense of insecurity that is a complete mystery to the person himself. It is as though everything which had seemed worthwhile in life up to that time has lost its attraction. In addition, he suddenly becomes aware that half of his life is over. Looking back at his life up to that point, the question arises whether this is 'everything life has to offer'. The former system of values no longer seems to suffice. Some people have the feeling that they will have to change a number of things in the outside world very quickly in order not to miss the boat. They change jobs, break off their marriage or relationship, and want to make a new start. Usually this is an illusion: in the new relationship or new job, you come across yourself again. What is required is actually an inner reorientation. It is more a matter of doing things differently than of doing different things. The most important task for the forty-year-old is to bid farewell to the expansive phase from twenty to forty, when his task was to find his place in the world. All his efforts were aimed at achieving this. By the age of forty this place has been found, and the question arises: 'What now? Is all that is left in life repetition, perhaps another one or two promotions, but what then?'

Instead of aiming for more extensive power, importance and recognition – in other words: egocentricity – the new inner task is to develop the restraint to give space to others, and to be there at times when these other, often younger people, need this. Obviously it will be possible to continue in the expansive mode for a few years, but as you approach fifty, this will become increasingly forced and evoke contempt, pity or irritation in the outside world.

This stage of life, when the old ways are no longer appropriate and the new ways have not yet been found, is often seen as an important transitional stage which is comparable to puberty in terms of its vehemence. Often it is accompanied by even more pain because it is not seen as moving in an ascending line, but in a descending line. The life of a person in his forties is characterized by depression and inner turmoil.

Frequently he will restlessly seek for ways to escape from these problems with the help of alcohol, TV, erotic adventures and other excitement. It requires courage to recognise these problems for what they are, and to look for spiritual values which will give a meaning and purpose to life again. That is where the possibilities lie. Now that there is a decline in physical vitality as you grow older, there is space for spiritual and idealistic efforts. No one else can tell you what these might be. You have to find out for yourself. This usually requires a considerable confrontation with yourself which may have the character of a crisis. However, the force emanated by newly discovered ideals can result in a person in his forties finding a new balance, new inner security as he reaches the age of fifty, which gives life a new impetus.

Obviously a person of this age takes all the above problems with him when he goes to work, although most people have a strong tendency to conceal these problems, because they feel that they should conceal their weaknesses. In personal discussions, several managers told us about their great insecurity during this period, and of their fear that their superiors would notice.

Sometimes a person in his forties can feel extremely daunted by tasks which he easily took in his stride before. Everything may seem to be going very well, while the inner satisfaction in the work is declining. 'My appraisals are excellent, I have just been promoted again, but it all means nothing to me.' For a person in this transitional period, work can provide either a welcome support or be a heavy burden, and often it is both at the same time. It is a support because you have to be back in the office every morning at 8.30, talk to people etc. It stops you from being dragged down by insecurity, but it can also be a heavy burden because you have to maintain a pretence to the outside world about things which are not, or no longer, present inwardly.

Although the above is a general basic pattern, the attitude of people of this age to their work does vary. It depends on the development in previous stages, the nature of the work, the attitude of colleagues, and so on. Some of the different possibilities are listed below:

- the person in her forties who seeks a solution in external changes, who starts applying for jobs internally or externally, who wants to move to a different town, start a new relationship etc.;

- someone in his forties who unexpectedly and emotionally starts to ask principled questions during a meeting, and for whom this becomes very important. At the same time, he may reveal an attitude of indifference with regard to matters which were important to him before;

- the woman who suddenly starts to work much harder, almost 'throwing' herself at her work, and taking work home. This is sometimes accompanied by a domineering attitude towards others to conceal a feeling of inner uncertainty;

- the man who can no longer divide his private problems from his work: problems such as alcohol abuse, extramarital affairs, financial problems which are the result of trying to escape these existential questions at weekends or in his free time.

Sooner or later, this will have an effect at work. Just as every person goes through puberty in his own way, everyone also passes through a transitional stage around the age of forty: the so-called mid-life crisis. Approaching the age of fifty, everything becomes less turbulent. It may be that by this time the person has discovered a new perspective or approach to life, and can work on this. Because of this new philosophy and the basic attitude which accompanies it, he can again become immensely valuable for his organization.

The fifty-year-old

The way in which a person lives and works in his fifties depends to a large extent on the way in which he has gone through the preceding transitional stage.

If he did not discover a new perspective on life because he ran away from the problems or continued the expansive stage, he may become increasingly inflexible in his fifties. Younger people, particularly those in their thirties, become a source of irritation, both at work and in private life. A person in his fifties wants to be in a position of superiority over younger colleagues at work, or children at home. He cannot listen to their sometimes rather wild ideas, and responds with a negative attitude such as contempt, ridicule or criticism. At the same time, he idealizes his own past. In this way he can create an unhealthy atmosphere. His negativity is often reflected by the people around him, so that he finds himself in a sort of vicious circle from which it is difficult to escape. There is often a great tendency to look for a scapegoat to which he can attribute his misery and the failures of his life.

If a person has discovered a new meaning in life by the time he enters his fifties, this period can be a source of great inner peace and creativity. It is precisely because the sense of ego, the egocentric attitude, is less prominent in a person in his fifties, that there is space for a true interest in people and society. Previously his hobbies were often a way of proving himself, but now they are ways of devoting himself to a particular field such as music, art, nature, history or a craft. People in their fifties can become true confidants for their often older children and their friends, partly because they can leave younger people free to do what they like, and do not interfere in their lives. The house can become a place where there is space for young people who feel at home there, and where the older people are available for them without being overbearing. Nevertheless, it is very difficult for people in their fifties to accept their physical decline, particularly in our culture in which the body is so important. If the crisis experienced by someone in his forties was exacerbated by signs of physical aging, such as hair loss, going grey, or developing a beer belly, this can become even worse with real complaints and disorders by the age of fifty. The deteriorating body requires more and more attention, although there are enormous differences between people. A person who is not inspired by spiritual ideals is in danger of becoming caught up in a physical downward spiral. On the other hand, it is possible to stay young with 'spiritual strength'. Some people look better in their early fifties than they did when they were forty. It is a matter of freeing yourself from your body in a spiritual way.

The negative development outlined above means that at work a person in his fifties can increasingly become a liability for the organization. He opposes any change and innovation. ('We tried that in 1970, and it didn't work then either!') He becomes stubborn and set in his ways. Work, and the situation at work, becomes a burden to him, and he starts counting the years to his pension or early retirement. As stated above, younger people are a constant threat. At first, the fifty-year-old will battle against them, but when he starts to lose the unequal struggle more and more often, he will resort to mockery and cynicism, tyrannising others by insisting on his rights. Small things, like smoking, open windows, taking a telephone call can lead to constantly recurring conflicts in a department.

On the other hand, positive development may mean that these people become an important support for the organization. They no longer feel the need to strengthen their own position, so they are able to be far more objective. Such a person in his fifties can stand back, surveying the broad picture, and is therefore able to think in a truly policy-oriented way. Because he no longer needs to prove himself, he is an ideal leader. Furthermore, he is able to take difficult, and if necessary, hard decisions, not on the basis of all sorts of subjective considerations, but because they are necessary for the organization. This person will feel less at home in a hectic environment, where there are ten things happening at once, and fast, short-term decisions have to be made. It is an art to find and create a place in an organization where the positive qualities of this stage of life can be made use of best. It goes without saying that in this respect, the traditional starting points of the present systems of salaries and pensions are a great obstacle.

The sixty-year-old

Our modern society, with its fixation on the vitality of youth (young, wild and free), reckons that at sixty, you are old, and this means you're 'out'. What advertisements or fashion magazines show people in their sixties? But at sixty, a person is not really old, though he is increasingly often confronted with the finite nature of his own life, a life which takes place between two poles: birth and death.

In the first half of life, everyone is confronted with the task of forming a connection with the earth and material existence. By making an effort in this respect, a person can develop, and work is a fantastic opportunity in this respect. During the second half of life, he is increasingly confronted with the task of separating from this. Eventually, he will have to let go of everything which became part of him in that world: his work, position, relationships, financial possibilities...

That is why crossing the boundary of the 'compulsory working period' can be both restricting and liberating. Your life is no longer carried by your work. Increasingly, you are dependent on your own resources. At the same time, this freedom from 'compulsory work' can provide many new opportunities. Often you can find new energy in a connection with something that is still really important to you. At the same time, you make a start on the great step of letting go of life.

Compulsory education stops at sixteen, and the obligation to work at sixty-five. At the moment you can still take early retirement, though this will not be possible for much longer because the system is not viable in social and economic terms. The new trend is for an individual approach. For every job and every individual, partial or complete retirement will become possible before or after the age of sixty-five. In fact, it will probably become necessary. And yet, there are not many people in their sixties left in organizations. Many have left earlier, and draw an old-age pension or take early retirement. Those who remain often want to complete the sixty-five years as a point of honour. If you do not suffer from too many physical ailments, you can still do a great deal.

At sixty, you are not old. So why are there so few people of this age in organizations? The usual reason given is that, 'They cannot keep up, and the rate of change is too great.' This is probably true for many people, but haven't we drawn the wrong conclusion from this? Aren't the reactions of older people in organizations a way of measuring the way in which changes and innovations are dealt with? Older people give up, where younger people still have the energy and perseverance to keep fooling about. But there is a great price to pay: their motivation and their commitment to the work declines. In older people the breaking point comes sooner. They prefer to get out, and the organization is happy to let them go, so that things continue as usual. After all, doesn't the market, clients, competition and cost cutting mean that there is no choice?

For people in their sixties to stay in an organization, an individual approach is required. To what extent are you still able to work part-time or full-time? When can you no longer work? What are the priorities for people in their sixties, and what are suitable tasks for them? What should the organization's expectations be, whether they are dealing with paid work or voluntary work? Appeal to the strength and enthusiasm, the specialist areas and experience of older people, and relate the conditions to these. Make clear and concrete agreements. This means that the organization is also able to discuss matters when things are no longer viable. In this way, an older person in his sixties can continue to serve the organization with his experience in a vital and creative way for a long time.

The seventy-year-old

There is an increase in the number of people who are reaching old age. For some people, growing old starts at seventy; for others, not until ninety. Many slip away and reach a condition in which they merely seem to vegetate, becoming completely dependent on others. Others are able to remain active, and are self-supporting to a ripe old age.

For a while, the sense of being liberated from the obligation to work continues to have an effect. They start on new projects and go on long trips. Life is still a multicoloured tapestry of social contributions, for example, to an association or church, family, neighbours and friends, and of leisure interests.

Later on, you see the world of most people becoming smaller as they approach eighty. It is too much to continue with all the different activities and to maintain all sorts of contacts. At the same time, these contacts become increasingly important. There is more loneliness, as many people stop coming round or pass away. The circle becomes smaller and the dependence on it becomes greater.

Your end is approaching, but you do not want to look at it yet. Memories become more and more important. You can become lost in them. But people who manage to retain an interest in what is happening in the world by continuing to read newspapers, watching TV and talking about it, remain spiritually active. One person told us: 'I'm a person of my own time, and these younger people belong to their own age. I want to follow what interests them. I want to experience these changing times and relate to them. What is happening in the world, to others, to younger people, to me? Of course, there are many things I do not agree with, but what is their experience, what does it mean for them? At the same time, I must remain myself. Yes, I'm old-fashioned, I'm from an earlier age.' This attitude allows for the opposite to happen as well: younger people start to take an interest in these old people, benefiting from their mild wisdom. A person in his seventies can become an oasis of tranquillity, and at the same time a hopeful example. Although the world becomes smaller in terms of the area of action, it actually becomes wider and freer because of this inner activity. But it is not presented on a plate. You have to exercise your mind, for example, by training your memory, remembering where you have put your key, or by taking bridge lessons.

The eighty-year-old
There is a growing dependence on an ever-smaller circle of people. The daily periods of activity become shorter, while periods of rest are longer. Very often the transition to these years is characterized by a significant physical event, such as breaking a hip. Life literally becomes more unsteady, more vulnerable and less secure. It is a difficult period in which a person is able to do less and less of what he wants. Everything that has to be abandoned has a definitive character, and this makes it even more difficult. There is a decline in the active life in the outside world, and if inner activities are not continued, there is not much left. At the same time, the ability to remain mentally active also declines. There is a conflict with the constantly approaching final boundary. Eternity makes you pull in your sails. The art is to accept this without surrendering entirely. There is always room to do those things which are close to the heart, albeit in a smaller, more modest way. Who to visit, and who not to. What to do and manage for yourself, and what to leave for others. It is a matter of restricting activities in terms of their scope, and this means that the quality of these activities can be very great. At these few moments, the person may experience a heightened intensity of life. People who see this happening feel gratitude and a sense of wonder. They see the struggle and the pain of the approaching end, but as one eighty-year-old told us: 'It's good that nature has organized things in such a way that you can prepare for departure.'

It is true that we cannot escape death. That's not so terrible. After this, we go and stay for a long time with a Host who is so fascinating that time completely stands still and becomes eternity.

Godfried Bomans

When you stay with someone, this comes to an end, and then you go home. Usually, your home has changed in the meantime, just as you have.

Crisis and transition in the course of life

In our time, people are confronted with changes in their environment much more than previous generations were. There is a great increase not only in the number of changes, but also in the rate at which they take place. Moreover, the nature of the process of the change itself is subject to change. For example, while the beginning and end of a process of change in a reorganization were relatively clear in the past, both the point of departure and the progress and final goal of this process are shrouded in mist nowadays. Many organizations are now involved in their third or fourth merger. The last merger has barely been completed when the next one is at hand. The same turbulence can also be found in other areas of life, both in the micro-sphere of private life and at the macro-social level.

In our time, innovation and change are the order of the day, and make high demands on those who are involved in these processes in a guiding capacity. In the technical material world we can make changes without having to take into account the inner life of things, simply because they do not have one. But if the changes affect people in their private life or at work, they can react to this very strongly and lose all confidence in themselves and their environment.

That is why it is important to make a distinction between external changes and the inner process people go through as a result. For example, transferring to a different job in the organization may only take a matter of days, while the inner processes for the person concerned could take several months.

This inner process is described here with the word 'transition', which means 'moving across'. Thus a transition is the inner process of crossing over when people undergo far-reaching changes in their lives.

Changes which lead to transitions do not come only from outside, but also from our own inner world. For example, puberty, and the so-called mid-life crisis, are such transitions. But there are many more moments in the course of life at which we have to bid farewell to old ideas, attitudes or behaviour, and have to take on new tasks.

Although transitions sometimes take place almost imperceptibly, they are often rather like a crisis, accompanied by strong feelings and emotions which can temporarily paralyse us. This does not always have to be visible to the outside world, because we often try to hide it from others and from ourselves. Many people are ashamed of these feelings, especially in the world of work. They are afraid – sometimes quite justifiably – of being considered fusspots, or worse still, to be branded as a 'wreck'.

An insight into transition and crisis situations can help you to recognise and understand your own feelings and emotions so that you can deal with them in a more conscious way.

A closer look at the process of transition

In ancient cultures and in the cultures of some Third World countries, the transition from one period to the next is – and was – expressed in ritual activities or ceremonies. For example, when the harvest had been brought in, the end of the season was marked with celebrations. This also happened at the end of a year or the end of a ruler's reign. The initiation rites of boys and girls on the brink of adulthood are very well known. They were removed from their family and the community to which they had belonged up to that time, and had to spend a long period of isolation in a lonely place in the jungle or desert. The young person would sometimes have to undergo all sorts of deprivations and face many dangers, sometimes for months on end. If he survived, he would be taken back into the community, but now with a different role.

According to William Bridges, a Dutch researcher, called Arnold van Gennep, had discovered at the beginning of this century, that almost all these rites comprise three stages, viz., separation, transition and reincorporation. The separation was a symbolic death experience. The transition was a sort of neutral zone where the old lifestyle was put aside in complete solitude and a new inner attitude had to be found. The stage of reincorporation meant the return to the community, and learning the skills and customs which went with the new social position.

Our own culture has abandoned such rituals apart from a few vestiges, of which many people no longer understand the original significance. These old cultures can teach us to be aware that it is necessary to let go of the old before starting on something new, and that there is an interim period of chaos between the end (farewell) and the new start, a sort of psychological no man's land in which a person is strongly confronted with himself, and in which a new basic attitude is born.

Changes succeed each other at a rapid rate. Neither we nor the organizations we work in devote more than a minimum amount of attention to coping with this process of transition, but what was expressed in the rites of ancient cultures is such an essential element for mankind that we ignore it at our peril. The consequences of ignoring it have become gigantic in our time, and manifest themselves in lack of motivation, stress, illness and disability.

The following description of the process of transition relates the insights of William Bridges who bases his work on 'the rites of passage' in ancient cultures, to the work of Elisabeth Kübler-Ross. She devoted herself particularly to the process of mourning which people undergo after the loss of their loved ones.

Following Kübler-Ross's pioneering work, it was discovered that people experience the same sort of processes in other situations of loss: incurable disease or amputation, divorce, losing a job, retirement etc. These processes are also found in situations which do not appear to be loss situations at all, such as pregnancy, moving house, and even promotion. However, a closer look reveals that these situations also contain elements of loss: leaving behind a carefree life, an old home and neighbourhood, an old familiar group.

Ill. 3: *Mood image*

Ill. 4: Support exercise; *Development*

Ill. 5: Support exercise; *Observation*

Ill. 6: Support exercise; *Turning point*

Ill. 7: *The Four Seasons,* ca. 300 x 100cm, 1860-62, 21-23 yr. Musée de la Ville de Paris, Petit Palais

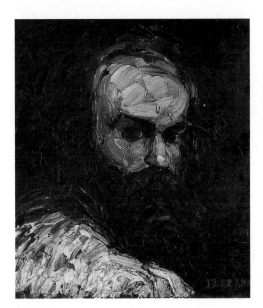

Ill. 8: *Self portrait,* 45 x 41cm, ca. 1866, 27 yr. Private collection

Ill. 9: *Head of an old man,* 51 x 48cm, ca. 1865, 26 yr. Musée de Orsay, Paris

Ill. 10
Paul Alexis reads Zola,
52 x 56cm, 1869-70,
30-31 yr. Private collection

Ill. 12: *Melting Snow at L'Estaque* or *The Red Roofs*, 73 x 92cm. ca. 1870, 31yr.
Private collection

Ill.11 *Two Card Players,*
97 x 130cm, 1892-93,
53-54 yr.
Private collection

Ill.13: *The House and Tree on the Road to the Hermitage, Pontiose,* 65 x 45cm, 1873-74, 34-45 yr.
Private collection

Ill.15: *The Sorrow of Mary Magdalen*
165 x 124cm, ca,1867, 27 yr.
Musée d'Orsay, Paris

Ill.14: *The Descent of Christ into Limbo,*
170 x 97cm, ca. 1867, 27 yr.
Private collection

Ill.16: *The Bathers*
205 x 245cm, 1906, 67 yr.
Museum of Art,
Philadelphia

An insight into the process of transition begins by recognizing this element of loss. Sometimes this is balanced by a 'gain' which compensates for the loss. This applies particularly when the person concerned wanted the change to happen himself. Yet when you find yourself in the new situation, you will feel the loss, though you probably think it would be wrong to complain. What you wanted, helps you to get through. However, if the change is imposed, or simply happens to you, the experience of loss can be extremely strong and more difficult to cope with.

Changes which are the result of growing older often have a similar character of loss. An adolescent may experience the loss of his childhood, a thirty-year-old the loss of his youth. At certain moments in your life you can experience the loss of vitality, but also the loss of innocence and confidence.

The following illustration is a diagram of the process of transition. The horizontal line is the axis of time, the vertical line represents the mood of the person in a process of transition. The process of transition can be subdivided into three different stages: the end or farewell, the transitional stage, and the stage in which there is a new start. These three stages are described in sequence below.

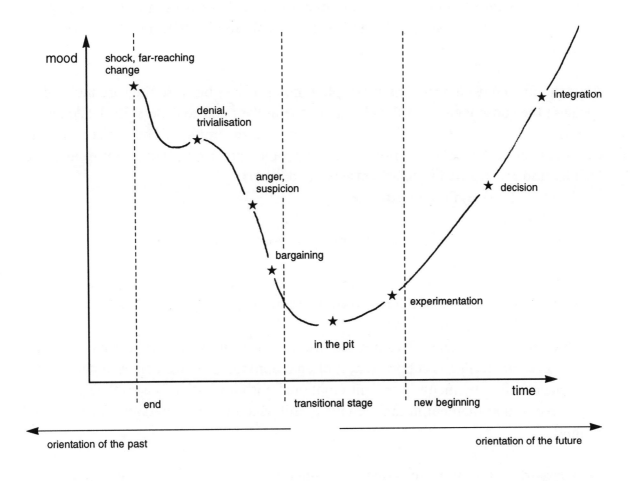

1 *Transitions begin with an ending*

The transition starts by taking leave of an old familiar situation. Often we can have strong links with this situation without realizing it. It comes as a shock when it suddenly comes to an end. This shock will be all the stronger if the old situation determined our identity to any extent, for example, when someone for whom work is all-important finds that she has been dismissed.

'It was as though the earth disappeared from under my feet.'

'My whole world caved in.'

'It was as though I died, became cold and stiff. My blood stopped flowing.'

These reactions are most usual in response to a change which comes from outside: bad news from a doctor, the announcement of a divorce, hearing about a company closure. This shock effect can also be caused by an inner change as a result of your own individual process of development ('I suddenly realized: this can't go on, this has to end, this is definite; and at the same time I was overwhelmed by tremendous sorrow'), but usually these transitions are more gradual, with a vague sense of restlessness or dissatisfaction.

People react very differently to far-reaching changes from outside. Some become terribly angry; others seem to be paralysed and do not say anything, while still others feverishly look for solutions to the new situation. The shock is usually emotionally overwhelming. An outwardly calm and reasonable facade is often merely an illusion concealing the pain of the departure.

After the first confrontation, many people's mood revives because they are inclined to trivialise the consequences of the change to themselves and to others. In the American literature this phenomenon is known as 'minimizing the impact'. This is the result of the character of the transition process; most people have a strong aversion to negative feelings and are inclined to tell themselves and others:

'I'm O.K., it doesn't matter to me.'

'We'll get over it.'

'Life goes on. You mustn't think it really troubles me.'

People convince themselves that it won't be so bad, and that everything will pass. They consult selective sources of information: 'Peter has heard the director say that this department will continue operating.'

Of course, this aversion does not remove the uncertainty, fear, shame and so on, but because the feeling is suppressed, it often reappears unexpectedly at other, often very inconvenient moments: a violent emotional outburst which is completely misplaced at that moment in that situation, and which is not understood by the people around.

With regard to transitions resulting from inner development, people also often convince themselves that things will pass, and that it is a temporary matter. One woman said of her marriage: 'We come into conflict almost every day, and the whole atmosphere seems to be poisoned by irritation. But I know that the base is sound. It must be the busy time we've had for the past few weeks which is against us. In a few weeks' time, things will be what they used to be.'

After a while this hope usually proves to be in vain, and harsh reality once again imposes itself. Many people feel anger and suspicion well up, and this is aimed against those who they see as being responsible for their misery; the doctors who should have seen it coming much earlier; the personnel department who have treated you as a cipher; the organization you worked yourself into the ground for, and from whom you get no thanks at all; the husband or wife for whom you have always been available, and who is now trading you in as though you are a used model.

With regard to inner developmental processes, the cause or reason for the dissatisfaction is also often blamed on the outside world: lack of understanding, millstones, no space, no response, lack of direction, or unclear job or task descriptions.

In nine out of ten cases the discussions arising from this are spectacularly unfruitful. The person who is attacked has the understandable tendency to defend himself. The other person feels even less understood because of this usually rational defence, and is reinforced in his feeling that he is being exploited and is misunderstood. The tragic aspect of this stage of the transition – and of the following stage – is that all sorts of good advice and possible solutions are ignored. On the one hand, the person concerned is crying out: 'Well tell me, what should I do now?' On the other hand, he rejects every answer. Bystanders soon have enough of this and turn away, so that he feels entirely abandoned.

People who took the initiative for themselves to make the change, such as a divorce or changing a job, will have a more inwardly oriented reaction during this stage of the transition, such as doubts about whether they have done the right thing; they experience self-recriminations and blame themselves: 'What on earth have I embarked on?' 'What am I doing to myself and others?'. Sometimes people have a tendency to tell others how good the old situation was. Some people in a new job go on for months saying: 'Do you know how they did that where I used to work?'

At the end of this first stage of the transition, you become aware that anger and aggression do not help. The angry words have been spoken dozens of times, and inwardly repeated hundreds of times. Feelings of guilt and self-recrimination have gone round and round, but remain a dead weight inside you. Other people around you have gone deaf to your complaints and recriminations. You feel that you are quite alone, and have landed in the deepest point of the transition, literally in the pit. You have hit rock bottom.

2 *The stage of transition – it's all crisis*

As in ancient cultures, the middle stage of a transition can also be seen in our own time as a period of confrontation with the self, and a time of reflection from which you can emerge as a different person. This does not happen automatically. Letting go of what you acquired in the past so that the seeds for the future have a chance to grow is often a heavy test.

Only now do you become aware that the original situation is over for good, and that things will never be as they were in the past, though at the same time you have no picture of the future. At this stage your behaviour is listless, indifferent and apathetic. The daily tasks at work and/or in the family are a heavy burden which fill you with apprehension. Inwardly you feel insecure and depressed. Periods of hope and despair alternate with one another, and you can experience a suffocating sense of loneliness. You feel that the world around has little or no understanding of your inner needs, and you are inclined to shut yourself away from others, with the result that you become increasingly isolated.

This middle stage of transition can have the character of a life crisis. A characteristic aspect of this is that the coping skills which you have used in your life up to then are no longer sufficient to deal with the situation you are in now. In her book, *Crisis as opportunity,* Verena Kast describes a crisis as a situation in 'which there is a great imbalance for the person in the crisis in the subjective importance of the problem and the available possibilities for dealing with it.'

It is clear that none of the familiar range of responses are of any use, all the existing possibilities to deal with the problem seem to have been exhausted:

– other people's advice is well meant, but does not help you get any further;

– getting angry and confronting others: this may give some relief, but seems pointless in the end;

– listing all the matters at hand, analyzing them and coming up with alternatives: it makes you feel even more hopeless.

What should you do? You feel impotent, and at the same time you are entirely taken up with the problem situation. It is not out of your mind for a moment.

With regard to this stage, William Bridges writes: 'Wheat grows at night and the neutral stage (i.e., the transition stage) is the nighttime of the whole transition process.' Underneath the surface of impotence and hopelessness, the seeds of further development are growing, invisible and undetected. These can sometimes emerge in a feeling such as: 'Things cannot go on like this.' 'Anything is better than remaining in this situation.' 'I must give up all hope of a solution from outside and do something myself.' Or 'I will have to break with all sorts of ideas, norms, wishes and expectations from the past, and start following new, unknown paths.'

These are the first signs of a turning point. You have to become active yourself by taking responsibility for your own life; by moving on under your own steam from the lowest point where you are now. Often it isn't clear at all where the path is leading. You will have to learn to do this: taking steps without knowing in advance exactly where they will lead you to. It is a process of trial and error. There will always be a response from the real world when you take a conscious step, and this answer can lead you to take the next step. In this way, the path will gradually become visible. Often you will only be able to tell with hindsight whether you have done the right thing.

At first, the strength of your own 'Self' is still weak, but as a result of these processes, it will become stronger and stronger, so that you can increasingly rely on it.

Transitions will continue to form part of our lives up to the last transition when we die. But because the Self is challenged by the process of transition, it will become stronger and stronger when it accepts this challenge, so that it will be able to deal with the following transitions in a more conscious and fruitful way.

Not all transitions are dealt with and concluded fruitfully. You can remain stuck in this stage or in the previous stage because your Self lacks the strength to take responsibility and to take the next step. The result can be that you give up and become embittered. You no longer see the meaning of life, and your interests fade. You want the outside world such as the members of your family or your boss to do what you want. The dissatisfaction which results when this does not work is systematically blamed on the world around you, and the following transitions reinforce this even further.

An understanding of the process of transition and talking about it to others can help to prevent these negative effects.

3 *The stage of a new beginning*

When the seeds which germinated in the previous stage ('Anything is better than this. I must do something myself.') become stronger and relate more to conscious understanding, a person will start to take first steps. He will perform small experiments which sometimes have a positive and sometimes a negative result. It is important not to be discouraged by negative experiences, but on the contrary, to convert these into positive learning results. In a study, a negative result is also significant. Thus it is important to learn to evaluate your experiences. This means that you ask yourself:

– What did I want?

– What did I do? How did I act in the specific situation?

– What is the effect? What effects did I observe in myself and in the world around me?

– What can I learn from this?

– What does this mean for the next step in concrete terms?

During this stage of experimentation, you will again make contacts with other people, though these are of a very different character from those in previous stages. The difference can probably be characterized best as follows. In stages 1 and 2, you usually call upon others to become active on your behalf. You are dependent on them, and actually expect someone else to deal with your problems. (We would like it to be clear that there is nothing wrong with this; sometimes it will produce results, but very often it will not. This is one of the causes of the crisis.) In stage 3 the basic attitude consists of undertaking something and becoming active yourself. You no longer present the problem to someone else, but use the other person to help you or to provide information, without being dependent on him.

The inner decision to truly connect with a new situation is usually only made after the stage of experimentation, although you may appear to have been in the new situation for a while, for example, in the case of a transfer to a new job, or living alone after a divorce. Forming this new connection is the real task of this third stage. However, you will only be able to achieve this new connection if you have passed through the preceding stages of the transition properly. Otherwise you will not have the inner freedom to form the new connection. When people fail in a new job, a new position or a new relationship, this is often partly the result of unfinished business from previous situations.

In addition, there may obviously also be objective factors in the new situation which make this inner connection more difficult. For example, this can be the case after a merger when you are suddenly confronted with a completely different culture or different style of management.

The new connection becomes apparent in your behaviour from your efforts, motivation and interest in people and things in the world around you. People often start to look better physically, and they start to enjoy and take pleasure in life again.

Finally, there is an integration of the new situation into the personality as a whole. Skills, experiences and abilities from the past can be very valuable, though seen in a different light, and others may be pleased to make use of them. There is a new sense of identity. Many people in this stage feel a sense of relief, and are even grateful in retrospect for having gone through this transition. They feel that they have become more mature as a result.

What can you do yourself to deal with transitions in a fruitful way?

Above, we described the process of transition as it generally takes place. Of course, the question arises whether you can influence the course of this process yourself. We believe that you can, and give a number of tips below.

*   Transitions are a part of life. They are a condition of inner growth and development. Transitions accompanied by a crisis are therefore meaningful, even if their significance is not entirely clear at the time. Although other people may have a different response, it is important to remember that there is nothing wrong with someone who is in a transition.

Sometimes people say to someone who has just gone through a transition: 'It's good to see that you're quite your old self again.' This sort of remark indicates that they see a crisis as an undesirable disruption of normal life. The ideal behind this is: to be the same again, i.e., before the crisis. This shows that they do not have an understanding of the dimension of development in life.

Maintaining a positive view can serve as an important support during difficult transitions.

*   Always try and make a distinction between facts and feelings. Try to find an anchor for yourself in the reality around you. For example, ask yourself: what happened exactly? What was said precisely, and by whom? Who was there? A negative mood can sometimes shed a very negative light on the facts, just as the hope that everything will be alright can lead to a rosy view of events. In itself, the pure and objective observation of what is happening in the outside world will make you stronger.

★   The above is not an argument for suppressing and concealing feelings. Feelings are also a reality. You must take them seriously without being dragged along by them. Being dragged along by anger, despair or fear gets in the way of the learning process, but so does suppressing these feelings. It is important to let them be, to experience them consciously and if necessary, express them in words.

★   Do not look for solutions too quickly. Transitions take time, and you cannot hurry the process. In our culture there are few rituals left to mark transitions. Therefore we must do this ourselves. This means:

– take care of a farewell, of when you leave things behind, and try to find a form such as a ritual, that is meaningful for you;

– during the transition stage, take time to reflect on the past, and for a reorientation on the future;

– organize the new beginning by drawing up a plan, deciding on when to evaluate, and so on.

As children of our time, we are very solution-oriented, and most of us find it difficult to be in a problem situation when there is no solution. This can result in a panicky search for solutions which are not found, because you are not inwardly ready for them. In fact, you put the brakes on the transition process in this way, and it will take longer than necessary.

★   Make a conscious effort to move in the opposite direction if you are turning inward too much and are becoming fixated on your own problems. Focus on sporting and artistic activities, such as walking, cycling, swimming, jogging, or painting, pottery, making things for the home. In general, watching films or TV is less suitable because this tends to stimulate the inner world.

★   During the experimental stage, do not aim to achieve immediately visible results, but see this time as a learning period when you see how the outside world responds to your steps. For example: you could arrange a meeting with someone you know who has gone through a turning point in his life, and ask if you could talk to that person about his experiences. Often it is quite an achievement to take this step. There is an immediate resistance to anything which does not fall under the ordinary pattern of behaviour. What will that do for me? What will he think? I'll make a complete fool of myself, and so on. However, if you find the courage to take these sorts of initiatives, they can result in very instructive experiences and valuable contacts. Moreover, you will develop a new type of self-confidence.

⋆   Stay in contact with others. Find people who you can talk to. These may be professional people, but could also be your life partner, a colleague or a friend. However, watch out for pitfalls. Of course, you can ask someone else to listen to your pain and sorrow, but guard against repeating yourself and telling the other person for the umpteenth time how you have been 'cheated'. The best remedy for this is to always ask yourself after you have talked, what results it has had. These do not have to be concrete results; a sense of peace, relief, understanding, encouragement, or being able to cope, are just as valuable.

It seems like a paradox. On the one hand, you are quite alone in a transition. No one can take over from you. On the other hand, it is almost impossible for a transition to be fruitful without the help of others. You find the right balance by trying to be conscious of the help and support which you ask for or receive from others.

Rounding off

It is not only individuals, but also communities, such as families, organizations and so on, which are faced with many transitions in these turbulent times. In a social respect, such enormous changes are taking place that you might say that all of mankind is in transition. Mankind also lacks certain abilities, such as the ability to find a satisfactory solution for problems such as the environment, starvation in the Third World, and the peaceful cohabitation of different ethnic groups. Many people have pointed out that for mankind to survive, new developments are necessary in science, politics and the economy.

With regard to the inner development of mankind, many people see the appearance of Christ two thousand years ago as a transition to a new stage. At Easter, His death and resurrection are commemorated. The Easter festival can be seen as an archetypal example of the transition process. Suffering, death and resurrection are the basic elements of any transition.

Before His suffering, Christ prayed in the Garden of Gethsemane: 'If thou wilt, Father, remove this chalice from me.' In the transition process, we would also like to be spared our suffering, but Christ completed his prayer: 'But not my will, but thine be done.' This expresses a surrender which is also a part of every transition; the surrender to and acceptance of what comes to you, and being prepared to connect with this.

Crisis, an example

The vocation of an artist is to bring light to the depths of the human heart
Robert Schumann

In a crisis, it is easy to lose the connection with the light in your own heart. It is an art to stop this being extinguished under the waves of anger and sadness, the constricting grey-black blanket of despair and depression, and to guard it in a corner of your soul. It is difficult to rediscover it when you have temporarily lost it. For some people, this struggle for light is the theme of their life, and is visible in all their acts.

A person writes his own biography with his actions. For an artist, part of this biography remains visible in his works. His development is expressed in them. Would it be possible to say something about the inner struggle of a man, an artist, from his work?

Our colleague, Rob Otte, drew our attention to the painter, Paul Cézanne. He said: 'Cézanne is a man who transformed himself, and thus also the art of his time.' This was a sufficiently intriguing view for us to examine Cézanne's life and work.

Cézanne's work

During his career as a painter, Cézanne painted nearly everything there is to paint: he copied old masters, painted mystical tales, allegorical themes, nudes, portraits, still lifes and landscapes, in oils and watercolours, and on walls; from very small paintings *The Judgement of Paris:* 15 x 21cm to large canvases *The Bathers:* 205 x 245cm (Ill. 16).

If you take a chronological look at Cézanne's paintings, and follow their development, you discover a number of periods: from the age of 18 to 22, he is learning the art of painting according to traditional views; from the age of 22, he has a personal, emotionally charged style; from 28 to 35, he develops from emotion to Impressionism; from the age of 38, he devotes more and more attention to natural forms; from 49, his work is a synthesis of the different aspects of his painting career, and by the time of his death at the age of 67, he is once again starting to look for expressive forms. It is as though from the time he goes his own way, he struggles all his life to control the explosive emotional force, and he is increasingly able to do so.

Cézanne measures up to the greatest artists of his time, if only because of the varied nature of his work in terms of its size and themes. When he is about 21, he paints the *Four Seasons* on the walls of the living room in his parental home, and signs these 'Ingres' (Illustration 7). Jean-Auguste Dominique Ingres (1780-1867), was one of the most famous painters of the age, with a distinctive classical style. Comparing Cézanne's *Four Seasons* with his subsequent paintings, it is as though he is finishing with this classical art by signing the name 'Ingres'. 'Look, I can do it,' i.e., drawing and painting existing works of art and well-known themes, in accordance with strict ideas. He does this once, and never repeats it. From then on he increasingly goes his own way. However, he does not break with classical art completely. Later on, he still paints old masters and well-known themes, but does so in an entirely individual way.

As soon as Cézanne goes his own way, he paints mainly using a palette knife, thick layers of paint, broad brush strokes, and with a few dark, contrasting colours. During his early period (up to about 1872, at the age of 33), his paintings are often sombre and heavy. The paintings exude an erotic quality *(Lot and his Daughters, The Temptation of St. Anthony,* nudes) and violence *(The Abduction, The Murder, The Strangled Woman).* He also paints hair-raising pictures of death *(Skulls, Preparation for the Funeral, Portrait of Marie Cézanne)* and scenes bordering on delusion *(Contrasts, A Modern Olympia).*

Apart from this work, Cézanne paints beautiful portraits and still lifes which reveal much more peace, control and subtlety. This contrast in his early period is illustrated in a self-portrait (Ill. 8, aged approximately 27 years) and a portrait of an old man (Ill. 9, painted aged approximately 26). The self-portrait reveals the violent aspect, largely resulting from the use of the palette knife. The other portrait radiates an inward-looking smile, as though the old man has calmed Cézanne down. The bottom right-hand corner of the portrait of the old man reveals a strange detail. When you turn it on its side, you see a procession – in the kingdom of death? The difference between these two portraits and the *Four Seasons* is greater than the difference between them. The light glows, but does not shine any more. It is almost concealed and concentrated, though it draws the eye. The variety of colour is reduced to a few dark tones and a deathly white.

After the age of 33, the fantasy and violence disappears. The eroticism becomes increasingly muted, and the representation more transparent *(Second Temptation of St. Anthony, The Bathers* (Ill. 16)). He paints death in an intimate, warm way *(Three Skulls, Pyramid of Skulls).* In addition to portraits and still lifes (Cézanne's apples), he paints more and more representations from nature (such as the Mont Sainte-Victoire). His palette becomes more varied and subtle. He no longer uses a palette knife, his brushwork becomes more delicate, and his figures become stronger. The most striking aspect is that his paintings become brighter and more transparent, and the light no longer falls onto the work from outside, but comes to you from inside. We have chosen two pairs of paintings which reveal how far-reaching the change in his style was:

- *Paul Alexis reads Zola,* 1869-70 (Ill. 10, aged approx. 31), and *Two Card Players,* 1892-93 (Ill. 11, aged approx. 54)

- *Melting Snow at L'Estaque* or *The Red Roofs,* c. 1870 (Ill. 12, aged approx. 31), and *House and Tree on the Road to the Hermitage, Pontoise,* 1873-1874 (Ill. 13, aged approx. 35).

Going through his work, the central change which took place when he was about 33 is very striking. We have chosen two paintings which were made shortly before this change (Ill. 10 and 12) and one painting from a long time afterwards, to clearly show the contrast (Ill. 11), as well as one from shortly after this which already reveals the change, (Ill. 13).

What are we looking at? Take the first pair of paintings: *Paul Alexis reading Zola* and *The Two Card Players*. They are comparable social situations: two people doing something together. Both paintings are built up using three colours, but in the first painting these colours are used next to each other in a bright, powerful way, with great use of contrast. In the second painting there are much more subtle nuances, the colours are more subdued and there are fewer contrasts. In this painting the figures are also quieter, more austere and they move and vibrate less. The whole image is more peaceful, also because of the composition: two men are seated at the same distance from us with a table in between them and the sides of the edges of the table intersect in the middle of the painting at an imaginary distance. The back wall of the room is parallel to the foreground, which is formed by the tablecloth on the front of the table. This wall is also divided up in an orderly way with a horizontal line and vertical line.

The first painting is built up on a diagonal line from left to right: a dark curtain, Zola's red jacket, Alexis's white suit, the red cupboard behind Alexis against the dark wall. There is also a diagonal from right to left: the dark patch on the floor on the right, the white floor, the dark wall and the white chimney-breast with a painting. The white chimney breast gives an impression that you're looking out through a window. The painting on it brings you back into the space where the people are seated. This produces a dynamic effect.

The interesting paradox is that in the first painting our eyes are glued to the area between the two people at the height of their hands, so that they cannot move, while in the second painting our eyes wander around, moving everywhere despite the central perspective created by the edge of the table.

In the first painting, the light comes from a particular spot, from the left above the curtain, and falls on the figures and objects. It is as though it falls on the scene from outside the painting, but in the second painting the light is much more diffuse and present everywhere. Perhaps it is our own eyes which cast the light on the painting, or perhaps the light comes across to us from the painting.

The other pair of paintings were made closer to the turning point and reveal comparable aspects.

In the rest of Cézanne's work the transitions are far less obvious than in the two transitions described above, made when he was 21-22 and about 33 years old. The last transition is particularly fascinating. What do we know about Cézanne's biography and what happened when he was 33?

Cézanne's life

Paul Cézanne was born on 19 January 1839 in Aix-en-Provence and died there on 23 October 1906. He was a big, strong man and was extremely healthy. He had a wild, emotional character and powerful depressive moods. Two of the early statements by the friend of his youth, Emile Zola, who encouraged him to paint, reveal this: 'The slightest obstacle makes him despair. He is a man who pays with days of despair for every hour of hope.' And later he said: 'When he hurts you, do not blame his heart, but rather the evil demon which clouds his thoughts. He has a heart of gold which understands us because he is as mad as we are and just as much of a dreamer.' Cézanne learnt to paint in the traditional style at the Ecole Municipale de la Ville. He reveals his training in his work, *The Four Seasons*. His later paintings have a completely individual character and barely comply with the old rules of beauty. He alternates life in Paris, where Emile had persuaded him to go, with life in Provence, where he spends more and more time in the second half of his life, and where he finally dies.

People and nature play an important role in Cézanne's life. He was impossible socially, almost intolerable, but at the same time there were people around him who did not give up on him. He irritated everyone and could not be influenced. In the early days in Paris, Emile Zola wrote: 'Proving something to Cézanne is like forcing the towers of the Notre Dame to dance the quadrille.' His view of Cézanne's future was extremely gloomy: 'Paul may have the genius of a great painter, but he doesn't have the genius to become one.' He struggles with this childhood friend and stays in contact only because of the past, but feels desperate about it.

For a long time Cézanne is not at all interested in women. When he is 27, he says: 'I don't need a woman at all – it would just get in my way too much. Anyway, I don't know what they're good for – I've always been afraid to try.' Zola writes: 'He has a crazy desire for nudity, but has never possessed any.' There is also a story that Cézanne would place a black hat and white shawl next to his nude model to give himself support while he was drawing or painting. Apart from the theme of eroticism, violence and death, and delusions and emotions are central elements in his work at that time. The public hate this, and his paintings are rejected from exhibitions. This serves only to provoke him.

When Cézanne is 30 he meets Hortense, a model, and lives with her. When he goes to stay in 1871, a friend from Aix-en-Provence, Achille Emperaire, can not bear to spend more than a few nights with Cézanne and Hortense in Paris. He finds Cézanne abandoned by all his friends. In the spring of 1872 Cézanne, Hortense and their four-month-old son join Camille Pissarro in Pontoise, a village outside Paris. He is 33 years old. They live there with the painters who were first called 'Impressionists' in 1874. During this period, two people are very important to Cézanne.

The first is Pissarro, ten years older than Cézanne, who has an incredible influence on him. Later, Cézanne says about him: 'Perhaps we all developed from him,' and in an exhibition at the end of his life he introduces himself as 'Pissarro's nephew'. They had first met in 1861/1862 in the Atelier Suisse in Paris. Pissarro saw in Cézanne an aspect of the 16th-century painter, Paolo Veronese, and he is the only one who always continues to believe in him. From the time that Cézanne comes to live in Pontoise, Pissarro would take him outside and say: 'One should have no other master than nature', and 'We should paint what we see and forget what there was before our time.' In those years they work together a great deal and would paint the same scene seated side by side (e.g., Ill. 13). Under Pissarro's influence, Cézanne's technique changes: he no longer uses a palette knife, but paints with finer brushstrokes, a broader palette of colours and more nuances. Cézanne starts to change in Pontoise. Before that time he didn't have the patience to study nature, and obstinately chased his dreams. Later he is to say: 'Art can only be developed in contact with nature.'

Six months after his arrival in Pontoise, Dr. Paul Gachet comes to live quite near in Auvers. He is the second person to play an important role in Cézanne's conversion. He lets him pay with paintings for his services to the colony of artists. Gachet places constraints on Cézanne's unbridled mania for painting by saying: 'Paul, that's enough, it's finished now.' Setting boundaries means finding the strength of form. Cézanne sought this form. Later he is to say: 'Everything in nature is based on the sphere, the cone and the cylinder.' He also says: 'When the colours are richest, the forms are the most perfect.' He sought form through colour, as illustrated beautifully in his many apples.

Nature is balm for the soul. People who are oppressed by an inner mood can be taken outside and their attention can be drawn to what they can see and hear. Take them out of their inner world of feelings and emotions and direct their perceptions at what is outside them. When you let them go they fall back, but by doing this repeatedly, you can break through the mechanism and they can start doing it themselves.

We have often experienced how effective this sort of help can be. What Pissarro did for Cézanne is rather similar. By concentrating on what he saw in nature, Cézanne was more and more able to use his emotions to serve his painting. Before that time it was as though his painting had been subject to his emotional world. What Gachet did was of comparable importance. He showed Cézanne the boundaries which the painter had not been able to place himself. Cézanne was helped by Pissarro and Gachet to manage his painting more and more effectively. This was very necessary.

The mystery of his conversion

In about 1867, when Cézanne is 28, he paints a scene on the wall of the living room in his parental home based on the 16th-century painter, Sebastiano del Piombo, *The Descent of Christ into Limbo,* as well as a scene entitled *The Sorrow of Mary Magdalene* (Ill. 14 and 15). The scenes were painted next to each other, and some people believed that originally they formed a single work. It is the only time in his life that Cézanne paints Christ, although he has had a church upbringing and becomes a conservative churchgoer later in life. Behind Christ, there is a man in the painting carrying a heavy beam like that of a cross. There is also a line of light showing the break of dawn. On the left, at the bottom of the painting, there is a deformed, blind man, and behind him a woman with her hands folded, as if she wants to support him. But this could also be a gesture of prayer, a prayer to Christ to help this man. Christ bends forward as He descends, and reaches out to the man's head with His hands, as though He wants to touch him. In *The Bible,* being touched by Christ or touching Him is a very special event and people were cured by this.

Mary Magdalene is one of Christ's intimate friends. She is cured by Him and is present at the Crucifixion. Mary Magdalene's sorrow in Cézanne's painting reinforces the imagery. This is Easter, the mystery of Golgotha.

What is the meaning of the fact that Cézanne paints this work of Christ at the age of 28, and then experiences such a conversion when he is 33? In looking for an answer. our thoughts go in three directions.

The rhythms of life

For many people, the age of 28 is an important time in their biography. People who married young and have already started a family or who found a permanent partner or working relationship, break out or go through a difficult period. Others who have studied for a long time or have had a free lifestyle with no obligations, struggle to find a permanent partner or have children and start a family, or start on a more permanent career with the steady routine this entails.

We have also found that many people go through an existential time when they are 33. Some people indicate that at this age they had an experience which made them think of Christ, realized that He died at this age, they heard His voice or had an inner image of Him. Others become aware of the finite nature of their life, experiencing death as something close to them, whether or not they were in any real physical danger of death. Others again have certain spiritual experiences accompanied by difficult physical or psychological circumstances.

On the basis of a spiritual view of mankind, you can see the life of man as an experiential route from his spiritual core which comes to earth and becomes more and more connected with the earth during the course of his life, until sooner or later it suddenly or gradually separates from the earth. In this view, the period from 28-35 is a time at which people have descended furthest into 'earthly existence'. They become embroiled in obligations or material commitments, such as a demanding job, small children, building or converting or furnishing a home.

Now it is dark in the earth. Without light, you cannot go down into caves or into mines or into the troughs of the ocean floor. It is important to keep the light. This reveals the struggle which people go through during this 'earthly' period. It may be a great or a small struggle not to be destroyed and to conserve the inner light. In the end, you can do this only on your own steam. The more you are successful. the more the inner light becomes powerful and also visible to others.

Rembrandt

Of course, it is interesting to find this in Cézanne's paintings, but what about other painters? We have barely started to look at these, but we did briefly examine one painter, Rembrandt, because the light and the New Testament are clear subjects in his work. Looking at the reproductions of Rembrandt's work in different books (Haak, Mastenbroek) in chronological order, the following things become clear.

Rembrandt created his New Testament paintings from 1627 (at the age of 21) to 1647 (when he was 42). During the middle period from 1632/1633 (when he was 26/27) until 1639 (33), there are only images of Christ during the active period of his life between 30 and 33, the period between the Baptism in the Jordan and his Ascension after Golgotha. In the years before and after this, Rembrandt mainly painted scenes of Jesus as a small child.

We also know that in 1634 (when he was 28) Rembrandt married Saskia, who had a number of miscarriages until the birth of Titus in 1641 (when he was 35) and that she died in 1642.

Walking through the exhibition: *Rembrandt, the Master and his Workplace* in 1993 in the Rijksmuseum in Amsterdam, we saw that the light in Rembrandt's work became more and more introspective between the birth of Titus and Saskia's death. The light was less focused on the scene and came more from within.

Christ

A great deal has been said and written about Christ. So much so that for many people, Christ is dead, the events of 2000 years ago meaningless, and everything that refers to Him even leads to revulsion.

For other people, Christ is very much alive, although He is present in a different way from His presence at that time. For them, the events at Bethlehem and Golgotha constitute one of the greatest mysteries of the history of humanity and of the development of the earth and the entire cosmos. This secret is so great, and at the same time so intimate and vulnerable, that there are no words to describe it. To talk about it in a material way evokes revulsion.

Thus it is not an easy situation to simply talk about Christ. And yet we do this, knowing that it is impossible, with an inner attitude which could be comparable to Cézanne's words in the following quotation:

> *Nature is not on the surface but in the depths. The colours are an expression of these depths on the surface; they rise up from the roots of the world.*

When you read *The Bible,* besides admirers, there were many people who thought Christ was a strange character. In the last twenty-four hours before His death He was completely abandoned by His friends and even by God whom He called his father. Christ may have been emotional but He certainly was not out of control. He does not give this impression, despite this despair in His cry on the cross: 'My God, my God, why hast thou forsaken me?' He nevertheless did what He had to do: 'It is done.'

According to tradition, Christ was crucified and buried and rose from the grave after three days. He then spends another forty days on earth, but is able to move around in earthly time and space unfettered. He is there and He isn't. He suddenly appears in a room when the doors and windows are shut. His figure after Golgotha is described as a figure of light like that of the angels. The light radiates from inside out of this figure. It is no light falling on His body. His body is clearly made of another substance which is not subject to the laws of nature. This may be difficult to understand let alone accept for a scientifically trained mind. But what Christ experienced, and what happened to Him can be seen as the archetype of an existential biographical crisis.

Ultimately, it is up to you whether you go through such a transition and become a new person. You can let go of the old familiar life and begin on unknown new things. However, this new aspect is often still too vulnerable to be touched, particularly by people from your old life who do not know you in your new guise.

This can also be recognised in Christ. He said to Mary Magdalene on Easter morning: 'Do not touch me.'

When you touch someone, it is as though you are holding that person still for a moment, holding him within his limits. It also requires strength to be touched. Before Golgotha, Christ noticed straightaway when he was touched. Perhaps he felt the energy of his healing powers being tapped. People were cured by touch. In our world the touch of anything you have just acquired hurts as though you are not yet strong enough, as though it is not yet solid enough. If another person keeps you in the old state by touching you and does not see the new things you have acquired you can experience this as an injury and a restraint. Obviously Christ was aware of all this with regard to Mary Magdalene.

The sad thing about Cézanne's childhood friend, Emile Zola, is that he never saw the 'new' Cézanne. He lived so much in the past that in his book, *L'oeuvre,* he described all his disappointments with Cézanne in the failed painter Claude Lantier. The latter recognized himself in this character and was hurt and wrote: 'I thank the author of *Les Rougon-Macquart* for this friendly gesture and ask for permission to shake his hand, thinking of times passed.' At this point, Cézanne and Zola were respectively 47 and 46 years old. For Cézanne, it was the end of an intense friendship and his letter was the last in a long series. It is an example of the pain you can suffer when people around do not recognise you in your new identity.

Is the reference to Christ and the process of his change when he was about 33 too ambitious? Who can say? Cézanne went to church, though like many other people with a Christian upbringing, he did little about religion at this stage of his life. Could the parallel nature of the two processes and the existential moment of the 33rd year of his life be seen as the Christ moment in Cézanne's biography? Both became different people with a greater inner light radiating from within. This can be seen in Cézanne's works.

Cézanne was actively involved in this process of transformation of the material he used and of himself. This sort of thing never works without a struggle. It is possibly man's one great task. There is an old Persian saying which makes reference to this:

> *Carry the sun to the earth.*
> *Oh man, you are placed between light and darkness,*
> *Be a warrior for the light.*
> *Love the earth until it becomes a shining gem,*
> *Recreate the plant, recreate the animal,*
> *Recreate yourself.*

Cézanne achieved an aspect of this and he is not the only one. This gives us hope. At the same time Cézanne became the 'father of modern art', as John Rewald concluded in his biography of the artist.

Transforming himself and becoming the father of modern art – if you wish to renew your art, you will have to work on yourself.

Looking at people

During the first bars of Mozart's *The Magic Flute,* Ingmar Bergman wanders through the audience with the camera in the film with the same name. He focuses on face after face, of young and old, man and woman, yellow, brown, black and white, in profile and full frontal, and diagonally from below or from above, all entranced by the opera. This is repeated again and again, and every time the camera comes to rest on a young girl's face, a blonde, ten-year-old Mona Lisa. The camera forces you to look as the director wants you to. Look! – and see what I see: everyone is under the spell of the magic flute.

Look! – and see people. Getting to know people starts by seeing them, but what do you see? There is so much to see. Looking only at the eyes:

> eyes close together, or wide apart
>
> high up in the face, or low down
>
> blue, green, brown, almost black
>
> eyes with a red glow or a washed-out expression
>
> protruding eyes, slit eyes, sunken eyes
>
> hollow eyes, light, shining, dark
>
> big, cheerful eyes, wide-eyed
>
> sombre pupils turned inwards

On the one hand, this tells you something about someone's external physical appearance (sunken eyes), while on the other hand it says something about their inner psychological state (hollow eyes). Our language describes the way in which people look at each other: 'as cunning as a fox', 'as slippery as an eel', 'looking broody'. These say something about the inner world, while expressions like: 'as strong as an ox', 'piggy eyes', 'as swift as a gazelle', say more about appearance. At the same time, man is compared with an animal in these expressions. There are also other possibilities:

lily-white skin, sturdy as an oak	(plant)
as steady as a rock, iron constitution	(earth)
starry-eyed, moon-faced	(cosmos)

What do you see when you look at people? Their external appearance and inner mood? An animal, plant, stone or star?

Or can you see more? Can you see the specific aspect which belongs to this one person? And can we give this a name and identify it? A name is a very personal thing, and it is important that other people know this personal thing:

> *my mother has forgotten my name*
> *my child does not yet know what I am called*
> *how can I feel safe?*
>
> *call me, confirm my existence*
> *let my name be like a chain*
> *call me, call me, address me*
> *oh, call me by my very deepest name*
>
> *for those I love, I want to have a name*

Neeltje Maria Min

How can you be safe without a name? Confirm my existence with a name which goes with who I am. I am. Looking at a person can mean seeing his or her: 'I am'.

Is this most intimate aspect of a person the essence? It cannot be seen by everyone or approached by everyone – sometimes not even by ourselves. Is this how a person distinguishes himself from everything and everyone?

Or is man nothing special? Thousands of people have the same name. Or do you look at man as a combination of different aspects? A coincidence from many unlimited possibilities? Man is a seemingly unique outcome from many different possibilities. A throw with a large number of dice with many, many sides, like a golf ball with a huge number of tiny surfaces. It will roll to a stop on one of them.

What is a human being? You look around in the street and it is immediately clear: there's a person. As a species he is easy to distinguish from other living creatures. When you spend more time with someone, the individual, essential aspects become clearer. Sometimes this takes a lifetime and at funerals you try to create a picture of the person in the coffin and try to express the essence of his life. But it is always a search, even when you are looking at yourself – the riddle of man.

However, what you see when you look at people depends on the glasses you are wearing. Rather like Ingmar Bergman's camera. By going to the cinema, you put on these glasses. But when you look yourself, there is also something that guides you, an inner orientation which you can call your view of man. You can discover another person's view of man from the way in which he looks, as in Bergman's images: 'All people can fall under the spell of the magic flute.'

Each one of us has a view of man, whether we are conscious of it or not, partly handed down from the past, partly chosen ourselves. Without it, we get lost in the wide range of perceptions around us.

Ingmar Bergman allows us to experience this: more and more images of human faces are passed over, more and more quickly so that you come into an inner chaos and are in danger of losing the connection with the film. But then the camera stops again to focus on the face of the young girl, full of devotion and intense commitment. This is the support he gives us.

We need an inner orientation so that we do not lose ourselves in looking at people and looking at ourselves. What is the support we choose? Which view of man?

Views of the human being

What is the inner orientation of people when they look at other people? How do they talk about them, what do they show, and what view of man does this reveal?

When you look at TV or pick up an arbitrary newspaper, you can become engrossed in the dreadful things which people do to one another: three burning bodies that were set alight, someone who has raped his own child, the mugging of an old woman in the street, in broad daylight, the muggers breaking her wrist and pelvis. The destruction of a mosque, threats to immigrants, the acceptance of bribes, tax evasion. Does this not show how bad people are by nature, and how they are always tempted to be evil? That you have to be careful of your fellow human being and of yourself, and that you should be suspicious of people? If you allow people to be free, something will go wrong. Keep man under control, because rules and restrictions are necessary.

It is difficult for us to break through these images and see other examples. A woman steps through a circle of spectators and sees a little girl lying down surrounded by onlookers, her body broken by the wheel of a lorry. She kneels down, takes her hand in hers and talks to her as she lies dying. An old man whose gangrenous foot has to be amputated is visited in hospital by people from the street where he lives, a different person every day. Despite the setbacks, the threats and the misery, despite the hopelessness, a man opens his house to travellers, the homeless and drug addicts. There is room to be there, to be accepted as a person – it is a place for contact and warmth, a place which provides food and shelter. Don't these images indicate that man is essentially good? Circumstances cause people to behave in strange ways. Perhaps we should improve them. A heart of gold could beat in an apparent villain. Basically you can trust people. Give him your trust and it will be returned to you.

Apart from these images of good and evil there are other orientations in the ways in which people speak about others and what they show to others:

Orientation to the world which we made ourselves

– The technical mechanical world; the head of a person is seen as a computer, the nerves as information cables, the heart as a pump, the digestive system as an oven.

– The physical, chemical world: man is seen as a reactor, a subtle balance of physical and chemical processes, temperature, humidity, hormones, adrenaline and other substances.

– The psycho-social world: man consists of a system of values, norms and patterns of behaviour which are determined by the family, schools, profession, industry, society, history and our own time.

Orientation to nature which is simply there

- Looking at a stone, plant and animal: man is genetically determined, a product of genes, DNA codes, evolution.

- Looking at heat, light, water, air and earth: man as a warm or light-hearted personality, moving like water or strongly grounded.

- Looking at the stars and the signs of the zodiac: man as a creature of the sun, as a Mars or Venus character, the strength of an Aries, the courage of a Leo, the lonely heights of a Capricorn.

- Looking at light and dark. She always radiates light, he is the personification of gloom.

Orientation to ourselves, our existence, 'being there'

- The fact that I am here and therefore exist has a purpose in itself. In concentration camps in the Second World War, Victor Frankl tried to make people aware of this and this helped them to survive.

- 'I am not my father, I am not my upbringing, I am me, and therefore different' – this is also an example of this orientation. With these remarks you pick up the thread which belongs to your existence in this world.

- And Jung said: 'After the age of 42, you are responsible for your own views, responsible for your own way of being.' But doesn't this start much earlier, and very gradually?

Orientation to an invisible world

A number of people struggle with the existence of this world. Others deny it and others believe in it unconditionally. At either end of life you can come much closer to it. An old man sitting on a bench in the evening sun; he is alive but he is no longer really there. And a child when it has just been born is alive, but not yet there. What is it that awakens in you and with which there can be a dialogue? When a child is born, we experience that someone has arrived on earth, and when someone dies, you feel that he is departing and leaving his body. Elizabeth Kübler-Ross, who worked with the dying throughout her life, writes about this in her books and lectures on it in her courses. She also speaks about near to death experiences. At the end of a dark tunnel, people encounter a being of light which they sometimes identify with Christ and which is waiting for them lovingly and sends them back either with or without a task for them to fulfil. Others were awaited by members of their family who had died or friends or other people close to them.

Kübler-Ross also tells the following almost comical story about a pair of twins. One sister is on her deathbed in hospital; the other is living far away. News comes to the hospital that she has died, though to spare her, the dying sister is not told about this. She dies too, but a moment later she sits up and angrily and indignantly shouts at the people standing around, asking why they haven't told her? Then she falls back and dies definitely.

Elizabeth Kübler-Ross, Rudolf Steiner and others also describes what happens to people when they leave their body for good. Briefly it could be said that there is a period of departing from this life and processing its experiences, followed by a period of preparation for the next life. It is like taking off your clothes and after deciding to return to earth, putting on other clothes. You can arrive at these non-sensory perceptions by means of many different exercises. The central elements in doing so are an unprejudiced interest, the intellectual discipline of natural science and boundless love of everything you come across during your search.

When you follow people who look at life in this way, you can discover a new content for old, worn out or veiled concepts – ideas such as the hereafter, heaven and hell, going back to the father and 'I am who I am'. This last idea is a reference to the essence of man which is unchanging throughout all his travels. You cannot grasp it, but you can follow its trail by looking at a person's deeds, and it continues to develop on all its travels.

Another important question is to what extent man's fate is pre-determined and to what extent he is able to determine the direction of his own life and where his responsibilities lie. Again there are two opinions, because this is what the different images or views of man come down to.

According to one view, it is the DNA code, your upbringing and other circumstances in life, the stars, your karma or even the task which God has given you which determine who you are, what you can do and what future awaits you. Your responsibility is to accept this and live in accordance with it.

The other view allows room for an independent 'self', with its own will which allows you, in relation to others, to determine the direction of your life rather like a coachman driving his coach. In this case, you are responsible for taking hold of the reins. In this view the future is open and depends on your own deeds and your own choices.

Without pretending to be exhaustive, we have indicated a number of orientations which you can rediscover when you look at people The many different possibilities invite you to decide on your own view.

How do we see things?

Our own view of man is strongly influenced by the ideas of Rudolf Steiner. Steiner was born in Austro-Hungary, in the part which is now Croatia, in 1861. For a long time he lived and worked in Germany, founded the Anthroposophical Society and developed the Goetheanum in Dornach near Basle as its centre. He was well known as an expert on Goethe and had close links with the European cultural heritage, i.e., with its Graeco-Roman and Judaeo-Christian roots.

We would like to explain that we see man as a person walking on the borders between yesterday and tomorrow, between thinking and doing, and between what is externally perceived and inwardly experienced. This walking on borders is someone who travels in an area, as it were, where land and water come together, for example, by the sea. One moment he will be walking on dry land with his feet firmly on the ground, the next moment the sea is washing against his legs, the water sucks in and pulls, and the ground is moving under the soles of his feet. In this land in between the walker is dependent on his own resources. When the tide comes in, he can become stranded on a sandbank. He will not get very far if he has no knowledge of the sea and the beach and doesn't respond alertly.

Man lives in three border areas.

Between yesterday and tomorrow

'Plan, do, control!' This is a slogan of dynamic management. The slogans radiate the confidence that you can control life despite the fact that things are always different from what you thought. That is exactly why it urges: plan the future, do what you intended to do, and control what is happening. This means: control the past. You could also say that you learn from the past and make plans so that you can do things better the next time. One person may be better at describing the past, while another person is better at finding new ideas for the future. One may be impatient and unable to wait to start on something new, while another person says: 'Hang on a minute, didn't we agree that...' or: 'We tried that a few years ago...' In every group, department or organisation you will find these two forces at work. Sometimes one is predominant, sometimes the other.

They are also present in the life of a person. In young people the force of the future is predominant while the past plays an increasingly larger part for old people. However, every person has his own lifestyle. One person finds it difficult to leave things behind and hangs on to the past. Another person constantly tries new possibilities and finds it easy to make new connections. One person falls down exhausted into a sleep and then jumps out of bed to greet the next day. Other people find it difficult to sleep. The day continues to mill round and round in their head, and they find it also difficult to wake up and shake off the night. Man lives through day and night waking and sleeping. There are morning people and evening people, night people and day people living in light and dark. This may change through life. It can also be a basic pattern: more at home in the night (in a literal, emotional and spiritual sense). But every person is subject to the rhythm of day and night and to the effects of the past and the attraction of the future. Man lives here on earth in the area of time between yesterday and tomorrow.

TIME

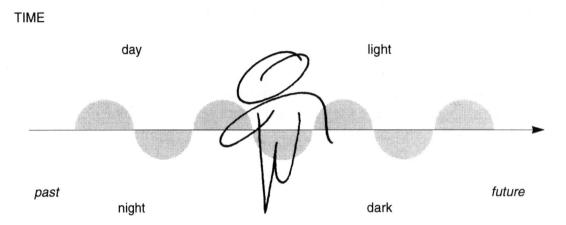

day   light

past   *future*

night   dark

Between thinking and doing

'Think at first then act upon, but in acting think on there'.

With these words, Guido Gezelle touches upon an everyday insight which can lead to great misunderstanding and even conflicts because thought and action do not always go together and can lead to tension both within one person and between people. For example:

– 'He makes lots of promises, but it is as though he has forgotten them the moment he goes through the door. Of course, that suits him very well, but I'm not going to take it any longer! We can't go on like this.'

– 'She has fantastic ideas, you can always go to her for those. She knows how to enthuse everyone, but when you see what comes of her ideas – nothing! At least if it's up to her. She just doesn't get it together. It's up to other people to realize her wonderful ideas.'

Or:

– 'She doesn't know what she's doing! It's always the same. She doesn't think beyond the next minute. What is she interfering for anyway? I can do it myself. Moreover I always have to clear up the mess she manages to make.'

– 'He's unbelievable, the things he gets together. We talked for years and nothing happened. One idea after the other foundered. And as soon as he arrives, things really start happening. He gives us no time for thinking. Things went well straight away. The first morning after his arrival, I'll never forget, we came in and our desks were no longer in their place. He had changed everything. 'Why?' we asked furiously. 'I wanted to get you moving', he said. 'Where?' we called out. 'Forwards', he called back. He couldn't tell us where that was or what it would look like, but at least something happened and gradually things became clear'.

Apart from these strategic reasons why people do or do not do things, it is clear that some people are more at home in the world of ideas, while other people are more at home where the action is. There are thinkers and dreamers, as well as men of action. In other words: some people live more with the head, while others are better with hands and feet.

Thoughts can be spiritual and full of ideas. They come and go, they are volatile and sometimes they quickly evaporate. It requires discipline to concentrate on one thought and to develop it and give it concrete form. With our thoughts we take part in the world of the mind, the world of ideas and immaterial things.

With our hands and feet we are linked to the world of things, of material things. You cannot turn on your PC by thinking about it, and you normally get to the conference hall or the coffee machine with your feet.

Man lives between these poles: ideas and things, thinking and doing, mind and matter. A spiritual force is at work in him, but his body is made of earthly matter. When you look at a person you see his feet on the ground and his head in the air. Some people walk with their head in the clouds, floating over the ground, while others plough on, with their feet deeply rooted in the ground. However, every person knows both aspects, and is at home in the border area where earth and sky come together. This is where he lives between heaven and earth, travelling in the border area of space.

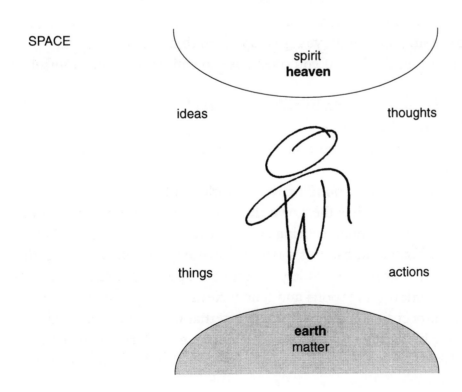

Between the inner and the outer world

Mrs. Sunshine came in laughing, a quarter of an hour later than we had agreed. She smiled apologetically and said, 'The gremlins were against me', describing one thing that went wrong after the other, a PC which had stopped working, a broken disk, a lost text, and so on. Slightly 'stressed' she started her car and drove off and then she heard a bang; she had a flat tyre. 'Oh well', she said, 'I'm here', and had a cup of coffee.

One minute to nine the door opened and Mr. Gloom comes in. 'Good morning, Ellie,' he said in a tired voice. 'Has Danny phoned yet?' 'Yes, he's just phoned. He didn't have much time', says his secretary, and the telephone rings. 'That'll be him,' cries Mr. Gloom, and walks to his room. When Ellie brings in the mail a little later, she finds him sitting there with a pained expression. 'Anything wrong?' she asks. 'Oh everything's against me today, of course Danny was too fast for me...' and so on.

These are two examples of the many different ways in which a person can relate to the world. One person loses his temper when he is abandoned by technology; another laughs about it. This is what happens in relation to other things, people, plants, animals – and, of course, the weather. The same things can make one person sad and melancholy, and another happy and light-hearted. In some people moods can change very suddenly: laughing one minute, crying the next. There are many factors which can determine the mood of the moment but when you know people for a while the basic patterns become visible.

Are you enthusiastic and full of energy so that you see the problems of life from a sunny perspective, or do you struggle against tiredness and inner lethargy and become down-hearted when things go against you? Or can you laugh about them and see the funny side?

Do you have the hide of an elephant so that little can touch you, or are you open and sensitive to what is going on around you, perhaps even thin-skinned, so that impressions from outside thunder in and you often have to withdraw to find yourself again?

Do you try to connect with the world by talking, and explain what matters to you, or listen to what is going on around you?

Do you look at the world in a suspicious and distrusting way, or do you trust people, and are optimistic?

Everyone has their own style of responding to the world, and their responses change in their own way. Everyone has their own rhythms, for example, listening for a long time and talking for a short while, or being active for long periods, followed by brief spells of withdrawal. You could call this a type of breathing. In this breathing, the alternation of observing what goes on outside you and your inner experience, thoughts and opinions, feelings, emotions, intentions and tendencies all play a role. As you get to know both sides, the aspect that is directed at the external world and your own inner world, you become better able to steer a course on the boundary. There are three layers of the soul available for this: thinking, feeling and the will, which allow you to relate to the world and other people. Man lives in this area of relations, on the border of inner and outer world.

RELATIONSHIPS

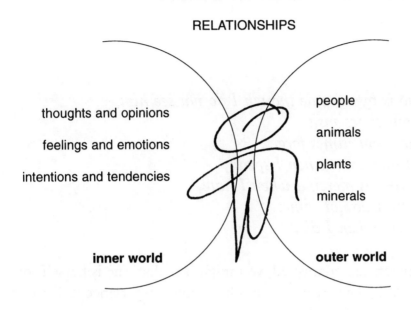

thoughts and opinions

feelings and emotions

intentions and tendencies

people

animals

plants

minerals

inner world　　　　　　　　　**outer world**

Being yourself

In the three areas of time, space and relationships man moves on boundaries. But he is also himself.

Sometimes people who are no longer in control, overcome by hysterical laughter, a fit of weeping or a terrible temper tantrum are told firmly to be themselves. This can have an effect and the person is able to take control again.

The opposite can be heard about people of whom it is said: 'She is imperturbable. She remains herself, no matter what happens'.

Being yourself, being your own person. We also say: 'You are fooling yourself' or 'I wasn't in control of myself.' Clearly there are two elements: you and your self. Many people have been -and continue to be – interested in this duality.

In Roberto Assagioli's psychosynthesis, these two elements are referred to as the 'daily self' (you) and the 'higher or transcendental self' (your Self). Assagioli sees the daily self as the centre of consciousness, which is not the same thing as consciousness. It is the conductor in the orchestra of our daily consciousness. The higher self or transcendental self, also known as the 'true self' is a permanent centre of a different order. In a sense, it is in an unassailable position above the daily current of events in and with the soul and the body. It is also seen as the entrance to the spiritual world. For this concept, Assagioli also refers to Jung's concept of individuation.

Carl Gustav Jung wrote about the 'conscious self and the Self'. He also sees the Self as an element of a higher order with eternal continuity, which can only be understood when it is approached. The conscious self is always connected to the social community and results in the 'persona' (which literally means mask) with which you function in that community. In the course of the process of individuation, the Self increasingly becomes the factor which guides the conscious self, so that it is increasingly liberated from its persona.

Juan Ramon Jiménez described this duality as follows:

I am not I.

I am
the one who is by my side though I do not see him
the one I sometimes visit
and the one I sometimes forget.
He is silent and calm when I speak,
he forgives and is merciful when I hate,
he goes where I do not come.
he will remain when I die.

When these two elements are connected, you might say that 'she is herself' or 'he is at one with himself'. That is the way in which other people experience it. It means that you are who you are, yourself.

'When I am myself I feel at peace.' This peace can easily be accompanied by activity but without the urge to be active. On the basis of his experiences in a concentration camp in the Second World War, Victor Frankl wrote: 'When all meaning is taken away from you and all the work for others and the ability to enjoy things, the only thing that remains is being yourself.' All that remains is the fact that you are. If you say this to yourself, you use the word 'I'. I am. This in itself gives meaning to existence. When people in the camp let go of this, they died in a few hours.

When someone is himself you can see this. 'There is a peaceful presence in everything he does', or 'What she says is real and comes straight from her heart.' At the same time, this person makes you experience an openness and interest in everything else in the world. Man lives with himself as he is, and with others as they are. He lives in the area of being. Man 'is' and can say 'I am who I am'.

BEING

I am

I am

But if you look at people in this way, who is it who says 'I am'? Is it possible to find out?

When you ask a little child: 'Who are you?' he may answer, 'Me'. The last thing that remains to you as an adult when you have mentioned all the roles that you fulfil is: 'I am I.' That is the person who is the same in all the roles and who can be found by others if they follow you, and look at what you do and listen to you. If you make an effort, you can also gain an idea of who you are in this way yourself. But you will never be completely successful. You will always be a riddle to yourself. It is a riddle that can be explored. Below, we will follow some of the many different ways of approaching it.

There have always been people interested in who man is. The Bible is an important example of this. In the biblical story of Creation, you find the following words.

The Creation begins: 'And God said, let there be light, and there was light.' It sounds powerful. God said something, and it happened. The word that creates is full of the will. Creation begins with the will.

The actual Creation took place in six days. In a sense, the second three days were a repetition of the first three, but were further elaborated and more differentiated with the Creation of man on the last day. The process of Creation was reinforced by this repetition, culminating in the Creation of man in God's own image. The story describes the consecutive creation of:

- light and dark, day and night (the element of time)

- water above and below, heaven and earth (the element of space)

- land, plants, animals and man and their interrelationships (the element of relationships)

- and finally, man created in the image of his creator (God).

However, God does not show himself, He is only heard. Later in the Bible, Moses meets God in a burning bush which is not consumed by fire. God instructs Moses to liberate the Israelites from Egypt. When Moses asks: 'Who are you, so I can say who sent me?' God answers: 'I am who I am.'

The biblical story of Creation also shows that plants exist for animals, animals exist for people, and people exist for each other. It relates that man, created in the image of God, is Lord of the earth and everything that lives on it. How should this concept of Lord be understood? Because of the consequences of the way in which we treat the earth, we have once again become conscious that this must have meant the Native American way of being Lord of the earth. In other words, an ecological consciousness.

Native Americans – Lesson 1

*Do not
use more
than you
need*

Loesje 13 May 1992

Cut trees and shoot game in order to live, but in such a way that the species survive. Ecological consciousness means acting in a way that is conscious of a biological balance and of the development of everything that lives, with an eye on the process as a whole. You could describe this as being a gardener, because a gardener looks after every plant as well as the whole garden throughout the year. And wasn't Paradise called the Garden of Eden?

Later in the Bible, in the *New Testament,* there is the story of Golgotha, which describes how Christ died and was resurrected. The Roman governor, Pontius Pilate, said: 'See the man', before handing Him over to be crucified. And Mary Magdalene, who was the first person to encounter the resurrected Christ on Easter morning first saw Him as a gardener. Rembrandt made a drawing and a painting of this which can now be found in Buckingham Palace in London. This painting inspired the following poem:

Christ as a Gardener

*One Rembrandt I knew well as a child,
the Christ with the big hat,
walking in the morning dawn.
And as the caption said:
He was a gardener.*

*And still tears flow down my cheeks,
when I see him standing in the garden,
and – a bit aside – in silent fright
she, the one who thought like me:
It was the gardener.*

*O childhood dream, green and gold –
no one took what I will keep.
The last gardens draw almost near,
and thinner gets the morning here.*

He is the gardener.

Ida Gerhardt

Illustration 17: Rembrandt, *Christ as gardener,* 154 x 146mm, ca. 1643, Rijksmuseum, Amsterdam

Christ as a gardener. In the Bible, he was also called the Son of God. During his life before Easter, he said himself: 'Anyone who meets me, meets him' referring to his father. Thus, the link is made between 'see the man', 'the gardener' and 'son of God', on the one hand, and 'I am who I am'. Man as a gardener, and as 'I am who I am'. Man who was created in the image of God and who does not know nowadays what to make of God or his son, Christ, but is looking for himself and becoming increasingly self-conscious. Perhaps you could say that the image of man could be found in the past in the invisible God of 'I am who I am'. Then you could discover that image in the encounter with His son, a man amongst men. And now man can find this image in himself so that he himself can say 'I am who I am'. Man is a person with an individual essence, a Self, which reveals itself by walking round in the world and doing something there. Seeing his acts and what he does in the course of his life, others gain an impression of who he is.

In the next chapter, *'Who am I?'*, we approach this question again in a different way. The question is too important to answer in only one way.

Who am I?

When you examine the course of your life by looking back at it, the question 'Who am I?' may occur as a sort of fundamental mood. In moments of strong emotion, aspects of yourself can become visible, also giving rise to this question. It often remains a rhetorical question because you know that you will not simply find an answer just like that. It is more just an expression of surprise or wonder than a real question for which you will try to seek an answer.

However, if you do, you will find in the first instance that you are on the brink of a bottomless abyss comparable to the infinite nature of the universe. This can be very frightening, but if you do not withdraw you can experience yourself as a microcosm. 'Know yourself' are the words written above the Temple of Apollo in Delphi. This goes beyond knowing your strong and weak points. It urges man to seek his deepest essence.

Is this a hopeless task? Discussions with other people about what it really means to be human often get bogged down or turn into a debate in which different conventional views oppose each other. As a result, some people become sceptical and consider that any discussion on these sorts of questions are pointless by their very nature.

In the past, many people sought and found answers in their faith or religion. However, in our own age many people feel a great need to work on these questions themselves, and on the basis of their own experience. But you immediately become aware that you reach a boundary. You realize that the normal range of instruments of sensory perception, rational thought and familiar views on man will only give limited access to the question 'Who am I?' We will have to let go of this type of thinking which is so familiar to us and venture into unknown areas.

To do this, it is necessary to learn to examine the small, seemingly imperceptible things: an observation, an experience, a feeling that you have, a thought or a question. It is a matter of taking these things seriously, of being open to them, assimilating them and 'allowing them to be', without immediately finding explanations or judgements for them. It is a matter of being patient, because this sort of study will not produce immediate results, as science does. Science has also had to develop over the centuries, and the results of science were also initially incomprehensible and unacceptable to the world at large. However, Rudolf Steiner says that the blossoming flower may appeal to us more than an imperceptible seed, but that this seed is the seed of the future and the flower will soon wither.

Although modern man likes to find his own way in this field, it is useful to allow yourself to be guided occasionally by people who are already at home there to some extent. They may be able to tell you something about their experiences and give indications of how you can proceed. You could consider these ideas as hypotheses. You do not have to surrender to these guides, but you can accompany them for a while. You remain yourself without becoming a blind follower. Going along with another person without prejudice also requires courage so that you can set aside all sorts of judgements, prejudices, ideas and thoughts which you developed in the past, without using them as a sort of wall to hide behind. A great deal of resistance to different approaches comes from the fear that you will lose your individuality as soon as you go along with someone else. However, this is not necessary at all. It is important to take note of how you respond inwardly, and especially emotionally, to these new ideas. Do you feel a sense of enthusiasm after a while? Are you encouraged to go on, or do you lose interest, find it dull and boring, and do you not wish to go on? In other words, the new ideas may bring something to life in you, or they may not take root, and die. With this approach, you can make use of guides and use their help to explore unknown regions without getting lost. In fact, it will also help you to become stronger.

Below, we will explore the question, 'Who am I?' on the basis of our own ideas. We invite you to come with us and look at this so that you will be able to develop your own view. In our exploration, we are helped by the 'spiritual science' founded by Rudolf Steiner in the first quarter of the twentieth century, which he called anthroposophy.

Body, soul and spirit
In the view described in more detail below, man is seen as a threefold being with a physical level, a psyche or soul, and a spiritual essence. It is possible to look at man in other and more detailed ways from a spiritual point of view, but this threefold view of man is the most elementary.

I am a physical being
'Who am I?' I stand in front of the mirror and look. 'So that's me, this nose, ears, hair, arms, legs and shoulders.' Some people stand in front of the mirror for hours on end when they are young, pulling all sorts of faces and grimacing at their reflection, satisfied or dissatisfied with what they see. Later on, they may still do this. Toon Hermans asked whether you ever look at your own face for a long time and finally turn away with a heartfelt 'yuck'. Possibly sometimes you feel that you hate your own face.

Our head, and particularly our face, is our most individual aspect. It is the most characteristically formed part and identifies us most clearly as an individual, distinguishing us from all other people. But the rest of the body is also unique, if less strikingly so. One example is the fingerprints on identity papers. Research has shown that our organs are also very individual: the heart, liver and kidneys and so on, and even every individual cell. People can often be identified by their teeth, even after a long time.

The way in which we move is also extremely characteristic: our way of walking, the gestures we make with our hands, and so on, particularly when this is spontaneous and not the result of practice, such as soldiers marching. Your movements make you visible

314

in a different way from your face. Sometimes you feel how visible, and therefore how vulnerable you are when you move, and when others are looking at you. That is why seeing yourself on video can be quite a confrontation.

Our body also has a front and a back. The front has an open character and is turned towards the world. The back is closed and turned away from the world.

We rarely reflect on the miracle of our body. The structure of our skeleton, the operation of the digestive, respiratory and circulatory systems, the way in which the senses work, the nervous system and the brain – all these things reveal an impressive wisdom of which we understand only a fraction. We are barely aware of what is happening inside our body. Food is digested, assimilated into the blood and released without our being conscious of it. This applies to countless processes in the body. As a result of medical and biological science, we have an external knowledge, but we do not really know anything about our body from within.

You can learn to know your body better by doing sport and also by listening more carefully to 'what your body has to tell you.' By observing the signals that it produces and, if necessary, taking these into account in your behaviour, you can do justice to the individual character of your body.

We are linked to the earth through our body. It is made of earthly materials which are kept 'in shape' as long as we are alive, but which fall apart and go back to the earth when after our death this forming process no longer exists. Then the body, abandoned by the other parts of our being, becomes subject to the laws of nature just like all other earthly materials.

I am a socio-psychological being

We human beings have a soul, i.e., an inner world. We have thoughts and opinions, feelings and emotions, wishes and desires. And yet for many people in our time it is very difficult to get to know this inner world.

Roberto Assagioli, the founder of psychosynthesis, a modern school of psychotherapy, wrote in the foreword to one of his books, that if a man from Ancient Egypt were suddenly placed in our own age, he would be dumbfounded at first by everything which modern man can do: about the radio and TV, our airplanes and rockets, our medical knowledge and expertise. But when he had recovered from his amazement, he would be astonished by the almost complete ignorance of this modern magician about what is happening in his own soul. Therefore it is not surprising that for many people, the question 'Who am I?' is nowadays mainly directed at this area. Therapy and training sessions are aimed at trying to help people to find their way in their own inner world. You need someone else who can act as a mirror or confront you with these things.

Although the soul is our own personal inner world, it is not possible to conceive of it without the outside world with which it constantly interacts.

When we are observing and thinking, it is as though we bring the outside world in. We collect impressions, have ideas and construct intellectual models which reflect the outside world in our inner world. It is a movement from the outside world inwards.

On the other hand, there is the will and all its variations, such as instincts, drives and desires, as well as longings, intentions and motives. The outside world is approached and set into motion with inner impulses which result in action. The will reveals a movement from inside outwards.

Feelings and emotions form a central area between thinking and the will. With our feelings, we are constantly in contact with the outside world. Feelings can be very vehement and intense, or they can be barely perceptible. They can be divided into two basic orientations: feelings of sympathy with a tendency to link to the outside world, and feelings of antipathy with a tendency to stand back from the outside world or even shut it out. Both these tendencies are essential to man. He must be able to form a link with the world around him, and enter it to some extent. But he must also be able to take his distance and stand apart. In fact, this is necessary to be able to think and judge. The area of feelings and emotions is the area which people consider to be the most intimate and closest to who you really are. Other people experience you as a sincere and honest person if your feelings are reflected in your actions, and if you show what you feel.

The Greek philosopher, Plato, called thinking, feeling and the will, the three horses of the soul which draw the human chariot. It is important to prevent any one of these horses from predominating, so that either of the other two do not come into their own. According to Plato, the task of the charioteer is to control and steer these three horses.

In Plato's philosophy, this charioteer is man's Self, which should not therefore be identified with thinking, feeling and the will. The Self is a spiritual entity which stands above the soul.

The shadow or doppelgänger – an intermezzo

Before looking at man as a spiritual being, we would like to point out an obstacle that you encounter when you examine your inner world: the confrontation with your 'doppelgänger'.

It is as though you come across a being that is the antithesis of what you would really like to be. It is a negative image of yourself, and you may be disgusted by it. For example, you see how small and insignificant you are, you see your secret thoughts or uncontrollable passions and desires, your inner emptiness or lack of love, and you experience the painful discrepancy between 'what you really are' and the way which you present yourself to the outside world. 'If they only knew who I really was.' Moreover, you feel certain that this self-image is real, and not merely a passing and gloomy feeling.

When you are confronted with your doppelgänger, you become aware of a number of negative characteristics and qualities which together make up a figure. You realize that this figure belongs to you. Previously you may have suppressed this figure and seen yourself as you show yourself to the outside world. It is often the case that other people see aspects of your doppelgänger more easily and clearly than you do yourself. These impressions become particularly clear in confrontations and conflicts, but also in appraisals or development interviews. The first response is usually one of defence and rejection. You do not recognise yourself in what the other person confronts you with. Of course, that image is often not very pure either, because that person's doppelgänger is also involved. In conflicts, people often encounter each other's doppelgängers.

It is important to take your doppelgänger seriously, but not to identify with it. It does belong to you, but you have other aspects. Bernard Lievegoed often said: 'Where there is shadow, there is light'. Thus, when you experience your own shadow you can be sure there is also a light side.

The confrontation with a doppelgänger again invites you to examine the question 'Who am I?' But who carries out this examination? When I say: 'I wonder', who is actually doing the wondering?

I am a spiritual being

This brings us to the third aspect of the three sides of our image of man: to the Self, or the spiritual essence of man. The word 'self' refers only to one person, and that is my Self. The Self is described in many ways, both in scientific and non-scientific literature. It is considered by virtually everyone as the aspect which makes us unique, and which expresses the thing which makes you different from all other people. Some see the Self as a unique result of all the forces of nature and nurture.

In our view, the Self is not something which arises in some way from the dimensions of man described above, but something which is added to these as an entirely new element, which has a great influence on the body and the soul. Furthermore, a distinction should be made between the daily self and the higher Self.

The day-to-day self is the self that goes shopping and says things like: 'I don't feel very well today' or 'I didn't think very much of that football match.' The higher Self gives the purpose and direction to your life, determines the values and ideals of your life and is ultimately responsible for your morality.

The influence of the higher Self can become stronger in the course of your life. Sometimes this influence is very slight, and the way in which you relate to life does become a product of your nature and your environment. However, it is the Self that distinguishes man from animals, which are one with their nature and surroundings. As the Self becomes more active in life, it becomes stronger and can oppose nature and the environment, so that its influence on life becomes greater.

The Self's area of operation is the soul, and within the soul, the Self is linked above all to the will. Man's Self is characterised by the will, or in other words: in your will, you can learn to know your Self.

We pointed out earlier that in transition and crisis situations a great demand is made on the Self. In these situations you may become aware of your Self. Then you can feel as though you are rooted in a deeper reality than your thinking, feeling or will. You experience that there is a spiritual force working in you, and that the Self has taken the reins and is starting to drive Plato's horses of the soul. However, it is not only in moments of crisis, but also in so-called top or peak experiences, that you can experience the quality of the spiritual world within you. Finally, it is possible to strengthen the connection with the higher Self in everyday life as well, by means of practice and training.

Once again, the body, spirit and soul

The body, spirit and soul are not separate areas in man. They are intensely interpenetrating. The Self has an effect on the soul. It can train and guide thoughts, it can help you to see your emotions objectively, and transform them into an organ of perception, it can purify the will and direct it at supra-personal ideals. However, the soul can also be disturbed, so that the Self no longer has access to it. This means that a person becomes spiritually sick. In fact, this is not really a correct description because the spirit or Self cannot be sick; it is merely that it is unable or not sufficiently able to carry out its guiding influence.

The body is closely linked to the soul. All sorts of psychological influences affect the body and can even make it sick, as shown in psychosomatic illnesses. Treating only the physical complaint is unsatisfactory, if the psychological factors are not dealt with as well.

The two higher parts of our being express themselves through our bodies. It is said that 'the eyes are the windows of the soul'. Our individual essence is visible from our attitudes and movements.

These three parts of man cannot be divided, and can at best be distinguished. However, this distinction can help you to observe yourself and others more accurately.

Karma and reincarnation

The question: 'Who am I?' is the sort of question to which there is never a definitive answer but which constantly gives rise to new questions. Thus the view of the guiding function of the Self can immediately evoke the question why it guides my life in one direction and not in another. Many things that have happened in your life are things you do not want, and which just seem to happen to you, while other things which you would like never happen. People say things like: 'I didn't ask to be dismissed,' or 'I really don't want to be in conflict with my boss again and again.' Sometimes it is said that the course of your life is a question of fate. But what exactly is fate?

Many modern views about man and his fate on earth arise from the traditional and contemporary eastern philosophies in which the doctrine of karma and reincarnation have a central place.

Man is seen as a being with numerous lives on earth behind him and many yet to come. In contrast with about thirty years ago, this philosophy is no longer viewed with scepticism. It is openly discussed and written about. There are many types of training and therapy in which people are supervised in their search for roots in previous lives. In anthroposophy, the doctrine of karma and reincarnation was reintroduced by Rudolf Steiner and linked to Christianity, and moreover, Steiner developed methods of spiritual science to carry out research into this field.

In this view the essence of man, the Self, has a spiritual nature which means that it is linked to, and derives from the divine spiritual world. The word 'incarnation' (becoming flesh) indicates that the Self connects with the body so that it can live on earth. Its development has come to a provisional end in the spiritual world. In order to continue this development it needs a new earthly life. In this life, the Self wishes to have certain experiences. For this to be possible, the Self carefully prepares for the forthcoming life on earth. It does not do this alone. In the spiritual world the Self is also linked to other people with whom it makes arrangements for the forthcoming period on earth. Other spiritual beings also participate in this preparation and the creation of the body is an important aspect of this. Man's Self is a creature of the will, it chooses for this forthcoming life and wants to do something with it. However, when it arrives on earth and is born in human form, he 'forgets' this pre-birth plan. However, the Self does steer a course through life, on the one hand, on the basis of the unconscious depths of the physical body, and on the other hand, on the basis of the 'social body' of the human community and encounters with others.

You are not aware of the Self steering this course. What happens to you in life is usually incomprehensible to normal daily consciousness. It often doesn't seem to be your own choice. On the contrary, you suffer it or even fiercely oppose it. However, it is not impossible that this opposition was actually aimed at, that in this way you develop something in yourself as you had intended, even before you were born.

You can become aware of an aspect of this course by looking back at the course of your life. It is above all the theme of your life that can indicate the direction of the decisions which are at the basis of your earthly life.

Up to now we have spoken only about the spirit (Self) and the body in this description of reincarnation and karma. What is the place of the soul in this?

The physical and spiritual dimensions form a polarity in man. When there is a polarity, the two poles are connected in such a way that one pole cannot exist without the other, and they interpenetrate, just like light and darkness.

The forces working from within the body and the Self come together in the central area where they form the inner world of man, the soul. The soul itself also contains many polarities, such as thinking and wanting, love and hatred, sympathy and antipathy, joy and sorrow and so on. In the soul, it is possible that you sometimes feel the painful polarity between body and spirit, for example, between your ideals and values on the one hand, and the passions and lusts of the body on the other.

This is what Goethe's Faust said:

> *Two souls, alas, are housed within my breast,*
> *And each will wrestle for mastery there.*
> *The one has passion's craving crude for love,*
> *And hugs a world where sweet the senses rage;*
> *The other longs for pastures fair above,*
> *Leaving the murk for lofty heritage.*

Translated by Philip Wayne, Penguin Classics

It is not only the forces of the body and the Self that have an effect on the soul. Forces from the outside world and particularly the relationships with other people also have a great influence on the soul. In fact, the development which we pass through on earth is, to an important extent, owed to other people. It is an illusion to think that you have developed by yourself to become who you are, all on your own. At most, you were open to what the world around you had to offer. We ourselves also have an effect on the development of others, even though we are usually not aware when and where this happens. What we contribute to each other's development is based on the 'agreements' which we made before birth in the spiritual world. If you look at it this way, the relationships which you have with other people during your lifetime are seen in a different light, and this includes the relationships at work with colleagues, with your superiors, other employees and clients. It is not only the people you get on with that are important to you, but also those who make life difficult for you or even those that hurt you.

You can stay out of these people's way and (for the time being), put aside an aspect of your development, or you can meet the challenge and examine the personal development which this relationship represents for you. Your own choice is fundamental in this.

During the years of childhood and youth, the soul gradually appears in parallel with your physical development. When your body has finished growing, the development of the soul continues, now directly guided by the Self which previously indirectly steered you through the fabric of social relationships.

During life on earth, the soul is therefore the actual field of operation of the Self, and the area in which our development takes place. After death, the Self assimilates the fruits of the development of the soul.

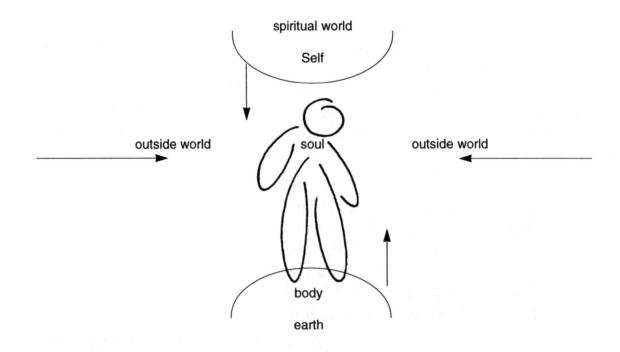

At a certain moment, life on earth comes to an end and a person dies. This is necessary, because the development you go through on earth is inevitably one-sided and limited. In one life you cannot be both a man and a woman at the same time, both European and Chinese, a beggar and a prime minister. For every person there are countless areas which have to be ignored in life. After death, new developments are possible again. The physical body remains behind and merges with the earth. The soul-spiritual being, released from the physical body, continues to exist in the spiritual world, where the experiences of the soul are assimilated by the Self and used to prepare for the next life on earth.

Our plan before birth and the choices we make for it, are closely related to the fruits of our previous lives. For example, if you had little interest in the outside world and in other people in your previous life, you will want to catch up on this in your next life, perhaps with the help of some painful experiences. This interrelationship between successive lives is known as karma.

Our acts, feelings and thoughts from previous lives, and above all, the effects of these on ourselves and our environment, have an effect on this life, just as what we do in this life has consequences for our next life. This interrelationship is comparable to the interrelationship in everyday life. When you get up in the morning, you do not start the day with a clean slate. You pick up the thread from the previous day and are faced with the consequences of your acts in the preceding days, or even earlier. At the same time, you do things on such a day which have consequences for the future.

Does this view allow you to be a free person in this life on earth? The circumstances we find ourselves in, and the encounters with people are determined, after all, to a large extent by karma, which means by the choices we made ourselves in the spiritual world. Our karma presents us with the facts of our lives. Our freedom lies in the way in which we deal with these facts and what we make of them.

The search for the answer to the question 'Who am I?' cannot be concluded without looking at the comprehensive developmental processes of mankind and the world. Mankind as a whole is also going through a process of development in which it is possible to distinguish different stages and eras. This development has been guided for a long time by divine 'spiritual' beings. However, gradually they have retreated and left man to guide himself. As an individual, you are part of this development of mankind. Every person born in this age is subject to the influences of quantitative, scientific thought, but also affected by the discussion provoked by this way of thinking in recent years. Thus, apart from our own individual karma, we form also a part of the karma of mankind. We are children of our time. The zeitgeist means that in this incarnation we can have experiences which we have never had before, and which we will not be able to have in subsequent incarnations either. In general, the next incarnation takes place only when conditions on earth have thoroughly changed.

Therefore we are the contemporaries of all people living on earth at present, and share in their destiny. We are subject to the spirit of the age, but at the same time we can join in the task of developing the age that we live in. It is important to gain an insight into this developmental task and to find your own relationship to it, because the purpose of your existence on earth lies not only in yourself and your own development, but also in the value which your existence has for others and for the development of the world. Each one of us is responsible for development as a whole.

The developmental process of mankind is literally concerned with developing love to the full. The earth must become the planet of love! We are still an incredibly long way away from achieving this ideal. We can hardly conceive of what it means. A great deal of what we call love is concealed selfishness. True love has nothing to do with sentimentality, romance, or being nice to each other. Love is a creative force, comparable to the sun, which allows seeds to grow with its light and warmth and brings nature alive. Love is a moral sun which allows people to create new life and renew the earth. We believe that with His life and death, Christ revealed love as the highest ideal in a visible and tangible way. In this way, a high, divine being gave man the chance for love to triumph on earth. Man will have to realise this with his own free will, and there is still a great deal to be done.

Afterword
David Megginson

Alexander Pope suggested that the proper study of humankind is ourselves. This direct, uncompromising, challenging and loving workbook provides a powerful means to pursue this study.

My experience of working with the material here has been filled with wonder and a sense of growing personal empowerment. The process has not been sudden for me. It was cumulative. It came from doing the exercises as well as reading about them and the tips and explanations that accompany them.

There seem to me to be four levels of using this book for one's own development. Firstly, you could just dip into it. This might yield little, as the exercises and questions – the seven stars – are sequential, and their power is increased by approaching them in order. So, a second approach would be to read the workbook from end to end. This would be more likely to yield insight and benefits, but would still leave you at risk of feeling, and being disconnected from, the words. The significant inner work would begin at the third level which would involve reading the book in sequence and doing all or most of the exercises. This provides an opportunity for us to experience the inner movement of our lives and to allow the questions to take root in our body, soul and spirit; and hence to work on us. Finally we can use the book in conjunction with others – having them help to characterize what we draw from doing the exercises, and to deepen our insights and our inspiration. This partnership could be with a peer where the help is mutual, or with a mentor whose role is to help, or in a group – which, again, might be organised on a self-help basis or might be facilitated.

The manual provides a 'mentor between covers' for people wishing to deepen their sense of living their destiny. It also offers a splendid range of tools for mentors to help others. It seems to me that it is crucial to the effective and principled use of this material that mentors themselves have used it in considering and laying hold of their own lives. If you are about to be helped by someone else who has introduced you to this material, it will be very instructive to spend some time asking them what use they have made of it and how it has affected their own development.

There is the lovely story of Gandhi who was asked by a woman, who had queued with her son for hours to see him, if he would tell her son, who ate sweets all the time, to stop. She said only his instruction would stop the boy and save him from damaging his health. Gandhi asked them to return in a fortnight, and, grumbling, they went off. A fortnight later they returned and the woman reminded Gandhi of her request. He turned to the son and said 'Stop eating sweets'. The woman said 'Is that it?' Gandhi replied that she had said that if he told the boy to stop then he would. She said, 'Then why didn't you tell him a fortnight ago?' 'Ah,' replied Gandhi, 'a fortnight ago, I was eating sweets'.

If your mentor does not pass the Gandhi test, then join with them as a peer, or find someone else, or go it alone until you seek out and find the right person to be with you on your quest.

My own use of the workbook is just beginning – so do not ask me to mentor you through it yet. However, I have found much already that has stimulated and strengthened my swimming in the currents of my life. From the early exercises, I drew a strong insight about the consequences of not pursuing a path which I wanted to do, but which I was experiencing resistance to following. The bleakness of the consequences have strengthened my resolve, and led to my increasing my commitment to this demanding path. The results are already palpable. The recurring theme of addressing the one question that life is asking, or we are asking of life, has been demanding and difficult, but heartening. It has been refreshing to see how my questions have changed during the course of my life so far, and to enlarge my sense of how they might change some more in the future.

I have also gained a lot of practical tips – including tips on giving tips! The process of characterizing as a way of giving constructive feedback I have found particularly useful. The exercise of characterizing a birch tree and a beech tree illuminates beautifully for me the skill of characterizing rather than judging. One of my personal research interests is in the distinction between planned and emergent learning strategies, and the materials here which explore the difference between waiting and planning, and the alternative of using scenarios, address this issue and offer me a framework for enriching what I have to say. The section on connectedness also spoke to my condition, as the task of living in a connected way is at the centre of my mission for the next period of my life.

So, how might a mentor use this workbook? The first step is to use it oneself, on one's own development. If this is done with thoroughness and openness, it seems to me it is highly likely that mentors will find their own ways of using the material, and that these ways will come from the responsible depth of our being.

It seems to me that mentors who want to help their learners to make a significant difference for themselves run two risks. On the one hand, they can become slavish followers of a technique – where they are bound to a sequence and to a way of addressing the questions which they are tempted to say we all face. I am reminded of the creativity trainer who insisted on taking all his participants through the same 20 creativity enhancing processes. On the other hand, as mentors, we can fall prey to a sort of windy portentousness, full of sound and fury, but signifying little, because it is not grounded in our own experience of life and the questions that this raises. This book offers a middle path for mentors which helps us to avoid both of these traps. We have here many strands of a developmental model of how to grow as a human being, which can provide a frame, a thread, to trace the developmental path. At the same time, working with this material provides us with practice in asking those earth-shattering questions, and then building on the answers, or on the blocked silence which emerges in response.

One of the exercises in this workbook asks us to identify the sources of inspiration in our lives, and I thought about many of the books that had inspired me. I felt sad that such a high proportion of them had come for the 1960's and early 70's. As I thought more about it, I was relieved to identify more books that I have read recently which are feeding me at a deep level again. I suspect that the availability of books is not the issue, but a readiness in oneself to be open to them. Then as I sat some more, thinking about this matter, it came to me that this book itself is one of the small but precious group of illuminating manuscripts which has touched me and enriched my life.

Bibliography

Fintelman, K., *Die Mission der Arbeit im Prozess der Menschwerdung*, Stuttgart, 1992.

Frankl, Viktor E., *Medische zielzorg. Inleiding tot logotherapie en existentieanalyse*, Utrecht, 1959.

Frankl, Viktor E., *Man's search for meaning*, New York, 1975

Gerhardt, Ida, *Verzamelde gedichten*, Amsterdam, 1985

Goethe, J.W., *The Green Snake and the Beautiful Lily*, in Allen, Paul/Allen, Joan, *The Time is at Hand*, New York, 1995.

Gombrich, E. H., *The Story of Art*, Oxford, 1982.

Gowing, Lawrence, *Cézanne. The early years (1859-1872)*, London, 1988.

Groot, Arjen F. de, *Kunstenaars over kunst*, Soest, 1986.

Guardini, R., *Tijdperken des levens*, Tiel/Den Haag, 1959.

Haak, Bob, *Rembrandt. Dessins*, Paris, 1975.

Haak, B., *Rembrandt, zijn leven, zijn werk, zijn tijd*, Den Haag, 1982.

Johanson, I., *Christuswirken in der Biographie*, Stuttgart, 1992.

Jung, C.G., *Het ik en het onbewuste*, Katwijk, 1981.

Hesse, Hermann, *Mit der Reife wird man immer jünger*, Frankfurt a.M., 1990.

Hesse, Hermann, *Jedem Anfang wohnt ein Zauber inne. Lebensstufen*, Frankfurt a.M., 1991

Hopson, Barrie et al., *Build your own rainbow. A workbook for career and life management*, Leeds, 1984.

Kast, Verena, *Crisis als kans*, Rotterdam, 1987

Kortweg, H., *Nog vele jaren. De symboliek van elk levensjaar*, Cothen, 1992.

Kübler-Ross, Elisabeth, *On Death and Dying*, London, 1975.

Kübler-Ross, Elisabeth, *Lessen voor levenden*, Bilthoven, 1969.

Kuiper, P.C., *Ver heen*, Den Haag 1988.

Kwant. R.C., *Filosofie van de arbeid*, Antwerpen, 1964.

Lauenstein, Diether, *Wetmatigheden in de menselijke levensloop*, Rotterdam, 1978.

Leber, S. et al., *Arbietlosigkeit. Ursachen und Auswege*, Stuttgart, 1984.

Lefébure, Marcus/Schauder, Hans, *Conversations on Counselling*, Edinburgh, 1990.

Levinson, D.J. et al., *Seasons of a Man's Life*, New York, 1978.

Lievegoed, B.C.J., *Phases: Crisis and Development in the Individual*, London, 1979.

Lievegoed, B.C.J., *Development phases of the child*, Edinburgh, 1990.

Mastenbroek, Mark, *Licht op Rembrandt*, Zeist, 1992.

Meer, Annemarie van der et al., *Levenswerk. Stuurmanskunst in de levensloop*. Zeist, 1993.

Meer, H. van der et al., *Biografische schetsen*, Amsterdam, 1990.

Min, Neeltje Maria, *Voor wie ik liefheb wil ik heten*, Den Haag, 1966.

Moers, Martha, *Die Entwicklungsphasen des menschlichen Lebens. Eine psychologische Studie als Grundlage der Ewachensenbildung*, Ratingen.

Moody, Raymond A., *Life after Life*, New York, 1976.

Mulisch, Harry, *Mijn getijdenboek*, Amsterdam, 1985.

Pedler, M. et al., *Managing yourself,* London, 1985.

Peeters, H.F, M. et al., *De menselijke levensloop in historisch perspektief,* Assen/Maastricht, 1986.

Prick, L.G.M., *Demonen van de middag,* Baarn, 1984.

Prinsenberg, Gabriël, *De tocht door het labyrint. Biografisch werken als methode voor sociale beroepen,* Driebergen, 1992.

Rewald, John, *Cézanne. The Late Work (1895-1906),* London, 1978.

Rewald, John, *Cézanne. A Biography,* London, 1896.

Rümke, H.C., *Levenstijdperken van de man,* Amsterdam, 1973.

Schöttelndreier, Jerry, *Life Patterns,* Stroud, 1992.

Selles, G. et al., *De Mid Career Crisis. Vooraf gewaarschuwd vooraf gewapend,* Den Haag, 1985.

Senge, Peter M., *The fifth discipline. The art and practice of the learning organization,* New York, 1994.

Sheahy, G., *Passages,* New York, 1977.

Sleigh, Julian, *Crisis Points,* Edinburgh, 1990.

Sleigh, Julian, *Thirteen to nineteen. Discovering the light,* Edinburgh, 1989.

Spencer, Sabina A./Adams John D., *Life changes, growing through personal transitions,* San Luis Obispo, California, 1992.

Stanislavsky, Konstantin, *Lessons for Actors,* International Theatre Bookshop, 1985.

Stein, Murray, *In Midlife. A Jungian perspective,* Dallas, 1988.

Steiner, Rudolf, *Human development and recognition of Christ,* Dornach, Schweiz, 1967.

Steiner, Rudolf, *De wetenschap van de geheimen der ziel,* Zeist, 1993.

Steiner, Rudolf, *Knowledge of the Higher Worlds,* London, 1990.

Steiner, Rudolf, *Theosophy,* New York, 1995.

Steiner, Rudolf, *Karma of Vocation,* New York, 1985

Steiner, Rudolf, *Door de poort van de dood. Teksten en meditaties,* Zeist, 1993.

Treichler, R., *Soulways: Development, Crises and Illnesses of the Soul,* Stroud, 1996.

Voorhoeve, Bert, *Op doorreis naar jezelf. Beelden op de levensweg,* Zeist, 1991.

Wais, Mathias, *Biographiearbeit und Lebensberatung,* Stuttgart, 1992.

Washbourn, P., *Fasen in het leven van de vrouw,* Rotterdam, 1985.

Welman, A.J., *De menselijke levensloop. Een psychotherapeutische benadering met behulp van sprookjesbeelden,* Zeist, 1990.

Zwart, C., *Op zoek naar een nieuwe cultuur van de arbeid,* Rotterdam, 1992.

Editor's note: We have tried to trace as many of these books in English as possible. Some may be out of print in English, or re-published under a new title.

How to contact other people using *Workways*

You can use *Workways* individually. You may also be drawing on *Workways* to mentor or counsel other people. Some readers will be working in self-managed groups. If you want to meet and link up with others, please send us a postcard with your name, address, telephone/fax number for our card index of *Workways* users.

Please tell us:
- Do you want us to send details of *Workways* workshops which we will offer from time to time as requested?
- Do you want to be put in contact with other *Workways* users in your area?
- Do you want help setting up a group?

Send your postcard to Workways, Hawthorn House, 1 Lansdown Lane, Stroud, Gloucestershire, GL5 1BJ
(Tel. 01543 757040   Fax. 01453 751138)

How to get a Workways group going in your organisation

If you want to get a group going, experienced Workways mentors and facilitators are available to assist. They can develop in-house mentors for one to one work, small group facilitators, or help self-managed groups get going.

Feedback and learning

We welcome feedback, evaluation and dialogue concerning your use of Workways. Opportunities to share this learning are offered, so that the Workways process can be improved.

Martin Large, Hawthorn Press, April 1997

Other books from Hawthorn Press

The Enterprise of the Future:
Moral intuition in leadership and organisational development
Friedrich Glasl

Friedrich Glasl describes the future of the modern organisation as a unique challenge for personal development. Every organisation, whether a business, a school, a hospital or a voluntary organisation, will have to develop closer relationships with the key stakeholders in its environment – its suppliers, customers, investors and local communities. Our consciousness as managers needs to expand beyond the boundaries of the organisation to work associatively with the community of enterprises with whom we 'share a destiny'.

216 x 138mm; 160pp; Social Ecology series; ISBN 1 869 890 79 5

Eye of the needle:
His life and working encounter with anthroposophy
Bernard Lievegoed

A man of wide ranging interests, Lievegoed combined his profound inner, spiritual research with his pioneering social, medical, educational and management work to produce a number of fascinating books. *The Eye of the Needle* illustrates the dynamics between the inner and outer worlds – and of Lievegoed's ability to work with these dynamics.

216 x 138mm; 103pp; paperback; Social Ecology series; ISBN 1 869 890 50 7

In place of the self: How drugs work
Ron Dunselman

Why are heroin, alcohol, hashish, ecstasy, LSD and tobacco attractive substances for so many people? Why are unusual, visionary and 'high' experiences so important to users? How can we understand such experiences? These and others questions about drugs and drug use are answered comprehensively in this remarkable book by Ron Dunselman.

216 x 138mm; 304pp; hardback; Social Ecology series; ISBN 1 869 890 72 8

More precious than light:
How dialogue can transform relationships and build commuity
Margreet van den Brink

Profound changes are taking place as people awaken to the experience of the Christ in themselves. The author is a social consultant and counsellor and offers helpful insights into building relationships. She shows how true encounter can be fostered.

216 x 138mm; 160pp; colour cover; Social Ecology series; ISBN 1 869 890 83 3

New eyes for plants:
A workbook for observing and drawing plants
Margaret Colquhoun and Axel Ewald

Here are fresh ways of seeing and understanding nature with a vivid journey through the seasons. Detailed facts are interwoven with artistic insights. Readers are helped by simple observation exercises, by inspiring illustrations which make a companion guide to plant growth around the year. This shows how science can be practised as an art, and how art can help science through using the holistic approach of Goethe. A wide variety of plants are beautifully drawn, from seed and bud to flower and fruit. The drawings are accompanied by helpful suggestions which encourage readers to try out the observation and drawing exercises. Dr Margaret Colquhoun researches into plants and landscape. Axel Ewald is a sculptor. The book is the outcome of their teaching and research work.

270 x 210mm; 208pp; paperback; colour cover; black and white illustrations. Social Ecology series; ISBN 1 869 890 85 X

Sing me the Creation
Paul Matthews

This is an inspirational workbook of creative writing exercises for poets and teachers. It provides over 300 exercises for improving writing skills and developing the life of the imagination. Although these exercises are intended for group work with adults, teachers will find them easily adaptable to the classroom. Paul Matthews, a poet himself, taught creative writing at Emerson College, Sussex.

238 x 135; 226pp; paperback; Learning Resources and Rudolf Steiner Education series; ISBN 1 869 890 60 4

Tapestries
Betty Staley

Tapestries gives a moving and wise guide to women's life phases. Drawing on original biographies of a wide variety of women, informed by personal experience and by her understanding of athroposophy, Betty Staley offers a vivid account of life journeys. This book helps readers reflect on their own lives and prepare for the next step in weaving their own biographical tapestry. To be published in Summer 1997.

A companion book to *Tapestries* will chart the twelve senses, the four temperament, the twelve philosophical viewpoints and soul types. This will be published in Autumn 1997 in the Biography and Self-Development series

Tools for transformation: A personal study
Adam Curle

This exploration of mediation, development and education draws on case studies from disparate cultural and geographical sources, reminding us of our participative relationship with the fabric of life. Specific issues include approaches to violence, negotiation, the nature of democracy, consensus management, community development, non-violence and learning for life.

210 x 138mm; 224pp; sewn limp bound; Conflict and Peacemaking series; ISBN 1 869 890 21 3

Vision in action
Chrisopher Schaefer and Tÿno Voors

'This book is excellent – a well-written exposition of organizational development and the problems that groups tend to encounter as they progress. I highly recommend it to anyone in the field.'   CAROLINE ESTES, Co-Founder of Alpha Farm and Master Facilitator

'This well thought-out book breathes life into the worn-out concept of vision. One finds in it an enlivening imagination of how to develop new initiatives. Like all worthwhile advice, it is based on hard-won life experience. Work with this book and you will find real help in developing small organizations.'
                ROBERT MICHAEL BURNSIDE, Director, Organization Development Products,
                Center for Creative Leadership

'Vision in Action explores and facilitates the vital process of social innovation.'
        HAZEL HENDERSON, author of *Building a Win-Win World: Life Beyond Economic Warfare*

'This is a very helpful book, full of examples, exercise, and case studies. The last section, Signs of Hope, describes many wonderful ways in which we are indeed creating a better world. Read it!'
                RACHAEL FLUG, CEO, Diaperwraps, Inc.

'Socially-oriented initiatives and small organizations play a vital role in a healthy, evolving society. *Vision in Action* offers important and practical perspectives that capture this essence.'
                WILL BRINTON, President of Woods End Laboratory

'Many readers will find *Vision* a valuable source of inspiration and help.'   JAMES ROBERTSON

Vision in Action is a workbook for those involved in social creation – in collaborative deeds that can influence the social environment in which we live and where our ideas and actions can matter.

This is a user-friendly, hands-on guide for developing healthy small organizations – organizations with soul and spirit. Chapters include: Starting Initiatives; Getting Going; Ways of Working Together; Funding Initiatives; Vision, Mission, and Long-Range Planning; Fund-raising.

235 x 145mm; 256pp; paperback; Social Ecology series; ISBN 1 869 890 88 4

Hawthorn Press' *Social Ecology* Series is available in North America from:

Anthroposophic Press,
3390 Route 9,
Hudson,
NY 12534

Fax:(518) 851 2047   Telephone:(518) 851 2054

Anthroposophic Press' *Spirituality and Social Renewal* Series is closely linked, and includes such titles as:

H. Zimmerman, *Speaking, Listening, Understanding – The Art of Creating Conscious Conversation*

Orders

If you have difficulties ordering from a bookshop, you can order direct from:

Hawthorn Press,
1 Lansdown Lane,
Stroud,
Gloucestershire, GL5 1BJ

Fax: (01453) 751138   Telephone: (01453) 757040